A Leap
from the Clouds

ALSO BY JERRY KUNTZ

*Baseball Fiends and Flying Machines:
The Many Lives and Outrageous Times
of George and Alfred Lawson* (McFarland, 2009)

A Leap from the Clouds

The Balloon-Parachute Act and the Daredevil Heritage of Aviation

JERRY KUNTZ

McFarland & Company, Inc., Publishers
Jefferson, North Carolina

ISBN (print) 978-1-4766-8960-9
ISBN (ebook) 978-1-4766-4742-5

LIBRARY OF CONGRESS AND BRITISH LIBRARY
CATALOGUING DATA ARE AVAILABLE

Library of Congress Control Number 2022030340

© 2022 Jerry Kuntz. All rights reserved

No part of this book may be reproduced or transmitted in any form or by any means, electronic or mechanical, including photocopying or recording, or by any information storage and retrieval system, without permission in writing from the publisher.

Front cover image: Parachuting from balloons Buffalo, NY, Courier Lith. Co., circa 1900 (Library of Congress)

Printed in the United States of America

*McFarland & Company, Inc., Publishers
Box 611, Jefferson, North Carolina 28640
www.mcfarlandpub.com*

To those who fell to the earth
to entertain us

Table of Contents

Acknowledgments	ix
Preface: The Leap from the Clouds	1
One—A Lighter-Than-Air Enlightenment	7
Two—Show Ballooning and Aerial Gymnasts	19
Three—Disciples of Donaldson	26
Four—Tom Baldwin's San Francisco Leap	35
Five—Gold Rush in the Heavens	42
Six—The Craze Arrives in Britain	55
Seven—A Global Frenzy	66
Eight—A Carnage of Daredevils	78
Nine—Eldorado and the New York Balloon Company	91
Ten—Other Company Troupes	101
Eleven—Notable Parachuting Performers	119
Twelve—The Balloon-Parachute Act and Society	145
Thirteen—Kites, Gliders and Airships	153
Fourteen—Case Study of a Parachute Aeronaut: L. Guy Mecklem	168
Fifteen—Airplanes and Skydiving	183
Appendix: Notable Balloon-Parachute Era Aeronauts	195
Chapter Notes	213
Bibliography	223
Index	225

Acknowledgments

My writing journeys have often led me to interests in which I have had no prior education, experience, insight, or even a basic understanding. In this case, my interest in the balloon-parachute act was sparked while writing my 2009 book on Alfred and George Lawson. That book, primarily about two outlaw baseball promoters, introduced me to accounts of parachutist Coryell Bartholomew, who accompanied Spalding's Baseball World Tour in 1888–1889. A year later, while researching the story of Samuel F. Cody and Maud Lee, I ran into mentions of English parachutists Charles Baldwin and Auguste Gaudron. Even so, the history of ballooning, parachute development, and airships was new territory to me. The titles listed in the accompanying bibliography were required reading, so a first note of thanks is owed to those authors.

As the scope of this project took form, two email correspondents agreed to review my proposed outline, Michael Horan and Tom D. Crouch, both of whom, as authors themselves, can be found in the bibliography. I could not have found more knowledgeable or encouraging sounding boards. During my research, I discovered that writer Catherine Clarke happened to be working a novel based on the earliest parachutists in Australia, and we exchanged several emails tracking the elusive foreign tours of Park Van Tassel and James W. Price, along with the Freitas sisters and the Hawker sisters. She filled in many blank spots for me. Similarly, Gary B. Fogel's biography of Park Van Tassel came out just as I had completed a first draft. I was able to take advantage of several facts about Van Tassel that Gary had unearthed during his thorough research and used them to make edits to my text.

Finally, though I tried to include mentions of as many early balloon-parachutists as I could, there are dozens (if not hundreds) of others who were active from 1889 to the 1940s. Their descendants may know much about their stories, but my reliance on published and online accounts has overlooked many of these performers. Acknowledgment of the risks they took for a few moments of public entertainment is overdue; hopefully, those living now that know their stories will be inspired to bring them forward.

Preface:
The Leap from the Clouds

One of the stranger threads in the early history of aviation is the role played by a forgotten daredevil craze. Beginning in 1887, for over two decades one of the most popular outdoor public entertainments was watching a person jump from a balloon and drop to earth by parachute. This worldwide fad was popularized by an American circus acrobat, Thomas S. "Tom" Baldwin, and his hundreds of imitators. Though the public appetite for the balloon-parachute act waned in the early 1900s, it persisted as a commonplace event in rural America for several decades, lingering as a type of performing folk art at fairs, fetes, and thrill shows, long after the contributions its progenitors made to the advancement of aeronautics.

In terms of technology, the balloon-parachute act introduced little that was new. Lacking deployment via a parachute pack—which was developed years after the height of the craze—the stunt had no discernable practical application, even in the event of a catastrophic balloon failure. Most balloon-parachuting acts were conducted with crudely made hot-air balloons, inflated via a trench dug into the ground and then covered, forming a flue. At one end wood and kerosene were burned, releasing heat into the makeshift furnace. In a technological sense, this was a step backwards from the hydrogen or coal-gas balloons preferred by "scientific" balloonists. Gas balloons were smaller, could stay aloft much longer, and could drift much farther. The sole purpose of these "smoke balloons" was to carry a parachutist straight up (a few thousand feet) as quickly as possible, and then, once unburdened, turn over, deflate, and fall to the ground as close as possible to the spot where the ascent started.

The balloon-parachute act diminished in popularity after thousands of successful jumps had been made, but also after scores of incautious, unlucky, or unskilled "aeronauts" had been maimed or killed. Tens of thousands of spectators were traumatized by the sickening scenes of these accidents, yet the grisly incidents played only a minor part in the demise of the balloon-parachute act. A larger cause of the disappearance of this performance was the public's fickle appetite for newer aerial daredevil feats: airplane stunt flyers, wing-walkers, and—once the parachute pack was perfected—skydivers. In comparison to these, a drop from a floating balloon was a relic of a bygone era.

However, the evolution of the balloon-parachute act was anything but quaint. Years before Tom Baldwin made his first jump, balloon showmen were performing acrobatic routines from a trapeze bar suspended underneath their globe in place of a basket. If people today were to see this stunt, they would consider it to be far more dangerous and thrilling than a parachute jump.[1] Soon after Baldwin made his first jumps, new wrinkles were continuously added to the parachute act: parachuting pets; sham races between parachutists dropping from separate balloons; double-drops from separate sides of a single balloon; double-drops of parachutists in which one was suspended beneath the other; one parachutist deploying multiple parachutes in one drop; parachutists that descended astride a bicycle; balloons with a cannon suspended underneath it that shot out a human cannonball with a parachute; and the penultimate act: a parachutist who emerged from within a giant exploding pyrotechnic bomb shell.

The "Leap from the Clouds" (as the balloon-parachute act was often billed) did not disappear without a legacy. Many of the individuals involved in performing this stunt were intrigued by the challenge of navigable flight and pursued both lighter-than-air and heavier-than-air solutions. Several, like Carl Myers, Thomas S. Baldwin, A. Leo Stevens, Bud Mars, Horace B. Wild, Charles Broadwick, Leslie Irvin, and others, went on to make substantial contributions to aeronautics. Parachute and balloon work served as a proving ground for those fearless souls who craved the sensation of being airborne and were eager to attempt new aerial firsts. By the time that airplanes were first openly demonstrated in 1908, the public was accustomed to the idea that "ascensionists"[2] were determined, undaunted by mishaps, and often successful.

As ambitious and fearless as some of these early parachutists were, the larger share of them were otherwise unskilled, desperate for income, and often untethered to a stable family life or career. They arose from the ranks of (or were recruited by) professional balloonist showmen. Following the American Civil War, balloon promoters toured America, marketing themselves and operating in a manner akin to medicine shows, carnivals and railroad circuses. There was substantial overlap between the careers of entrepreneurial balloonists and other touring entertainment troupes, which explains why many of the first parachutists were former circus or stage acrobats—or eager wannabes drawn by the allure of that lifestyle. These balloon companies, like other touring performance circuits, were often forced by competition to operate on thin profit margins and were plagued by unethical business practices, lax safety precautions, and exploitation of their performers.

Many of the personal stories of these artiste parachutists contain the elements of sensational melodrama, but one can discern in the background of their colorful anecdotes some self-recognition that they were participants and witnesses to a momentous change—humankind was taking to the skies. However, they found little credit bestowed upon them. A staggering number of balloon-parachutists died while performing, and in the aftermath of each tragic event, few among the public mourned their loss, while many openly mocked their foolhardiness. None of the fallen were hailed as pioneers and few were honored with plaques or memorials. At the very least, they are owed a written sketch of their endeavors. Several of those unfortunates who attained their final fame from the balloon-parachute act are worthy of praise for their sacrifice, such as Charles Leroux, who provided Baldwin with the first non-rigid parachute; Edward Hogan, who died while testing the Campbell-Myers airship; and Daniel J. Maloney, who was killed while piloting one of John J. Montgomery's balloon-launched gliders.

Setting aside the balloon-parachutists who dreamed of navigable flight—and those who died while performing—the greater number gave up this risky vocation after a season or two and retreated to more conventional lives. They were likely content with their brief taste of glamour and their dance with risk, and they could take pride in the entertainment they had offered. Doubtless, they recognized that they had been luckier than those who were maimed or killed. Very few were later interviewed or wrote memoirs, but during their careers, they were willing to share some thrilling stories with newspaper reporters. Most of the first-person glimpses of their careers found in the following pages were culled from those contemporary newspaper articles.

The biggest mystery left by the balloon-parachute act craze was why it became a sensation in the first place, considering that parachutes had been publicly demonstrated decades earlier. There is no definitive answer, but three arguments come to the forefront: first, Tom Baldwin's variation of the act emphasized the human figure and the act of jumping, whereas earlier parachutists just stood in wicker baskets and cut loose their "car"; second, the later decades of the nineteenth century saw a great expansion of recreational venues available to all classes, with events managed by cadres of publicists and impresarios; and finally, this same period was marked by a new public appetite for daredevil acts of all kinds, perhaps as a reaction to the taming effects of progressive society.

The popular fascination for death-defying daredevil stunts has sometimes been likened to the bloodlust of gladiator games and other forms of violent mob barbarity. There is a kernel of truth to this comparison, as will be seen later in accounts of ugly crowd behavior when balloon ascents were cancelled. However, most psychologists agree that viewing death-defying stunts resonates with deep-rooted neural wiring within the human brain, though there is disagreement over the nature of that mechanism.

Evolutionary psychologists have suggested that we are transfixed by the sight of someone in mortal danger because we have an instinct to learn from that person's success or failure, to better our chances if we find ourselves in the same situation. Others posit that the response of onlookers is not selfish, but empathetic. We feel the same emotions that we imagine the person we are observing must be feeling, and we imagine that they must be feeling great fear, though rationally we know the danger is managed. Few fears are more visceral and primal than the fear of falling. Another suggestion is that witnessing a death-defying act is cathartic, in that seeing a horrible outcome averted relieves the onlooker's pent-up anxieties over their own troubles, much the way that watching a horror movie releases tension for many viewers. When this catharsis occurs in a crowd setting, it may serve to bond a community.

While appealing to primeval sensations may not require great art or science, the balloon-parachute act added an inspirational aspect, in that it proved that ingenuity could conquer even the fear of falling. There is a moral aspect to this as well: dangers can be overcome by bravery. In 1947, Julia Stevens, reflecting on the eccentric and reckless balloonists, aeronauts, and early aviators that her husband A. Leo Stevens had introduced to her, remarked, "They were a wonderful bunch of people, though; and their courage made aviation the industry it is today."

Some of those who performed the act were drawn into the young science of aeronautics, but even those whose motives were more mercenary described the sensation of being aloft in exhilarating terms. By far the most common question asked of the parachutists was "What does it feel like?" Invariably, they replied that the sensations of ascending and descending with parachute unfurled were both peaceful and wondrous. The mechanisms used for the balloon-parachute act only allowed very brief periods of freefall. Interestingly, not one balloon-parachutist described freefall as pleasant, and several described it as terrifying.

However, it can be assumed that many balloon-parachute aeronauts would have embraced freefall skydiving, had they had a chance to try it.

During the heyday of the balloon-parachute act, more methodical minds were working outside the realm of public entertainment to solve engineering challenges of powered flight. The Wrights, Otto Lilienthal, Octave Chanute, Samuel Langley, John J. Montgomery, Lawrence Hargrave, etc., studied and engineered wing shapes, light-weight frames, steering mechanisms, propeller design, and weight distribution. They employed models, wind tunnels, and tightly controlled incremental tests. A handful of those performing the "Leap from the Clouds," the "Jump from the Heavens," or the "Perilous Plunge" involved themselves in the advance of aviation that was led by these engineers, particularly with their work on airships and in developing the freefall parachute pack. Others became noted "Early Bird" glider, airship and airplane pilots and tested the limits of these new machines.[3] However, the vast majority of the balloon-parachute act performers served a more nebulous purpose: their descents lifted imaginations.

ONE

A Lighter-Than-Air Enlightenment

The invention of both balloons and parachutes was inspired through observations of nature. Embers and light debris are cast upwards over a fire, and leaves and air-borne seedings float to earth gently when dropped, according to their weight, design, and surface area. Any culture that developed textiles might have invented large-scale balloons and parachutes at some point, and, in fact, small-scale balloons and parachutes were conceived independently in different cultures at different time periods. For instance, several stories of bamboo hats and umbrellas being used as parachutes are found in China, dating back over 2,000 years. The French diplomat Simon de la Loubère related in 1691 that umbrella parachutes had been used for entertaining the king of Siam.

Yet, the first recorded instance of a human lifted into the air by a balloon is credited to Jacques Étienne Montgolfier in France in October 1783, and the first recorded parachute jump by a human occurred two months later (also in France), when Louis-Sébastien Lenormand jumped from a high tower.[1] Though these achievements are an impressive tribute to the intellectual atmosphere of the French Enlightenment, one must wonder whether earlier eras lacked surviving records to assert a prior claim or whether practical necessity discouraged the pursuit of such a seemingly impractical novelty.

The Montgolfier brothers were fabric paper manufacturers, with ready access to the main material of early balloons. Nearly a decade before realizing the possibility of balloons, Joseph-Michel Montgolfier built a crude parachute and attempted to use it from the roof of his house. Though he discarded that experiment, when he saw laundry drying over a fire billow upwards, he conceived the idea of an envelope of fabric, open at the bottom to capture the hot air—or gas—or whatever it

The first documented parachute use by a person: Sébastien Lenormand at Montpellier (Library of Congress, Control Number 2002717347).

was that he supposed was generated by the fire that caused the fabric to rise. In the span of just a couple of years, Montgolfier's experiments led to the first free balloon ascent of a human being.

Within weeks of Montgolfier's success, fellow countryman Jacques Charles ascended in a balloon using hydrogen gas, which had only been separated and identified as a discrete element in 1766. Hydrogen had the advantage of being much more buoyant than hot air and so required balloons that were much smaller than a hot air balloon; moreover, unlike hot air balloons, they retained their buoyancy, allowing flights of longer duration and distance. However, the cost and lengthy process of producing enough hydrogen for an inflation was a limiting factor, given that the main source was usually generated from capturing the reaction between sulfuric acid and iron filings.

In the months following Montgolfier's and Charles's ascents, another young French inventor, Jean-Pierre Blanchard, devoted himself to ballooning. He made the first balloon voyages in several European countries, as well as the first flight across the English Channel. Blanchard conducted several experiments with parachutes and in 1785 demonstrated the dropping of a dog to in a basket attached to a parachute. It should be noted that Blanchard raised money for his efforts from paying audiences attending his launches. Parachute drops of objects and fireworks displays were some features of his showmanship that drew crowds to his ascensions.

Jean-Pierre Blanchard died shortly after suffering a heart attack and falling fifty feet from a balloon in 1808, but his enthusiasm for spectacular ascensions was surpassed by his young bride, Sophie Blanchard. Sophie was a fixture at the court of Napoleon and his restoration successor, Louis XVIII, and served as France's official aeronaut to both rulers. Sophie eschewed the protection of a wicker basket and instead posed herself standing in a silver gondola, draped in ornate fashions. She realized that ascensions could offer spectators a dream-like tableau—a fantastic, supernatural vision. Sophie Blanchard's aerial stagecraft echoed across the decades of the nineteenth century.

Before his death, Jean-Pierre Blanchard claimed to be the first person to descend from a balloon via parachute, though what occurred was an accidental rupture of his balloon's fabric, which flattened against the upper netting of the balloon, forming a parachute. From that instance forward, many early balloonists reported a similar experience of surviving the catastrophic failure of their balloon envelopes.[2] If they were lucky, the balloon fabric collapsed into a parabola that braked their descent—but such instances were rare. In the late 1830s and 1840s, American balloonist John Wise designed his balloons with rip-panels to facilitate deflation, allowing him to also claim that he had intentionally parachuted to the ground.

In 1798, fifteen years after the Montgolfier Brothers' first ascensions, André-Jacques Garnerin, a student of the gas-balloon innovator Jacques Charles, made the first recorded parachute jump by a human

Sophie Blanchard's presentation during her ascensions set a new standard for ballooning as performance (Library of Congress, Control Number 2002716393).

from a balloon. He invented a reinforced fabric parachute, a break from earlier designs used by building jumpers that incorporated rigid panels. Most aeronautical authorities recognize Garnerin as the founder of parachuting. Garnerin made several jumps in Paris and repeated the feat in London in 1802. He used a parachute that was 23 feet in diameter,

One—A Lighter-Than-Air Enlightenment   11

measuring close in size to those used by Tom Baldwin and others at the end of the century. Garnerin's parachute had a small basket suspended under it; the parachute itself was suspended beneath the main balloon. It had ribs, like an umbrella, which were in a closed position when the balloon ascended. Garnerin would unfurl the parachute and cut loose

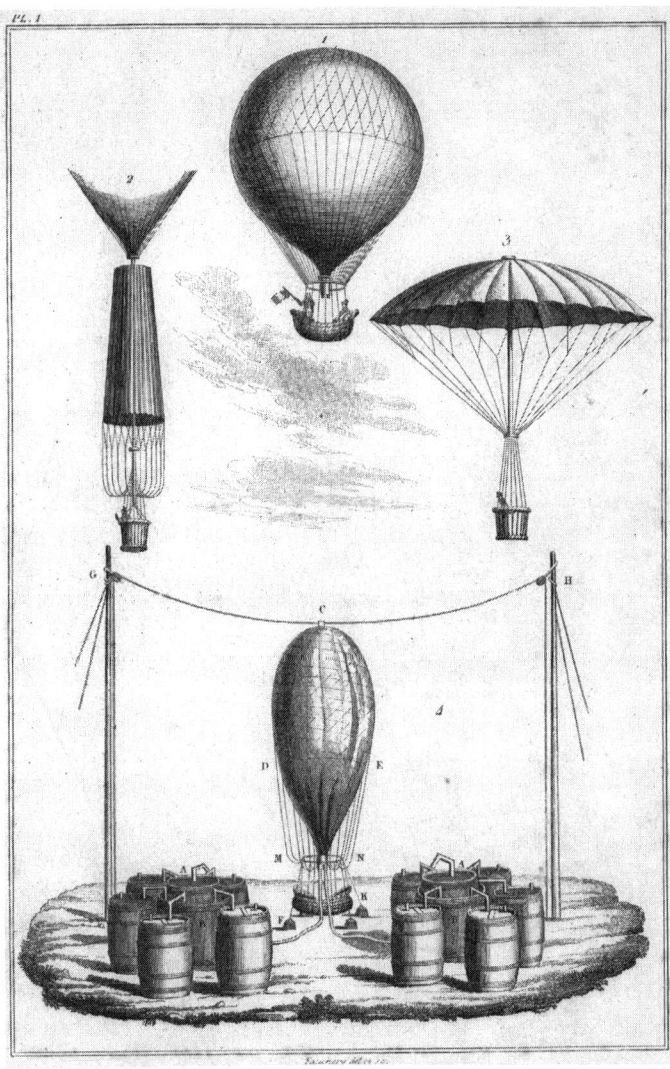

An illustration of the stages of Garnerin's balloon-parachute act: inflating a balloon with hydrogen (at bottom); balloon in flight (at 1); parachute attached to balloon (at 2); and parachute cut loose (at 3) (Library of Congress, Control Number 2002735900).

from the balloon. The abandoned balloon would rotate, deflate and fall to the ground; ideally, it would not travel far from the landing spot of the parachute.

Like the Blanchards, Garnerin embraced showmanship and created a sensation when he invited women to accompany him on his balloon voyages. However, it was not one of Garnerin's female guest passengers that made the first parachute jump by a woman; the credit for that feat belongs to his niece, Élisa Garnerin, who in 1815 capitalized on her uncle's fame. Between 1815 and 1836, Élisa Garnerin made over three dozen parachute drops throughout various European countries. However, because of Élisa's gender and the fact that none of her exhibitions were in English-speaking countries, her celebrity eluded universal acclaim.

Starting in 1818, Frenchman Louis Charles Guillé toured the eastern United States conducting balloon ascensions—the first American glimpse of balloons since Jean-Pierre Blanchard's demonstrations in the mid–1790s. Guillé amazed New York City crowds with a parachute drop over Vauxhall Gardens in 1819, an event that many residents recalled decades later. For New Yorkers, Guillé's demonstration was not

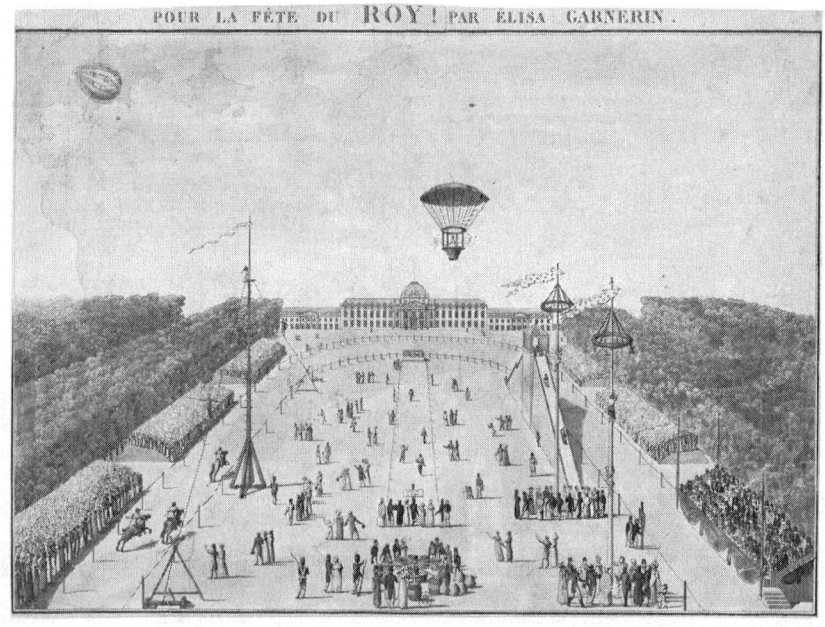

Élisa Garnerin (1791–1853), the niece of André-Jacques Garnerin, made nearly forty parachute drops in a twenty-year span (Wikimedia Commons).

only their first sight of a parachute, but also of a balloon. An eyewitness account appeared in the diary of merchant Jacob Harvey:

> The ascent was for a moment impeded by a few tall poplar trees which surrounded the spot, but upon clearing these, the adventurous Æronaut, swiftly advanced towards the ethereal regions, amidst the repeated shouts of the astonished multitude. The weather was rather unpropitious—a gust of wind from the North West accompanied by a slight shower, carried the balloon with amazing rapidity towards the Sea. Much alarm was expressed for the safety of Mr. G, in consequence of the rolling of the Parachute occasioned by its want of proper poizing—but he was too safely lodged, to be easily thrown out. In ten minutes he had reached the height of 1500 fathoms, when, fearing the effects of a gust, which was approaching, he disengaged himself from the balloon. This was the awful moment! And had not the Parachute, instantly yielded to the pressure of the wind, and unfolded itself, he must have unavoidably perished. The anxiety of the Spectators had become extreme, and great was their joy, at beholding the slow and majestic manner in which Mr. G descended from his lofty station. Half an hour's gentle "sailing," brought him once more to "terra firma," at a place on Long Island, six miles distant from Vauxhall Gardens. He returned to the City the same evening, and attended the Circus, where he was received with much applause.[3]

The flashy balloon ascensions of the early nineteenth century disguised the debate over the practical applications of aerial navigation. The lack of steerable balloons remained a problem that limited their utility, though they did contribute to the understanding of the earth's atmosphere and weather patterns. Given that balloons offered no predictable form of transportation, parachutes remained a novelty that reappeared sporadically between 1820 and 1887, resulting in both unheralded successes and horrific failures.

Élisa Garnerin was performing parachute jumps between 1815 and 1836, but following Guillé's exhibitions in the New York area between 1818 and 1821, no other parachutists gained prominence until the endeavor was taken up by an English watercolor artist, Robert Cocking. Cocking, after studying Sir George Cayley's essay "On Aerial Navigation," became engrossed with Cayley's description of Garnerin's parachutes. In his paper, Cayley suggested that an inverted conical shape would solve the problem of oscillation that Garnerin experienced. Upon reading this, Cocking followed that suggestion and drew up his own design: an array of three hoops, each larger than the one below, sewn together by fabric. The top hoop was 34 feet in diameter, a bit larger than Baldwin's first parachute.

Through his contacts in scientific circles, Cocking was able to convince England's premiere balloonists—Charles Green and Edward

Edward Spencer, who, along with Charles Green, owned the balloon "Royal Vauxhall" from which Robert Cocking attempted to release a parachute on July 24, 1837, with fatal consequences ("Edward Spencer," Smithsonian National Air and Space Museum [NASM A19680090000]).

Spencer—to take him aloft with his creation. Cocking stood in a basket underneath his parachute, which was suspended from the balloon *Royal Nassau* piloted by Green and Spencer. They ascended from Vauxhall Gardens, near London, on July 24, 1837. At 5,000 feet, the balloon began to lose lift, and 61-year-old Cocking was signaled by the balloonists to

One—A Lighter-Than-Air Enlightenment 15

cut the cord. Immediately after he did this, the parachute plummeted, while the *Royal Nassau* soared upward. The inverted cone did little to arrest the drop, and it was later learned that Cocking had not properly accounted for the heavy weight of its framework. The cone tipped sideways, and Cocking was dashed to the ground, dying within moments. Green and Spencer's reputations suffered, as did that of the aviation expert, Sir George Cayley, but the real fault lay in Cocking's failure to adequately test his design.

Less than a year later, a former British naval worker named John Hampton began making balloon ascensions in public exhibitions. In October of 1838, Hampton decided to add a parachute drop to his show, following Garnerin's design: canvas stretched over a stiff whalebone and bamboo parabolic framework. Like Garnerin, Hampton had his parachute suspended from an unmanned gas balloon; once he cut the parachute loose, the balloon was designed to tip over and collapse. Hampton made a successful drop at Cheltenham, England on October 3, 1838. He went on to make seven more parachute descensions throughout Britain before retiring in 1852.

The nineteenth-century's most accomplished aeronaut, Eugène Godard, came from a ballooning family, having acquired his aeronautical passion from his uncle, Marcel Andre Godard. The Godards began constructing balloons in the late 1840s. In 1849 Eugène met

Scenes depicting Robert Cocking and his inverted parachute design and his fatal crash in London (Wellcome Collection).

16   A Leap from the Clouds

Engraving of John Hampton's Ascent from Cremorne House, Chelsea, on June 13, 1839 (*The Mirror of Literature, Amusement, and Instruction*, Vol. XXXIII, January 1839).

with Britain's leading balloonist, Charles Green, who taught Godard the advantages of using coal gas instead of hydrogen or hot air: it was cheaper and more readily available than hydrogen, since many towns had a gasworks to provide illumination. Undoubtedly, Green and Godard also discussed Garnerin's parachute and Cocking's failure, in which

Green had played a part. Godard consequently made several impressive ascensions in France in the early 1850s and assisted Henri Giffard in constructing the first powered dirigible in 1852, though it could hardly be called a success.

Godard established himself as a rival to the theatrical balloon presentations of the husband-and-wife team of Eugene and Louise Poitevin. The Poitevins continued a tradition originated by Sophie Blanchard

Eugène Godard (1827–1890), among the greatest nineteenth-century balloonists, sketched by Eduard Kaiser (1820–1895) (Wikimedia Commons).

of using ornately decorated balloons. They drew attention to the suspended human figure by replacing the balloon basket with a platform, or a boat-like shell, or even a harnessed horse. The Poitevins employed a Garnerin-like parachute to make their descent, but it was their habit of sending aloft harnessed animals that brought them fame. Louise Poitevin was arrested in England on a charge of animal cruelty for dangling from a balloon astride a heifer. She was attempting to present a tableau evocative of Europa and the god Zeus, who disguised himself as a bull to abduct the young princess.

After competing with ascensions being made by the Poitevins in the early 1850s, Eugène Godard toured North America from 1855 to 1859, accompanied by his wife and a brother, Auguste Godard. Eugène Godard, like many early balloonists, was an astute showman. His tour of North America was designed to reap a profit, and he aimed to impress crowds with gigantic balloons and aerial stunts. Following each of his ascensions, Godard's troupe entertained paying crowds with an elaborate stage magic act. During some of his balloon ascensions, Auguste Godard would lower himself from the balloon basket to a hanging trapeze and would thrill crowds by performing acrobatic stunts while suspended from the bar.

In mid–July 1857, while in Philadelphia, the Godards were greeted by America's leading balloonist, John Wise. On this occasion, the Godards made an ascension and dropped a small dog attached by a harness to a parachute. Two months later, Auguste Godard descended from a balloon by means of a parachute which was suspended beneath the balloon basket. He sat on an exposed wood bar beneath the parachute's canopy.[4] The Godards repeated their parachute drop act several times during their North American tour. The aerial trapeze showmanship of the Godards made a lasting impression on American balloonists and entertainers, but the impact of their act was eclipsed by another Frenchman touring in the United States who shook the entertainment world with a daredevil performance of a different nature: tightrope walking. He was known as the Great Blondin.

Two

Show Ballooning and Aerial Gymnasts

French acrobat Charles Blondin arrived in the United States in 1855, performing at New York entertainment resorts and in his own touring circus. However, he gained worldwide fame four years later, in 1859, for a series of tightrope walks above the Niagara River Gorge. He was the first daredevil to do so, and he performed many stunts while balanced on the rope, such as carrying a man on his back. The success of Blondin inspired scores of American performers to take up wire walking. One of the first to do so was Harry Leslie, nicknamed "the American Blondin," who in 1865 repeated Blondin's feats at Niagara.

In the late 1860s, Harry Leslie teamed up with the former head of the Union Army balloon service, Thaddeus Lowe, to present an act in which he performed stunts on a trapeze bar suspended from a balloon. Leslie likely copied this act from the Godards, who had performed in America in 1857, but he also might have seen another French company of acrobats that had come to the United States, the Buislay Family. Auguste and Adolphe Buislay performed the balloon-trapeze feature many times in the 1860s, until Adolphe was killed during a performance in Mexico City in 1870.[1] A wind gust hit his ascending balloon and crashed it into a post, knocking Adolphe off his seat and causing him to fall to his death.

Leslie was bested by a female acrobat, Leona Dare, who in 1872 introduced an act in which she suspended herself beneath a balloon by only a strap held between her teeth (and a hidden safety line)—a stunt she had earlier performed from a trapeze bar inside theaters. Dare's use of her traditional brief, form-fitting circus tights added sex appeal to her aerial acrobatics, setting a standard that would later be imitated by female parachutists.

At about the same time that Leona Dare rose to fame, Harry Leslie's balloon-trapeze act was surpassed by another male practitioner, Washington H. Donaldson. As a boy in Philadelphia, Donaldson was indifferent to his studies and instead haunted the city's low-brow theaters. There he rubbed shoulders with variety artists in venues that, decades later, would collectively be recognized as "vaudeville." In the 1850s, these stages included beer gardens, concert saloons, lecture halls, and small theaters. From these performers Donaldson acquired a repertoire of magic tricks, vocal impressions, ventriloquism, and acrobatic stunts. At age 17, while Donaldson was immersed in learning the entertainment business, the Godard brothers appeared in Philadelphia. There is no documentation that Donaldson was one of the thousands that viewed the Godard balloon trapeze act and parachute drop, though surely it would not have escaped his notice.

Daredevil Harry Leslie performs while suspended from Thaddeus Lowe's balloon over New York City ("Up in a Balloon," *Frank Leslie's Illustrated Magazine*, October 21, 1865, p. 76; House Divided: The Civil War Research Engine at Dickinson College, https://hd.housedivided.dickinson.edu/node/44604).

Two—Show Ballooning and Aerial Gymnasts 21

Poster for Leona Dare's performance at the Hippodrome in Paris, France, by Jules Chéret (1836–1932) (Wikimedia Commons).

By the time he was 18, Donaldson was headlining his own show of magic and ventriloquism at Philadelphia's Mechanics' Institute.[2] As adept as Donaldson was, in 1859 he was chagrined to find that it was a Frenchman, Charles Blondin, who had captured the imagination of the American public with his rope-walking act. Donaldson, inspired by both envy of "the Hero of Niagara," and by confidence in his own abilities, changed his act and made rope-walking the focus of his future performances. By 1862 (after a short enlistment in the Union Army), he was conducting funambulist exhibitions above Philadelphia's streets and parks and across the Schuylkill River. He was assisted in these exhibitions by his business manager and fellow actor-acrobat, Harry Gilbert.

In the years following the Civil War, Donaldson became recognized as America's most accomplished tightrope walker. While Donaldson was touring with his act in the western states, a local promoter found himself in debt to Donaldson and paid off the balance with the only collateral he had left: a balloon. Donaldson brought it back to his home in Reading, Pennsylvania, and made his first balloon flight there in 1871. From that point forward, ballooning became his passion. By default, his friend and manager Harry Gilbert also became a balloon enthusiast. Donaldson's new obsession brought him in contact with America's leading balloonist, John Wise of Philadelphia.

Wise, of Pennsylvania German descent, was the most active balloonist in the United States between 1835 and 1879, making nearly 500 ascents. Although he often performed ascents to entertain crowds, Wise had a keen interest in the scientific aspects of aerial navigation. He performed many experiments on atmospheric conditions and was the first to detect the high-altitude prevailing west-to-east wind current, later recognized as the jet stream. In 1859, Wise and John LaMountain made an unsuccessful attempt to cross the Atlantic by balloon but still traveled a record

Portrait of John Wise, one of the most notable American balloonists of the nineteenth century (Rare Book Division, New York Public Library Digital Collections).

1,500 miles in the effort. During the Civil War, Wise volunteered his talents to conduct battlefield observation by balloon, but he left his service appointment in the Union Army abruptly after one of his balloons was mishandled. Leadership of the balloon corps was given to his rival, Thaddeus Lowe.

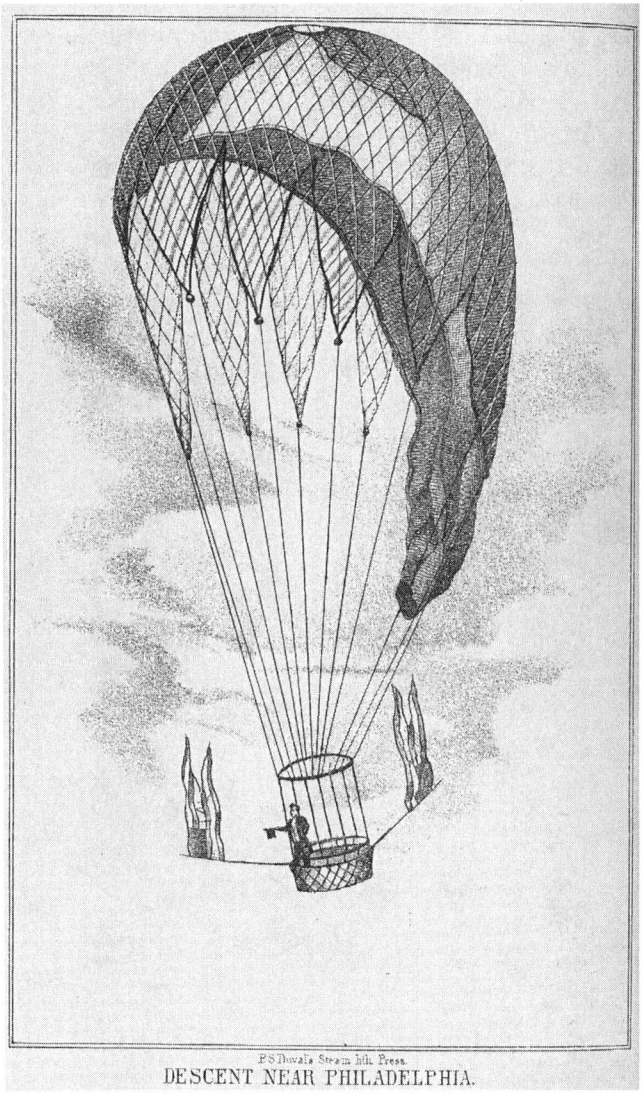

John Wise demonstrating a balloon rip panel could collapse an envelope to form a parachute within the netting (Rare Book Division, New York Public Library Digital Collections).

Wise was also intrigued by parachutes and made tests comparing Garnerin's umbrella design against Cocking's inverted cone. As mentioned earlier, Wise had designed his balloons with a rip panel so that the netting could contain the uninflated balloon fabric if it ruptured, making a parachute. On one occasion he confirmed this feature worked by unfortunate accident, but on other occasions Wise claimed that he intentionally caused this to happen. Wise carried the first United States mail by air and made deliveries of mail via parachute. In 1850 he wrote the standard layman's text on aviation, *A system of aeronautics, comprehending its earliest investigations, and modern practice and art*.

Wise's new acquaintance, Washington H. Donaldson, made 139 balloon ascensions between 1871 and 1875, many of which were conducted with no basket. Instead, Donaldson perched on a trapeze bar dangling under the balloon, like Harry Leslie. It is likely that Donaldson purchased some of his balloons from Wise, who manufactured them in Philadelphia. The two men discussed aerial navigation, with Wise telling Donaldson of the existence of a prevailing west-to-east current that could make long voyages possible. In June 1873, the two men signed a contract with the *New York Graphic* to pilot a balloon built to their

W.H. Donaldson's final ascent from Chicago before being lost over Lake Michigan (*Harpers Weekly* 19, August 7, 1875, 637; author's collection).

specifications across the Atlantic.[3] Wise later pulled out of the effort over a disagreement on construction materials, but in 1874 Donaldson followed through on the project, though it ended in failure after a storm forced Donaldson and his partners down over Connecticut.

Starting in 1874, many of Donaldson's ascensions were sponsored by P.T. Barnum, conducted either at Barnum's New York Hippodrome or coinciding with Barnum's traveling circus venues around the country. In July 1875, Donaldson and a newspaper reporter ascended from Chicago and headed eastward over Lake Michigan. The craft was caught in a squall and was never seen again. The reporter's body washed up a month later, but the balloon and Donaldson were never found. John Wise wrote a pamphlet about Donaldson's tragic last voyage. Ironically, Wise himself was lost in a balloon over Lake Michigan four years later. A body was recovered but was never positively identified as Wise. Several commentators believed that Wise had surrendered some of his scientific reputation by working with showmen like Donaldson.

Three

Disciples of Donaldson

The death of the popular W.H. Donaldson only seemed to create a vacuum that other balloon-trapeze acts rushed to fill. Those best positioned to fill public demand were touring show balloonists, working independently or in conjunction with a circus. Show balloonists proliferated in the 1870s, especially in the Ohio Valley and Great Lakes border states: Western New York, Ohio, Michigan, Indiana, Illinois. Geography and population trends made this region ideal for ballooning: relatively flat topography, well-connected by rail lines, and dotted by towns and small cities that depended on touring groups to provide their entertainment. This section of the United States became the hotbed of American ballooning in the 1870s and 1880s and gave rise to the new American practitioners of the balloon-parachute act.

Several circuses adopted the use of balloon ascensions to attract crowds. Circus balloon ascensions were made using either coal gas (supplied by the gasworks of a city being visited) or by hot air. For the needs of a traveling circus offering evening performances in rural areas, a hot-air balloon launched aloft for a flight measured in minutes was sufficient to attract a crowd. Circus hot-air balloons were launched using techniques that differed little from those the Montgolfiers had used a hundred years earlier: a canvas envelope slung between two poles, with its opening placed over a makeshift chimney, fed by a trench pit-fire.

A quick survey of the most well-known show balloonists of this hotbed region serves to provide context to the subsequent explosion of the balloon-parachute craze. While the following sketches do not present a complete account of all show balloonists of the post–Civil War era, they do include those who attempted to transition from the balloon-trapeze act to the parachute act.

Western New York State

Like Donaldson, balloonist Ira Allen of Dansville, New York, got his start as a ropewalker, performing locally just prior to the Civil War. Undoubtedly, he was inspired by the acclaim showered on Blondin at Niagara, not far distant. Allen was a Union Army scout during the war and was credited with many heroic exploits. After the war, he returned to performing on the wire and appeared in several circuses: Pullman & Hamilton; Ringling; Washburn; Grady; and Forepaugh. He purchased a war surplus balloon in 1875 and introduced ballooning to his brothers Martin Allen and Comfort "Curt" Allen.[1] By 1884, Ira Allen had made over a hundred ascents and experimented with dropping farm animals and pets from his balloon via parachute.

Inventor Carl E. Myers of Frankfort, New York, was a grudging entry into show ballooning. A former banker, telegraph operator, and photographer, he developed an interest in hydrogen balloons in the late 1870s. Myers developed several patents for balloon fabrics, put into use at his "balloon farm" in Herkimer County, New York. While Myers was more interested in scientific ballooning, he could not ignore the commercial windfall that others were reaping with their primitive smoke balloons. In response to the trend for balloon acrobatics, Myers recruited several female aeronauts to make ascensions, including his wife, Mary (as "Carlotta"), Helene A. Thiers (Mrs. Edward H. Thayer, trained by Harry Gilbert), Pearl McBain, and Lizzie Ihling Wise (niece of John Wise). Myers also hired other young balloonists acrobats, including William Rulison, John J. Frisbie, Nell Brayton, Edwin Claridge, William Wilson (aka "Del Dare," a nod to Leona Dare), and "Signor Pedanto."

Ohio

Following Donaldson's death in 1875, his partner and manager, Harry Gilbert, continued for several years as P.T. Barnum's balloonist. He also worked as the balloonist for Buffalo Bill's Wild West, and he took independent engagements at fairs, exhibitions, etc., for a time partnering with English balloonist Charles H. Grimley. During this period, Harry Gilbert made Cincinnati, Ohio, his headquarters. By the early 1880s, Gilbert was middle-aged and was obliged to hire two young, athletic variety show actors—Charles W. Williams and Samuel C. Young—to perform most of the balloon ascensions. Williams and Young often employed Donaldson's routine of dangling from a trapeze bar.[2] In 1883,

"Carlotta" (Mary Breed Hawley) and Prof. Carl Myers posed just prior to an ascension (Krainik Ballooning Collection, Acc. 1990–0009, ref1788, National Air and Space Museum, Smithsonian Institution).

Gilbert introduced a young female aeronaut, known as "Louise Bates," to make the solo balloon launches.[3] "Lulu" was a teen-aged German immigrant that Gilbert and his wife adopted, allegedly after Louise's mother had died.

Another circus agent, Oscar Hunt, was manning balloons for the Cooper & Jackson Circus and Menagerie in the early 1880s. He later settled in Cleveland, Ohio, and made balloon-trapeze ascensions throughout Ohio over the next several years, accompanied by his wife, who was known professionally as Lottie Leon.[4] Hunt was born in 1854 in California to Australian parents—a fact worth noting due to the career of his future partner, James W. Price. Hunt genuinely enjoyed exhibiting to the public and sharing his love for ballooning with the young people of Cleveland.

Two brothers introduced to ballooning by Hunt were Albert Leo Stevens and Frank Stevens.[5] Despite their Anglican-sounding names, the boys were born to two German parents, Franz Hoefner and Anna Louisa Waldheger. Their father died when the boys were young, and their mother remarried to another German resident of Cleveland, Alois Schutt. Just before their father's death, the older boy, Albert Leo, was handed over to the care of a shady promoter of a touring acrobatic company, Walla Leonard, who provided four-year-old Albert with the stage name "Prince Leo."

Young Albert was prodded into performing a tightrope routine on a Philadelphia theater stage for several months, before word of his harsh mistreatment reached his mother in Cleveland. The promoter Leonard was lightly rebuked by a Philadelphia court, but found another unfortunate boy who took over the stage name "Prince Leo."[6] This second Prince Leo was rescued from a New York City stage by the recently-formed Society for the Prevention of Cruelty to Children—a case that generated sensational headlines for exposing the routine abuse of young performers.[7] Back home in Cleveland, Albert Leo Stevens did not abandon his stage name or his talent for acrobatics, but he also did not perform in public again until he reached age eighteen. He was then brought under the management of a local amusement venue promoter, George W. Baird.[8]

Also in Cleveland in the late 1880s was Owen J. Brady (who later used the spelling Bready), a shooting-gallery operator in his twenties. Brady later recalled that he worked as an assistant for a ballooning showman (Hunt or George W. Baird?) and observed that the promoter of balloon ascensions also received the lion's share of the profits, compared to the aeronaut. Brady soon found an amateur aeronaut to partner with, his roommate, Hubbard "Frank" Vandegrift. Together they toured regionally from 1885 to 1888, performing the balloon-trapeze act, with Vandegrift making most of the ascents, but occasionally relieved by Brady himself.[9]

A further Ohio-based professed disciple of W.H. Donaldson was a man who went by the stage name Harry Warner. His real name was John Wesley Biggerstaff, and he came from a respectable family in Pickaway

County. He attended Ohio Wesleyan University and was on his way to becoming a physician like his older brother James, but instead Biggerstaff gave up the prospect of a safe and valued profession to pursue a career as a tightrope walker. He quickly became one of the best rope walkers in America, and in 1882 he ascended and descended the Niagara gorge suspension bridge along its guy wires. In 1883 he performed a new act, appearing on a trapeze bar dangling under a balloon, emulating W.H. Donaldson. Harry Warner claimed to have worked with Tom Baldwin; this may have been possible, given that both were ropewalking and performing the balloon-trapeze act at about the same time (1882–1884) and both were active in same region of the country.[10] However, at least one of Warner's claims was false: whenever he was interviewed, he maintained that he had been born and raised in Canada, but in truth he was a native of the regional hotbed of American ballooning, the Midwest states of Ohio, Michigan, Indiana, and Illinois.

Michigan

To the north, Edward D. Hogan established himself as the first representative of what was to become another hot-bed city of ballooning and parachuting: Jackson, Michigan. Hogan made his initial balloon ascension in 1880. He spent one year, 1882, under contract as balloonist for the James T. Johnson circus, but the troupe was handled so shabbily that Hogan opted to become his own manager, securing engagements at fairs and exhibitions in several states. Hogan, too, on occasion performed "daring and difficult feats" on a trapeze.[11] In 1884, he rigged a balloon with a harness to lift a wagon (manufactured in Jackson) and flew it over thirty miles of countryside, thereby laying a claim to be the first to convey commercial cargo by air. Recruited to assist Hogan were his brothers, William Hogan and John Hogan.

Illinois

One of the first circus impresarios to conduct regular balloon ascensions was George DeHaven, who was active from the late 1850s to the 1890s with over thirty different circuses, including several under his own name. DeHaven, who was most often based in Illinois, is credited by many with launching the first circus tour by rail and with introducing Roman hippodrome-style horse races. In the early 1880s, he spotted an acrobatic young railroad worker in Quincy, Illinois, named Thomas

Edward D. Hogan's publicity stunt on behalf of a Jackson, Michigan, wagon manufacturer (Krainik Ballooning Collection, Acc. 1990–0009, ref1763, National Air and Space Museum, Smithsonian Institution).

S. Baldwin. Baldwin, born in Decatur, Illinois, in 1857, had been left fatherless in 1861. In the independent years of his youth, Baldwin had earned money as a lamplighter, newspaper employee, and book salesman, but in his free time, he practiced acrobatics in the sawdust piles of nearby lumberyards.

DeHaven invited Baldwin to join his circus, and, in addition to performing a rope-walking act, soon assigned him to be one of his balloon aeronauts. During a DeHaven show in Chillicothe, Ohio, Baldwin went aloft in a balloon for the first time on a trapeze bar and performed stunts. Baldwin later selflessly credited W.H. Donaldson with originating this act, perhaps unaware that the Godards, Harry Leslie, and the Buislays had presented it much earlier. In 1879, after a circus he was in disbanded in Texas, Tom Baldwin and a friend, Harry Victor, barnstormed northward performing tightrope demonstrations in city streets and passing a hat to collect money. At Columbus, Ohio, a rope snapped while they were performing; Victor was seriously injured, but Baldwin escaped with bruises.

In the early 1880s, no less than nine men were actively performing the balloon-trapeze act who all hailed from a single Midwest city: Springfield, Illinois. They were close in age (born between 1852 and 1862) and knew one another: Uel E. Hurd, who performed under the name Ned Hathaway; Joseph B. Gomes; Ira N. Fisk; Thomas Jewell; J. Daniel Headley; Eleazer M. Wood; William M. Smith; John L. Gillock; and James W. Price.

Fisk could be found making ascensions at fairs and resorts in the late 1870s, employing a trapeze bar in place of a basket. Fisk's career as a balloonist and carnival show manager spanned five decades, visiting small towns and fairgrounds in the Ohio River Valley. John Daniel "Dan" Headley and his brother James started making ascensions in 1877, about the same time that Fisk first became active. Headley was severely injured when his balloon collapsed during an ascension in 1881, and from

Thomas S. Baldwin during his years as a performer (*Representative Men and Homes, Quincy, Illinois* [Quincy: Press of Volk, Jones & McMein, 1899]; author's collection).

that point forward, he hired a series of younger men to perform the trapeze act. Those assistants had a string of bad luck: Charles Walcott, who was with Headley in 1883 and 1884, was injured during a storm and spent five months in a Nashville, Tennessee, hospital. Headley's 1885 helper was 20-year-old Peter Carroll, who landed in the Ohio River and drowned. Finally, in 1887, his young partner Randall Blakeslee lost his grip 400 feet from the ground and plummeted into the fairgrounds at Mercer County, Missouri, in front of thousands of onlookers.[12] Headley retired from the balloon business at that point, though his legacy lived on in the subsequent career of his former assistant, Charles Walcott.

Price, Hathaway, and Gomes got their start as balloonists in the early 1880s, several years after Fisk and Headley. Hathaway was originally a railroad brakeman and Gomes was a sign painter, but as young men both abandoned their conventional jobs for performing. In the summer they each toured separately as balloonists and during the rest of the year often performed together in minstrel and medicine show companies.[13] Hathaway recruited John Gillock into ballooning, while Gomes brought in partners Thomas Jewell, Eleazer M. Wood and William M. Smith to form a touring company. James W. Price, the youngest of the Springfield aeronauts, arose from a history of juvenile delinquency to begin ballooning in 1884, at about the same time his first marriage collapsed.

An aeronaut from Fairbury, Illinois, named Albert L. Tolbert faced nearly as much adversity in his domestic affairs as he did in performing the balloon-trapeze act. Born in 1856, by 1885 he was alternating farming and balloon ascensions from his home in Kankakee, Illinois. In mid–July of that year, an El Paso, Illinois, newspaper reported that a young woman had checked into a hotel there, sent a telegram to Albert Tolbert in Kankakee saying that she, his wife, was dying. She then retired to her room and drank poison. Reporters investigating her death found that Tolbert already had a living wife with children in Fairbury, whom Tolbert claimed he had divorced, and confirmed that he had, indeed, been married to the suicide victim.[14] No record of those marriages has surfaced.

Just days after this tragedy, Tolbert made an appearance in Chicago for a balloon "race" against William M. Smith, one of the Springfield aeronauts of the Gomes-Jewell company. Such races started with a command for the balloonists to inflate their balloons and then were judged by which aeronaut, hanging from a trapeze, let his craft climb the furthest. Tolbert, to ascend quicker, over-inflated his envelope. At 2,000 feet above the ground, the decreased air pressure caused his balloon to expand and burst. At 1,500 feet, he came down like a shot, hitting some telegraph wires—which may have saved his life. He fell on his back. When the first attendees reached him, he was still conscious and said, "My back is broken. I am going to die."[15] Reports suggested his spine was fractured. However, after a month in the hospital, he was released and suggested some supporter of Smith had sabotaged his craft. By 1887, Tolbert had returned to making ascents on the trapeze bar.

The West

Parker A. "Park" Van Tassel, a native of Ohio, was a Forepaugh Circus balloonist and advertising agent during the late 1870s. Advance publicity agents of the big circuses were the foremost marketing experts of that era, traveling through the country in their well-appointed custom railcars, and the Adam Forepaugh Circus was arguably the largest. Regardless, Park Van Tassel either opted to give up that high-profile vocation or was removed.[16] Instead, he acquired some old circus balloons and staged freelance promotional events in New Mexico, Colorado, Utah, and California. By 1885, Park Van Tassel had migrated to San Francisco, where he produced a series of regular balloon ascensions at area resorts. Van Tassel did not personally perform a trapeze act, but as a promoter, he was instrumental in Tom Baldwin's later career and notable for the world tours he conducted with other parachutists.

All those mentioned above constituted the first generation of presenters of the balloon-parachute act craze that began in 1887. Their careers would diverge wildly, but all would have acknowledged the debt they owed to Washington H. Donaldson, the great popularizer of balloon acrobatics. However, only one among this group was the first to be inspired to make the progression from the trapeze bar to the parachute: his name was Thomas S. "Tom" Baldwin.

Four

Tom Baldwin's San Francisco Leap

After leaving the employ of Adam Forepaugh's circus (around 1880) Park Van Tassel purchased a balloon in California and conducted several exhibition ascensions in the Sacramento area. He then had the outfit conveyed to Albuquerque, New Mexico, where he opened a liquor store.[1] Soon, Van Tassel abandoned that unsteady business and devoted himself to aerial showmanship. He made New Mexico's first ascension in 1882, then migrated his riggings to Denver. After conducting balloon ascensions in Denver, Van Tassel went to Salt Lake City and made Utah's first ascension. Though well liked in Salt Lake City, Van Tassel returned to California in 1885. In San Francisco, he attracted good crowds to his ascensions at fairs and summer resorts, but he was not the only balloonist in the city.

In 1886, another showman named Emil Leandro Melville materialized in the Bay Area.[2] Unlike Van Tassel, Melville was a fearless athlete, and he not only presented the public with a balloon ascension but also displayed the ever-impressive trapeze bar act while dangling underneath his hot-air bag. Park Van Tassel, by contrast, weighed 250 pounds, had unhealthy habits, and was incapable of matching Melville's dazzling gymnastics. Moreover, Melville had another novelty stunt: he carried aloft a pet monkey that he dropped by parachute from 2,000 feet.[3] Van Tassel faced a dilemma in coming up with ideas to compete with the extravaganza that Melville offered the public. Both aeronauts conducted their ascensions at one of the most popular coastal resorts in the Bay Area, the Cliff House.

Though not far from downtown San Francisco, the Cliff House was a favorite destination for weekend carriage rides. Featuring a canteen and restaurant, the site loomed over Ocean Beach. Its wide veranda provided observation spots where people could watch seals sunning on a rocky outcrop named Seal Rock, located 400 feet offshore. In the early 1860s, local promoters had pondered what they might do to match the crowd-pleasing feats of the Great Blondin at Niagara Falls. They concluded that a tightrope walk from the heights of the Cliff House out to Seal Rock would be a worthy spectacle. Circus performer James Cooke was enticed to make the attempt, which he successfully accomplished in September 1865. Between 1865 and the mid–1880s, the Cliff House saw several funambulists attempt the wire walk, making a name not only for themselves, but for the Cliff House as the premier venue for Bay Area outdoor entertainment.

In 1884, former circus-acrobat Thomas S. Baldwin embarked on a tightrope-exhibition tour of the West Coast and remained in the region for three years. Baldwin was undoubtedly drawn by the challenge of repeating Cooke's Cliff House-to-Seal Rock tightrope walk. Over the following three years, Baldwin was able to repeat that feat several times. It was while he was in San Francisco that Baldwin encountered balloon promoter Park Van Tassel, and from that meeting, a partnership was born. However, the circumstances surrounding the genesis of their joint venture remain in dispute.

By Park Van Tassel's account, he was the one responsible for coming up with the idea of a human parachute drop. He said that he found a dictionary or encyclopedia that had a picture of a parachute, from which he had a human-scale version constructed.[4] In contrast, Thomas Baldwin maintained that he, not Van Tassel, scoured public and private libraries for information on parachutes and that it was mainly his experimentation that resulted in a reliable design.

In September of 1886, Van Tassel and Baldwin took a small dog aloft and released it on their parachute from Van Tassel's balloon at Seal Rock Park. The device worked to perfection, leading Van Tassel and Baldwin to approach the manager of the local streetcar company about sponsoring Baldwin's jump. The price demanded was $1 a foot from an altitude of the manager's choice. Prudently, the man consulted the upcoming calendar of open dates for local events and selected Sunday, January 30, 1887, for Baldwin to attempt a leap from 1,000 feet, as measured by the length of tethered rope to the balloon. However, a parachute for a small dog was hardly the same as one needed for a man, and they needed help developing a scaled-up design.

A newspaper article published two weeks before Baldwin's first public jump suggests that the parachute they used was not designed from scratch by either man, but instead was provided by a trapeze artist who had recently performed in San Francisco. When a reporter from the *San Francisco Examiner* discovered Van Tassel and Baldwin conducting a manned test of their parachute in the confines of the city's cavernous Mechanics' Pavilion in mid–January 1887, he heard the following admission: "Further inquiry elicited the fact that the parachute was the patent of one of the two gymnasts who recently appeared at the Bush-street Theater, and was considered the safest thing of the kind ever invented.... Baldwin recently became enthused over a description of the workings of the thing as given him by one of the proprietors, and made up his mind to astonish the world with a big jump.... The parachute arrived a day or two ago, and yesterday was the first experiment of the new proprietors."[5]

The gymnast referred to by the *Examiner* was Charles Leroux, who was in San Francisco the week of January 9, 1887, at the Bush Street Theater performing a trapeze act with the Howard Athenæum Star Specialty Company.[6] Leroux, whose real name was Joseph Johnson, was from Waterbury, Connecticut, and had been a performing gymnast for about eight years. In the summer of 1886, Leroux had made headlines for a parachute jump from the bridge over Passaic Falls in New Jersey and jumping from the roof of the Dime Museum in Philadelphia. At one point he planned to make the Passaic Falls jump from a balloon but changed plans for reasons unknown. Leroux's parachute was small in diameter, which suited short jumps, but would have been dangerous from a higher distance. Leroux was not known to have made any jumps from a balloon prior to meeting with Tom Baldwin.

Leroux may have agreed to give his parachute to Baldwin and Van Tassel to let them be the first to take the risk. He surely could not have

Charles Leroux, an uncredited inventor of the balloon-parachute act (*London Graphic*, November 9, 1889; author's collection).

anticipated the fame and wealth that it brought to Baldwin. Left unknown is whether the testing done by Van Tassel and Baldwin resulted in modifications to Leroux's design. For instance, the parachute that Baldwin settled on for his first jump had a wider diameter than those used earlier by Leroux, and is it not known whether Leroux's parachutes had a vent at the crown.

Baldwin and Van Tassel's newly acquired parachute was different from any arrangement used in the past: it had no frame and no rigid skeleton. After making tests, Van Tassel and Baldwin settled on a design consisting of a circular, light muslin canopy about twenty-five feet in diameter with cord suspension lines leading down to a trapeze bar (Baldwin later just used an iron hoop to hang by his hands). To avoid the oscillation that plagued earlier parachutes, their parachute had a small circular vent at the top which served to stabilize the descent and decrease the likelihood of a rip in the fabric. In a departure from earlier parachute performances, the figure of the jumper would be fully exposed to view, not hidden in a basket. The parachute itself was not contained in a pack; instead, it was suspended from the side of the balloon by a light string, with all its suspension lines hanging limply down to the bar (or hoop) in the hands of the jumper.

Armed with their new parachute, Baldwin and Van Tassel were now prepared to make good on their promised exhibition on Sunday, January 30, 1887. The most evocative account of Baldwin's jump was found in the next day's edition of the *San Francisco Examiner*:

A Wonderful and Fearful Leap of 500 Feet

The magnet which drew such an immense gathering toward the Golden Gate Park yesterday was the published announcement that prof. T.S. Baldwin would make a parachute descent from a balloon, leaping from it while it was captive at an altitude of 1,000 feet.

Such a feat was never attempted in this city, the nearest to it being made the ascensions made from Woodward's Gardens some years ago, by a man who swung to a trapeze bar under a balloon inflated by heated air.[7]

No noticeable falling off in the usual Sunday contingent could be seen in the park proper, the crowds that thronged the vicinity of the music pavilion being fully up to the average. Added to these were fully 8,000 people of all sorts and appearances, gathered in groups, knots, and large crowds, on the sand lots at the Haight-street entrance to the park, while away on the surrounding hills, in every direction, were collected groups of spectators, each from its peculiar dash of high coloring giving a beautiful and pleasing contrast to the deep vernal green of the hills. As far as the eye could reach, black dots were visible, proving that the novelty and daring of the intended leap had a wide interest among all classes.

At 12 o'clock a party of men led by Professors Van Tassel and Whiteside

Four—Tom Baldwin's San Francisco Leap

began the preparations for inflating the balloon, the spot selected being directly south of the park entrance and opposite the P. and O. railroad depot. The balloon used was the "Eclipse," so well known in the past few years, as it has figured in several local ascensions of more than ordinary interest.

The balloon was filled to nearly its full capacity, holding about 35,000 cubic feet, and having, at the time of the ascension, about 28,000 feet. It was captive by means of a stout manila line leading through a "snatch block" and fastened around a heavy stake some distance off. To its side, up near the network, was attached a small block through which was received a light cotton line, one end leading into the car, while to the other was fastened the parachute with which the jump was to be made.

The parachute is, when expanded, very like an umbrella when opened, saving that the stick is not there. From its lower or wider end, at distances of a foot (its circumference [*sic*, diameter] being some twenty feet), are attached small cotton lines of the size of an ordinary clothesline. These are led together at some ten feet from the hoop which holds the parachute open to take the air, and from their combined ends is pendent a small crossbar from which the man hangs in his descent. The upper or smaller end is open some four inches in diameter and hemmed with leather to prevent its bursting, as the heavy pressure of air passing up through the aperture when the descent is in progress makes it liable to split, and therein lies the real danger of such an undertaking.

It was now 2:45 and the wind was a light breeze from the westward, not sufficient to throw the balloon ten degrees out of a perpendicular, while the genial

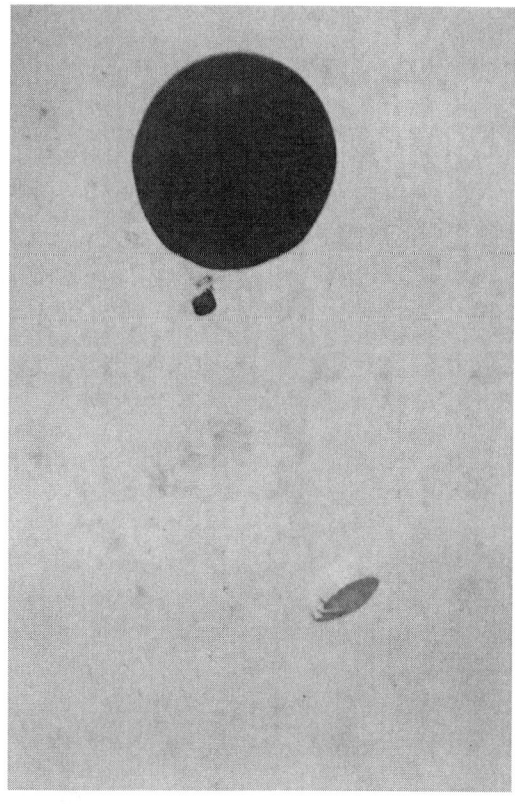

Tom Baldwin's January 1887 parachute descent at San Francisco (San Francisco History Center, San Francisco Public Library).

rays of the sun and the clear blue sky tended to make it as Professor Van Tassel tersely put it "a daisy time to go up."

All being in readiness for the act, the men holding the lines attached to weights that had held the balloon, closed in on the basket, and nothing but the rope by which it was to be captive held it. Professor Baldwin with an assistant jumped nimbly into the car, and at a signal from Baldwin the men eased of the rope and the balloon gradually rose. Good judgement had placed the parachute on the east side of the balloon, thus allowing it to hang clear as the balloon careened toward the east more and more as its tether became longer. While ascending, the Professor was greeted with cheers from the men and the general waving of handkerchiefs from the ladies. Some of the timid of both sexes hid their heads and some their ears, as if to shut out the expected catastrophe. The crowds broke and ran at will to positions where it was likely he would fall, and the diversity of judgment displayed in this was ludicrous.

Arrived at a height of some 400 feet the line was made fast and hundreds cheered, while many, especially ladies, bowed their heads, and such remarks as the following were general: "Oh, dear gracious, is he coming yet?" "My goodness, goodness sakes alive, he'll be killed stone dead." "Oh, what a foolish young man," etc.

The Professor, meanwhile, carefully shook out the bottom of the parachute, standing upon the edge of the car to do so, and arranged each little line so that all should bear equally in the downward strain. All being in readiness, and the balloon almost perpendicularly over her fastenings, the word was given and out he shot, clear of the basket, making a graceful swing as he brought up under the tension of the parachute, which latter opened handsomely, and, catching the breeze, together with the momentum his leap gave it, it sailed slowly in a slanting line, coming down gracefully and landing the professor in a front yard of a small house nearby, among a bunch of shrubbery, none the worse for his descent. A stop watch showed the time consumed in the descent to be 4½ seconds. So gentle, indeed, was the fall that he did not lose his footing, and picking up his parachute he marched off amid uproarious cheers, the envy of the men and the darling of the ladies.[8]

A different account added that as he worked his way back to his launch point, the exuberant Baldwin flipped back somersaults and ran a fifty-yard dash to show the crowd that he was totally unharmed and boasted that he would soon repeat the jump from the full 1,000 feet.[9]

Baldwin and Van Tassel scheduled their second public parachute jump for Sunday, April 3, 1887, in conjunction with a baseball game at San Francisco's Golden Gate Park. However, during the inflation of the balloon envelope, a strong gust tore a rent in the fabric, ruining their plans. The next month, May 1887, Baldwin appeared at a balloon ascension of Van Tassel's sponsored by the *San Francisco Examiner* but was not there to attempt a jump. After that, the two men parted company, apparently in a disagreement over their financial arrangement. Tom Baldwin returned to his hometown of Quincy, Illinois. On July 4, 1887, he made a parachute jump from his own untethered balloon at a height of several thousand feet in front of a crowd of 30,000 people at Quincy's Fairgrounds. A newspaper item datelined from Quincy declared the performance "the most daring and thrilling ever attempted by man."[10]

Within a month, Quincy, Illinois, was reported to be gripped by a parachuting craze. Retailers were selling new products of every sort using the brand name "Parachute." Young boys were throwing themselves out of barn lofts and second story windows with umbrellas (resulting in several broken bones). Others made pocket-sized parachute toys using paper or cloth, and by August, the city's telegraph wires and trees were littered with the novelties. One report mentioned that a consumptive-looking Quincy blacksmith (originally from Jackson, Michigan) named Bartholomew had witnessed the event and immediately decided to sell his business and devote his efforts toward matching Baldwin's feats.[11] Baldwin's landing appeared flawless to the crowd, but in fact he was shaken hard by the impact and spent a couple of weeks recuperating. Regardless, Baldwin had made himself as famous as the Great Blondin and inspired as many fledgling parachutists as Blondin had tightrope walkers.

Five

Gold Rush in the Heavens

There was no immediate rush to imitate Baldwin's feat of January 1887. Nearly all the balloon-trapeze act showmen resided east of the Mississippi and had ceased their operations for the winter. Moreover, no photographs or detailed descriptions of the design of Baldwin's parachute were published, so other aeronauts were in the dark as far as how to duplicate Baldwin's act. Indeed, some may have questioned the veracity of the San Francisco newspaper reports, withholding judgment until Baldwin brought his act back east.

During the winter of 1886–1887, Samuel C. Young and Charles W. Williams had been pursuing their separate theatrical careers, with the expectation that they would meet again in Cincinnati, Ohio, to spend the summer of 1887 performing the balloon-trapeze act they had learned from Harry Gilbert. On the stage, Young was a comic singer who specializing in performing an ethnic stereotype: the dull-witted German immigrant. Williams was a talented ventriloquist, known for his very life-like mannequins. In January of 1887, both saw the newspaper reports describing Baldwin's jump in San Francisco and—as experienced balloonists—assumed that they could duplicate it. They had no details concerning the construction of Baldwin's parachute, but they did have had the benefit of the experience of their mentor, Harry Gilbert. Though the literature on parachutes was scant, they decided their best option was to imitate the design of the Godards and their predecessors and use a solid-ribbed parachute suspended underneath their balloon.

Both Young and Williams had theater commitments that delayed any aerial work until early summer, 1887. While construction of their parachute was underway, the pair resumed their balloon ascensions at Cincinnati's pleasure resort, Coney Island, on the banks of the Ohio

Five—Gold Rush in the Heavens

about ten miles east of the city. Named after the New York seaside resort, Cincinnati's Coney Island was developed in the 1880s by steamboat operators and featured food vendors, concerts, dancing, games, and carnival attractions. On July 4, 1887, Young and Williams conducted a balloon ascension and from their basket launched a spectacular fireworks display, but on the same day, 450 miles to the west, Tom Baldwin was making his revolutionary parachute descent at the Quincy Fairgrounds.

Young and Williams finally had their parachute ready on July 30, 1887. A crowd of less than two thousand arrived at Coney Island to view the event. On the ground, before launch, their parachute looked like a closed umbrella supported by a stout oak rod at the center. From the top of the rod, strong bamboo ribs were arranged to fold out, which, when extended, measured about twenty-nine feet in diameter. Stretched over the ribs was a light canvas fabric. Strong cotton suspension lines ran from the outer tips of the ribs to a basket underneath, where the parachutist would stand. The parachute with its basket was attached by a single rope to an iron ring that supported the balloon; once the parachutist cut the rope, the pilotless balloon would shoot upwards and soon tip over and fall on its own accord. Charles W. Williams was selected as the first of the partners to make the attempt at parachuting.

The pair inflated the hot-air balloon using the tried-and-true method: the balloon fabric envelope was suspended between poles, its mouth opening placed over a chimney, a trench fire was lit, and petroleum was poured on the fire to generate great heat. Williams placed one of his legs in the basket and the other outside it to keep the basket from bouncing as it rose above the ground. Once clear, he lifted himself fully inside. In minutes Williams had cleared the treetops and ascended to two thousand feet. He then pulled on the cord connected to a pruning blade, cutting the lone rope that attached the parachute to the balloon. The parachute and Williams in the basket underneath dropped like a lead weight. Women shrieked and many in the crowd closed their eyes, but after a couple of hundred feet, the parachute canopy opened, and Williams drifted to the ground in the basket. As it fell, the parachute oscillated like a pendulum, forcing Williams to maintain a good grip on the basket. However, he alighted without a scratch, becoming the first American aeronaut to successfully imitate Baldwin.[1]

A week later, on August 6, Samuel C. Young took his turn in the parachute basket before a crowd of about 1,000 people at Coney Island. His balloon rose over the Ohio River, and at 3,000 feet, Young cut loose. The parachute opened and he came down in the low branches of a tree on the Kentucky side of the river. He easily stepped out of the basket onto firm ground. Both the parachute and balloon were recovered undamaged. Now that both men had tasted success, they looked beyond Coney Island to more lucrative venues where they could attract larger purses. With the help of a New York theatrical agent, they booked a half-dozen engagements to make jumps at county fairs in Ohio and upstate New York from late August through September, including Sabina, Ohio; Washington, Ohio; Binghamton, New York; Watertown, New York; and Mexico, New York. However, attendance at Williams and Young's upstate New York engagements paled beside Tom Baldwin's August 9 drop at Rockaway Beach, Queens, New York, and his September 22 jump at the New York State Fair in Syracuse.

At the New York State Fair, Baldwin was seen by 30,000 people and made $1,300 for one jump.[2] In contrast, on the very same day, New York's Ira Allen had been scheduled to make his very first jump from a balloon at the Mount Morris (NY) Fair for a more modest $300.[3] As it was, Allen's underinflated balloon failed to ascend to an adequate height, and he would not make his first public jump until September 1888 at a fair in Weedsport, New York. Ira's brother Martin also made a jump during that same 1888 Weedsport fair.

Tom Baldwin's sensational Rockaway and Syracuse appearances must have irked upstate New York's most accomplished balloonist, Carl Myers. Myers was growing increasingly nervous over staging balloon acrobatics. In July of 1887 (just after Tom Baldwin's jump at Quincy), at Olean, New York, one of Myers' hired trapeze-act aeronauts, Edwin Claridge, hit telephone wires while ascending and was knocked off his bar. Claridge fell and was fatally injured, leaving an impoverished widow and four children. Myers had announced that another of his performers, "Del Dare" (William Wilson), would make a parachute drop at the Atlanta, Georgia, Exposition in September 1887.[4] Ultimately, Myers decided against allowing Del Dare to make the jump. Similarly, he made several announcements that his wife, "Carlotta," would make jumps in 1887 and 1888, but always found reasons to cancel.[5] By 1889, Myers seems to have entirely soured on attempting the balloon-parachute act.

Even so, it was one of Myers's former aeronauts, William Rulison, who built the gas balloon that Tom Baldwin used for at jump at Potsdam, New York, on September 24, 1887. This performance had originally been scheduled for September 22, but Baldwin was delayed in Syracuse; moreover, there was a problem generating enough gas at Potsdam to enable a jump to be made. In a demonstration of collegiality, Charles W. Williams came to Potsdam from Watertown, New York, with equipment and his expertise to assist Rulison in getting the balloon inflated,

Five—Gold Rush in the Heavens

and Baldwin was able to make the jump.[6] Dating forward, Williams and Baldwin remained on friendly terms throughout their careers.

From their New York State appearances in 1887, Charles W. Williams and Samuel C. Young returned to the theater circuits in October 1887, having made more money from their summer of parachute jumps than they had ever made in previous years. They did not resume their balloon-parachute act until June of 1888, but still managed to make thousands of dollars in a handful of appearances (Newark, New Jersey; Hamilton, Ontario; Ottawa, Ontario; Louisville, Kentucky; and back at Coney Island, Cincinnati, Ohio).

Another of Harry Gilbert's Cincinnati protégés—aside from Young and Williams—was his adopted daughter Louisa "Lulu" Bates. Bates had made dozens of solo balloon ascents since the early 1880s, but her first documented parachute drop had to wait until 1888's July Fourth celebration at Sidney, Ohio. There, she made the descent from 1,000 feet, using a basket rig like that used by Young and Williams. In doing so, she became the first recorded woman parachutist of the post–Baldwin era.[7]

A month later, in August, Bates returned to Cincinnati and made a few jumps at the Coney Island resort. She was joined there in late August by Albert Tolbert, the Kankakee balloonist. Tolbert had made his first parachute jump at Washington, Indiana, in June 1888.[8] Where Tolbert obtained his first parachute is a minor mystery since he worked independently, but Tolbert had known contacts with both the Springfield Illinois balloonists and with Harry Gilbert's protégés in Cincinnati. Possibly, he might even had obtained his parachute from Tom Baldwin.

After September 1887, Tom Baldwin returned from New York to Quincy, Illinois, for the winter. With his earnings, he and his brother Samuel established their own balloon and parachute factory. Over the winter of 1887–1888, Tom entertained offers to make parachute descents in Europe. One anecdote suggested that Baldwin had been urged to go to England to reap windfall earnings by William F. "Buffalo Bill" Cody, who, earlier in 1887, had staged his Wild West show there to enormous success. Once Baldwin committed to go overseas, his brother Samuel Baldwin took over the bookings of jumps on American soil. Sam made his first leap at Quincy, Illinois, in July 1888. In September he performed several successful drops at the Buffalo (New York) International Fair.

The Baldwin brothers also offered to give instruction to patrons of their balloon and parachute factory. Several of their clients went on to become regular practitioners of the balloon-parachute act, but two of the first were Edward White of Wichita, Kansas (stage name W.E. St. Clair) and W.H. Leroy of Chillicothe, Ohio. These two students came from very different backgrounds: White was a 25-year-old single son whose mother had remarried into a large family—White was anxious to break out of the shadow of his stepfamily as quickly as possible. Leroy, already in his mid-thirties, had been a circus ropewalker and acrobat for fifteen years and had once worked on the high wire with Tom Baldwin.[9] Leroy made parachute jumps off towers in 1888 but did not jump from a balloon until he went to Quincy in April 1889.

In addition to obtaining equipment from the Baldwins, Edward White (aka St. Clair) also spent a few weeks in 1888 as an assistant to Ohio's experienced balloonist, John W. Biggerstaff (stage name Harry Warner). Biggerstaff made his first leap from a balloon at New Orleans in June 1888. His erstwhile assistant White tried to make ascensions several times throughout 1888, using a gas balloon he had purchased from the Baldwins. However, he had trouble getting adequate gas supplies from municipal gasworks. Eventually, he was able to make his first ascension and parachute descent at a fair at San Antonio, Texas, in November 1888—one of the final jumps in America of that year.

A bit of mystery surrounds another probable early follower of the Baldwins named Thomas F. Langford. Langford hailed from a rural township in Illinois about thirty-five miles north of Quincy, but appeared in Wichita, Kansas, in July 1888 claiming to be one of the first four parachutists in America.[10] Langford used a gas balloon rather than a hot-air balloon, which was a hallmark of the Baldwins. Langford made many jumps in Kansas and Oklahoma from August 1888 through to the early 1900s, but it was strictly a sideline from his profession as a plasterer. However, he did go on tour one summer as a parachutist with a short-lived railroad show, Harry Hill's Historical Oklahoma Wild West.[11]

Although the Springfield aeronauts—Hathaway, Gomes, Fisk, et al.—were geographically much closer to Baldwin's base at Quincy, Illinois, they were perhaps more inspired to emulate the parachute drops of Williams and Young, since they were well-known balloonists who had been exhibiting for several years with the trapeze act. As late as May 1887, there was no evidence that Hathaway and Gomes thought of copying Baldwin. Indeed, Hathaway and Gomes were then part of "Dr. Ryder's Medicine Show," traveling peddlers of patent medicines giving free shows, in which Hathaway portrayed "Dr. Ryder" and Gomes was a ballad singer.[12] However, as the summer progressed, they returned to ballooning and soon caught the parachuting craze.

In mid–October 1887, Hathaway made his first jump from the height of 1,200 feet at Galesburg, Illinois. Like Williams and Young, Hathaway's first parachute was semi-rigid, with ribs, and was already unfurled when he launched from the ground. Two months later, in early

December, Joseph Gomes made his first jump from 2,000 feet not far from his home in Springfield. Ned Hathaway opened the year of 1888 with his second jump, performed at Sportsmen's Park in New Orleans, Louisiana, in January. This was the kickoff of Hathaway's frenetic year, veering back and forth between parachuting and stage work.

Hathaway, under the name Edward M. Hurd, joined Steele Mackaye's *Paul Kauvar; or Anarchy* production in New York in early 1888 playing the part of "Goujon, a corporal in the Bonnets Rouge." Impresario Steele Mackaye was an immensely romantic figure of the American theatrical world: soldier, actor, artist, innovative playwright, inventor, and dreamer. He undoubtedly served as an energetic role model for Hathaway. During Hathaway's thirteen weeks in New York, he also served as a talent agent for booking Springfield's most experienced balloonist, Ira N. Fisk, to do parachute drops in April and May (bookings that Hathaway may have originally intended to do himself). Fisk's first jump of 2,000 feet was on April 17, 1888, at the Lansdowne Park resort in Natchez, Mississippi.[13] From that success, Fisk returned north and made a higher jump at Paris, Illinois, employing the same type of rig used by the Cincinnati and other Springfield aeronauts.

As Ned Hathaway was completing his New York stage work in *Paul Kauvar*, he signed up with a recently formed circus, the Miller & Freeman United Monster Railroad Show, to do parachute drops several times a week during their touring season. Although a small "ten-cent" circus, Miller & Freeman had the distinction of being the first conglomeration to feature parachute jumps from a balloon. Hathaway opened the circus season in early April 1888 with parachute drops at Newark, Ohio, before the troupe moved on to Columbus and Springfield, Ohio. The handbills prepared in advance for the circus depicted Hathaway in mid-air, hanging on to a parachute no bigger than an umbrella; the artist had obviously never seen Hathaway's real parachute jump.

At Columbus on April 26, Hathaway's parachute descent drifted over the city streets. He just missed striking a church steeple and instead was dashed against the chimney of an adjoining building. He suffered a bone fracture in a lower leg and many bruises from the subsequent bounces made in getting to the ground.[14] On crutches temporarily, Hathaway entrusted the circus performances to his two assistants: John Gillock, who was another young man from Springfield, Illinois, and Charles E. Colby, a balloon-trapeze performer from Massachusetts. Colby had previously worked with experienced Boston balloonist George A. Rogers (himself a protégé of balloonist Samuel A. King) but had not made parachute jumps before joining the Miller & Freeman circus. Hathaway was responsible for recruiting his friend Gillock, but it is not known whether Hathaway had previously known Colby or whether Miller & Freeman found him on their own.

Gillock and Colby continued to fill-in for Hathaway's Miller & Freeman circus performances, while he returned for a few weeks to the *Paul Kauvar* production, which had gone on tour. Hathaway was likely the one who arranged for either Gillock or Colby (or both) to moonlight from the circus by making parachute jumps under the name "Carvalli, the Italian" at the Oakland Garden summer resort in the Roxbury section of Boston.[15] Like Hathaway, Charles Colby was sidelined by an accident that broke his leg in June 1888 while jumping for the Miller & Freeman show in Marlboro, Massachusetts; this left Gillock as the remaining aeronaut for the circus. The circus tour ended in mid-summer, and by mid–August Gillock (as "Carvalli") and a healed Ned Hathaway were performing regularly at the Nantasket Beach resort on Boston's South Shore.

Hathaway spent the following year, 1889, pursuing his theatrical career, but returned to New England in the summer of 1890 to perform several parachute jumps at New Hampshire lake resorts and at Nantasket Beach. By 1890, Hathaway had likely made more drops than any other person alive—but had little to show for it. He appears to have spent money as soon as he made it. In 1891, he relocated to the St. Paul, Minnesota, area and teamed up with a local printer, T.I. Cash, to form the Hathaway-Cash Balloon and Parachute Company. They booked some performances at St. Louis, Missouri, and at Du Quoin, Illinois, where Hathaway had once worked on the railroad.

On May 22, 1891, Hathaway ascended at Du Quoin to 2,500 feet and then cut loose. His parachute failed to open, and he fell head over heels, turning three somersaults, before finally getting the chute partially open at 500 feet. He hit the ground hard and lay motionless for a long time. He was taken to his hotel. Later that evening, he made an appearance and seemed to be recovering, but in fact he had suffered a permanent injury.[16] After a long convalescence, Hathaway was able to return to work as a railroad brakeman in Chicago, where he resided with a brother. He died in 1909 at age 57 at a home for invalids.

Joseph Gomes, the balloonist friend of Hathaway, made his first parachute jump in December 1887 at Springfield, Illinois. Gomes was still partnering in the show ballooning business with fellow Springfield residents Thomas Jewell, William Smith, and Eleazer M. Wood. The company had survived a scandal involving Gomes, who in 1886 had eloped with an 18-year-old Jewish woman who had been engaged to another man. The lovers were tracked down before they could take vows, but weeks later they eloped a second time and married.[17]

The Gomes-Jewell combination typically had two or three balloon units to make multiple bookings on the same date, and Gomes frequently took charge of one of them. Gomes made several more jumps in 1888, but also saw his assistant, William Hanner, make his first jump on July 6 at Butte, Montana.[18] The Gomes-Jewell partnership ended during the 1889 season, with the principals Gomes and Jewell going their separate ways. Hanner stayed with Gomes, while Thomas Jewell took on as a partner bartender and part-time aeronaut Harry Gruber and two young men: Charles Richmond of Springfield and Edward Baltz of Buffalo, New York. Gomes continued touring with a balloon-parachute act until 1892, employing Hanner and a Springfield woman named Viola Wheeler, aka "Nina Van Upgo." He appears to have retired from the business when his brother James suffered broken arms and a broken back after a fall at Peoria, Illinois.[19] Joseph Gomes then resumed his lucrative singing career, starring as the featured tenor of the biggest and most successful minstrel troupe of the latter nineteenth century, Haverly's Mastodon Minstrels. He died in 1919, survived by his wife Goldie—the young woman with whom he had eloped.

Though younger than most of the other Springfield aeronauts, Ira N. Fisk started his ballooning career in the late 1870s, a few years before Hathaway, Gomes, Jewell, etc. He likely learned the craft from the city's first ascensionist, John Daniel Headley. It is a minor mystery why Hathaway and Fisk were not partners in the Gomes-Jewell company, though Fisk, like Hathaway, may have had other career commitments. Fisk's bookings were sporadic, to the extent that Hathaway tried to help him contract appearances in 1887 and 1888. Fisk's first parachute drop was to have been in New Orleans in January of 1888, but Hathaway abruptly had to step in to take his place. However, as mentioned earlier, Fisk did make his first leap a few months later, in April 1888, at Natchez, Mississippi.

Unlike Hathaway, who appeared to lose all the money he made, Fisk immediately invested his income in the lease of a resort at East Lake, Birmingham, Alabama—a newly-formed man-made recreational park. There he took on a local assistant, William K. Perry, and taught him the balloon business, dubbing their venture "The American Balloon Company." Perry and Fisk made dozens of ascensions in 1888 and 1889, touring throughout southern states. In August 1889, Perry ascended alone at a fair in Mount Holly, North Carolina. His balloon burst at 500 feet, and Perry was mortally injured.[20] Fisk continued to make ascensions for the next few years, employing both men and women to make parachute jumps. One of the female parachutists he introduced was Grace Shannon, of whom more will be said in a later chapter.

Ira N. Fisk gradually cut back his ballooning business in favor of managing town and city street fairs. Though he still infrequently had assistants making parachute drops, he also devised a timer mechanism that cut loose a parachute that held a cage of farm animals and opened a cage door to let pigeons fly free. Fisk retired to Cincinnati, Ohio, where he passed away peacefully in January 1928 at age 68—having never personally suffered a serious ballooning accident.

The youngest and most intriguing of the Springfield balloonists was James W. Price, born in 1862. Price's ballooning career was both long in duration and global in scope, but his character—especially his treatment of women—was shameful. Yet somehow, Price managed to have connections with many of the era's most successful parachuting impresarios. Price took the name of his stepfather, having been born as James W. Sisk, an alias he employed when convenient. He might have often had that need, being sent to jail as a juvenile delinquent more than once. In 1883 he married and soon divorced a woman named Elenora Wing (whose name will make a surprising return in a later chapter). Price made his first ascension in Springfield the following year, despite the doubts of the city residents who knew his reputation and wondered about the reliability of his heavily-patched balloon. Price may have obtained it from fellow resident Ira N. Fisk since Price gave his name as "Fisk" on at least on occasion.

Between 1884 and 1887, Price made several ascents in towns in Southern Illinois, Missouri, and Kansas. In 1884, he hired a young local tightrope walker named Joseph W. "Montz" Bozarth to do acrobatics on a trapeze hanging from his balloon. Bozarth had a cousin, Ida Bozarth, whom Price romanced and then married later that year.[21] In 1886, they had a son, Clarence Price, who was often left in care of Ida's mother. Ida took the stage name "Mlle. Viola," which newspapers transformed into "Millie Viola."[22]

Price made his first parachute jump in May 1888, becoming one of the handful of performers that followed Tom Baldwin's lead that year.[23] A few weeks later, he and Ida joined Cleveland-based balloonist Oscar Hunt and his wife, Lizzie, to conduct a series of ascensions and parachute drops in front of large crowds in Chicago, Illinois. On July 21, 1888, Lizzie (who used "Lottie Hunt" or "Lottie Leon" as her stage names) jumped from 5,000 ft. into Lake Michigan from Cheltenham Beach. Both couples alternated making parachute jumps that summer throughout the Midwest. Ida Bozarth Price took her turn, but some of her appearances were cancelled due to illness. Whatever chronic condition she had is not known, but she fell seriously ill in the winter of 1888–1889 and died at her parents' home in Missouri that March. The boy

Five—Gold Rush in the Heavens

Clarence Price was raised by his grandmother and never lived with his travelling father. Clarence, like his father, turned out to be a delinquent youth, and he died at age 22 from a morphine overdose.

Oscar Hunt and James W. Price opened the 1889 season still touring together but split up later that summer. In place of Price, Hunt took on King Burke (real name John Stokes), who had formerly worked with the Bready brothers.[24] Like Ida Bozarth Price, Oscar Hunt became increasingly ill starting in 1889, and he finally succumbed to paralysis in January 1893. Newspapers attributed his condition to ballooning injuries. Since splitting with Price, Hunt had employed a young teen woman named Isabelle Acker who took Lizzie Hunt's place as the troupe's female aeronaut, using the stage name Elsie Vandell.[25] After Hunt's death, King Burke performed as a balloonist for Ringling Brothers circus and for the Sells-Floto Circus.

The Jackson, Michigan, contingent of balloonists entered the field of parachuting in April of 1888, when Edward Hogan made his first jump from the dizzying height of 10,000 feet. Hogan, unlike the Cincinnati and Springfield aeronauts, directly copied Baldwin's method of descent, employing a limp parachute hanging from the side of the balloon, and the jumper leaping from the balloon basket, which released the lightly tied parachute from the balloon. The crowd was shocked to see Hogan free-fall nearly 500 feet before his chute expanded. In terms of dramatic value, this method was much more thrilling than watching an already unfurled parachute cut loose.[26]

In August of the same year, 1888, Hogan and his assistant William W. McEwen signed a contract to make a series of parachute jumps at Rockaway Beach—the same location where Tom Baldwin had made a jump a year earlier. Hogan and McEwen took turns performing the stunt. Like Hathaway's engagements at Nantasket Beach south of Boston, Hogan's dates at Rockaway Beach, Queens, New York, provided thousands of eastern city dwellers their chance to see this new stunt.

Edward Hogan's friend and enthusiastic aeronaut student Coryell Bartholomew (the blacksmith who had witnessed Baldwin's first jump at Quincy in July 1887) attempted his first jump at La Grange, Michigan, on August 20, 1888.[27] Ed Hogan employed the traditional method of inflating his balloon, connecting the crown of the envelope to a cable strung between two tall poles. The poles (between 25 and 45 feet high) themselves were set in shallow holes and kept erect by taut guy ropes. As Bartholomew's balloon filled, winds buffeted the expanding fabric and increased stresses on the poles. As Bartholomew watched, one of the guy wire stakes pulled loose, and the huge wooden pole started to tip over. Bartholomew grabbed one of the guy wires to steer the falling pole away from the crowd of onlookers, but the log still crashed to earth and pinned two boys, aged nine and 15, under its enormous weight. By the time they were extracted, they were already dead.[28]

Bartholomew's bad luck continued a few weeks later, at an ascension at Centreville, Michigan. On this occasion, the poles held steady as the balloon inflated, and it was held to earth until the last minute by a crew of volunteers who each held a rope that tethered the vessel. Bartholomew barked the command to let go, and as the men did so, one of the ropes whipped around the leg of a holder named Sanborn. He was lurched upwards by his leg and dangled in the air as the balloon rose higher. Bartholomew tried to drop another rope to him so that he could pull himself up onto the trapeze bar, but Sanborn could not climb all the way up. Fortunately, Bartholomew was using a hot air balloon, and the cooling of the air inside the envelope, combined with the extra weight of the passenger, allowed them to descend to earth before the rope unwound from Sanborn's leg. Jokes were later made that suggested that while dangling in the air, Bartholomew had quizzed Sanborn about whether he intended to vote Republican or Democratic in the upcoming election.[29]

At any rate, Bartholomew finished the season with a successful parachute jump at the Western New York Fair, where he had been accompanied by his mentor, Ed Hogan. Based on that success, Hogan recommended Bartholomew for an interesting offer he had received. Albert Spalding, the sporting goods magnate, was looking for an act to accompany the champion Chicago White Stockings on a world tour. Spalding, with some acumen, guessed that foreign audiences might not clamor to see a strange sport, but would flock to a game that also featured a daredevil act. Hogan's commitments prevented him from accepting, but Bartholomew gladly signed up. By Thanksgiving 1888, Bartholomew set sail from California and arrived in Hawaii, where he was to rendezvous with the baseball players.

One can wonder whether Bartholomew checked in with Park Van Tassel before leaving San Francisco. Van Tassel had been deprived of his aeronaut, Tom Baldwin, in the spring of 1887. He searched without success for some man brave enough to make the leap, and he even hired one who was announced as his brother "Charles Van Tassel," but whose real name was Charles Oliver.[30] However, just before their first attempt, a boy in the crowd accidentally tore the parachute, forcing the cancellation of the leap. "Charles Van Tassel" may have accompanied Van Tassel to a subsequent engagement in Salt Lake City, but no further.

Van Tassel's impatience mounted as the 1888 season got underway, and reports streamed in from the east of the many aeronauts that

Coryell Bartholomew. Note that the high-contrast circus outfits also made it easier for spectators to follow the movements of the distant aeronaut (author's collection).

had successfully made the jump. Van Tassel's wife of three years (his third marriage), the adventurous Clara Coykendall, agreed to try a jump in Los Angeles on the Fourth of July. Park Van Tassel went up in his gas balloon with her and helped her make the leap.[31] Had not Louise Bates made her first jump in Ohio a few hours earlier, Clara Van Tassel could have claimed to have been the first female American parachutist. However, one parachute jump was enough for Clara, so Van Tassel still needed another aeronaut.

By November 1888, Thomas Baldwin and the first class of his imitators had completed scores of parachute jumps, with the most serious injury to any aeronaut being a few bone fractures. Nearly all who had attempted the feat had experience as balloonists or acrobats, or both. That run of good fortune was bound to fail and did so before the calendar year ended. The two Cleveland partners, Owen J. Brady and Hubbard Vandegrift, earlier in the year had successfully introduced the parachute drop into their ascensions, starting in August at a Hillsboro, Ohio, fair and in September at the Montpelier, Ohio, fair. By November they had worked their way down to Columbus, Georgia.

On November 22, Vandegrift made a launch and rose to 3,000 feet, but his balloon tore open. With luck, Vandegrift dove off the trapeze bar and was able to separate the parachute from the deflating bag. He fell a long way before the chute opened, but then drifted with the wind over the Chattahoochee River. Many aeronauts had come to prefer water landings, but usually planned to have boats ready for pickup. It is not known whether Vandegrift had experience with water landings previously, but he came down in the water and started shouting for help. A small launch rowed out to him, and Vandegrift tried to climb over the side, but only succeeded in partially capsizing the vessel. By the time the boatmen righted their vessel, Vandegrift had slipped under the surface and did not arise.[32]

Vandegrift's sad end was a portent of the dozens of deaths that parachuting would tally in the coming years. A full reckoning of the danger of the balloon-parachute act would not come until after the craze had spread around the world. The global herald of this strange new mania was, once again, Thomas S. "Tom" Baldwin.

Six

The Craze Arrives in Britain

In May 1888, Thomas S. Baldwin made one parachute jump in Minneapolis—a site hastily settled upon after a failed negotiation to perform in Chicago. He then sailed from New York in mid–June 1888 and was met in London by his English sponsor and promoter, the Great Farini, otherwise known as William Leonard Hunt. Hunt had been born in Lockport, New York, and resided in Ontario, Canada; he was known mainly by his showman alias in England and often assumed to be Italian. Baldwin would have considered it an honor to meet Farini, who, a generation earlier, had been one of the greatest ropewalkers in the world—a rival to Blondin. After retiring from performing, Farini managed several daredevil acrobats and patented devices used in their performances. He is credited with originating the "human cannonball" act, which employed a rubber-strap and spring-driven platform mechanism, not explosives.

British newspapers made a point of mentioning Farini in their first articles about Baldwin and stated that they had co-patented the parachute that Baldwin was using. Indeed, a British patent application drawing with both names on it exists; the features they were claiming as original were the rib-less fabric and the stabilizing vent hole at the crown of the chute. Charles Leroux, from whom Baldwin had gotten a parachute, was making balloon-parachute jumps in New England in the summer of 1888, likely unaware of any patent claims by Baldwin. The patent application was likely urged by Farini to stave off British imitators, but if so, that intent was doomed to failure.

Farini arranged for Baldwin's first jump to take place at London's Alexandra Palace, one of the city's leading entertainment resorts with spacious open grounds. By 1888, Alexandra Palace had been used for balloon ascents for over a decade. Indeed, the Banqueting Hall at

Alexandra Palace was home to England's leading ballooning concern, the Green-Spencer family, and the facilities were frequently used for events by the Balloon Society of Great Britain. If any single locale could be considered as the center of British ballooning, that place was Alexandra Palace. Tom Baldwin could not have wished for a better venue to demonstrate his new stunt.

On Saturday, July 28, 1888, a crowd of thousands gathered at Alexandra Palace to watch Baldwin's stunt. Among the spectators were members of Britain's aeronautical establishment, including veteran balloonists Spencer, Wright, and Norman. The *Pall Mall Budget* reported:

> To the balloon, which had neither car, ballast, grappling irons, nor any of the impediments usually carried by aeronauts, was attached by a slipknot a parachute (in its closed condition a shapeless mass). From the parachute depended a long rope, to which the string of the slipknot was tied. Grasping the rope with his hands and winding his legs around the lower portion, Baldwin gave the word to set free the balloon. It ascended like a rocket, and in less than half a minute had attained a great altitude. All eyes were bent upon the balloon, which was suddenly seen to leap upwards with increased swiftness. Then a deep silence reigned, for it was perceived that Baldwin was free of the balloon. He had pulled the slipknot, and for safety had nothing to trust to but the seeming bundle above his head. For the smallest possible space he appeared motionless—suspended between heaven and earth, like Mahomet's coffin. But almost before the mind could grasp the situation he began to drop. Faster and faster, for 200 or 300 feet—no one, not even the performer, could exactly fix the distance—he came down like a stone. Then slowly, the bundle or sack above him changed its shape. It expanded, and assumed the form of a Japanese umbrella. Two or three seconds more, and all danger, save any that might arise from the inability of Baldwin to hold onto his rope, was at an end. The pace of the descent slackened. With his new species of balloon Baldwin floated gently through the air, and, with the easy grace of a butterfly setting upon some tempting blossom, rushed *terra firma*. The landing place was near where he had anticipated—a large field with an avenue of trees between the racecourse and the houses that of late years have been erected on the verge of the Alexandra Palace premises. Directly his feet touched the ground, Baldwin set off at a brisk run toward the Palace, and, scaling a gate, was met by an enthusiastic crowd that had hurried to welcome him after his perilous trip through the air.[1]

Baldwin made over three dozen jumps in Great Britain over the next three months. In contrast to London, where on eleven occasions he drew huge crowds, in Edinburgh, Scotland, the paid attendance was slight. It was reported that there was indeed a large crowd of tens of thousands of people there, but the majority decided the vantage point from Calton Hill was just as good outside the ascension ground gates as it was inside and viewed Baldwin's jump without paying for the privilege. So impressed were the onlookers by Baldwin's feat that the promoter later reported he had received hundreds of envelopes with

Tom Baldwin at the Alexandra Palace, London, England, August 1888 (*Illustrated London News*, September 29, 1888; author's collection).

postage stamps and money orders as "conscience money" from the free spectators.²

Illinois aviation historian Howard Lee Scamehorn summed up the acclaim that Baldwin received:

> From England Baldwin traveled to the Continent where news of his successes brought demands for performances in almost every large city of every country. He continued on to South Africa, Australia and New Zealand.... Throughout the tour his performances were as profitable as they were daring and breathtaking; net profits from the trip reportedly totaled about $65,000. Royal families, government officials and societies conferred jewels, honors and titles on Baldwin; French scientific society presented him with a ribbon. The English composer Felix Burns dedicated his "Cloud Land Waltz" to the famed aeronaut, whose picture appeared on the ornate cover. In Spain the Archbishop of Barcelona presented Baldwin with a gold medal bearing the archiepiscopal arms on one side, and on the reverse an inscription in Spanish, "for bravery, daring and respect for religion."³

Baldwin had scarcely departed Britain to continue his world tour before England's own balloon showmen put forth their first Baldwin imitator, George Higgins. Higgins, in 1888, was a 37-year-old carriage driver who—in earlier years—had been a capable amateur athlete, competing in long-distance runs, sculling and pedestrian races. He was enthralled by Baldwin's feat and was confident that he could equal it. To that end, he tested a cloth parachute of his own making and made test jumps from a 40-foot ladder. Higgins approached a veteran balloonist (also in his late 30s) named Alfred D. Orton. Orton, too, believed that Baldwin's jump could be equaled, though he scoffed at Higgin's homemade parachute and quickly started work on one of his own design, much more like Baldwin's in construction.

On October 28, 1888, a visibly nervous George Higgins ascended in the Orton balloon *Eagle* from the Greyhound Pleasure Gardens in North London. He quickly rose 2,000 feet and then cast loose. The parachute took a while to inflate, but Higgins landed safely less than a mile away, heartily cheered on by the large (mostly non-paying) crowd. He was later awarded a medal by England's Balloon Society.

Orton and Higgins had a successful fall season, but their partnership soured over the winter, and by the spring of 1889, Higgins had acquired his own balloon equipment and severed ties with Orton. Instead, Higgins found a new partner in "Signor Henri Balleni," an older English funambulist who, in his heyday, had conquered Niagara Gorge in the wake of Blondin and Farini. Balleni was also an amateur balloonist and in 1877 had submitted a patent on a "navigable balloon." His real name was Henry Newbold, born in Warwickshire. However, Balleni's fame had faltered until he teamed up with Higgins, and he had eked out a living performing music hall comedy.

By the time they combined efforts, both Higgins and Balleni had abandoned wives and children. Higgins had earlier been married to a woman named Matilda Dovey and had four children by her but left them on their own shortly before his first parachute jump. He had run off with Matilda's younger sister, Emily, who was (like Balleni) a music hall performer. In early 1889, Balleni and Higgins convinced Emily to join their aeronautical team as "Emmie Devoy."

Similarly, years earlier, Henry "Balleni" Newbold had split from his first wife and in the 1890s was living with a much younger woman, Ada MacDonald, who became a headlining parachutist under the tutelage of Higgins and Bellini.[4] MacDonald also had a background in theater; she operated a studio crafting women's costumes for the stage. Combining her passions, Ada MacDonald invented an electric lamp rig that would shine down on a parachutist, illuminating the figure floating through the night air. Finally, in the early 1890s, the Balleni-Higgins troupe added a young male assistant, Walter Mizen, and another young woman, Jenny Dene.

The Higgins-Balleni troupe had a successful run for two years, until August of 1891. Several ascents they had booked that summer had to be cancelled at the last minute due to dangerous weather, so when they reached Kirkstall, Leeds, Higgins was determined to make good on that contract. They decided to do a double drop, with Emmie Devoy hanging from one side of the balloon and George Higgins on the opposite side. As the two aeronauts took their seats on the trapeze perches, a stiff wind buffeted the balloon, wrenching it from the grasp of half of the rope handlers and causing a tear in the balloon fabric. Seeing the danger, Devoy leapt off her seat, but Higgins was unaware of the problems and shouted at the other handlers to let go. The balloon drifted sideways with the wind, with Higgins hanging lopsided, since the counterbalance of Devoy's weight was gone. The balloon struggled to rise and hit some telegraph wires. Higgins' legs were flipped over and his grip on the bar loosened. He fell forty feet and hit a wooden wall with his back, snapping it in two. By the time anyone could reach him, it was obvious his injuries were fatal.[5]

The troupe continued to perform for a few more years in the 1890s under the direction of Balleni. However, on one occasion Walter Mizen refused to make an ascent because he deemed it too dangerous, putting him at odds with his manager. Also, Jenny Dene made night jumps using Ada MacDonald's electric rigging, exciting the jealousy of its designer. Under these internal pressures the troupe split, with MacDonald and

Mizen forming a new company and Balleni retaining the control of Jenny Dene and the electric "leap in the dark" (despite MacDonald's patent violation threats).[6]

The next parachute jump in Great Britain came from a scion of the country's ballooning dynasty, the Spencers. Twenty-one-year-old Stanley Spencer made several jumps in January 1889—but they were not made from a balloon, but from within the 100-foot rafters of London's Olympia Hall exhibition center.[7] The young generation of Spencers were anxious to capitalize on Baldwin's feat, but patriarch Charles Green Spencer was less enthusiastic—no doubt he remembered the damage done to his father's reputation for his role in the death of Robert Cocking. Using a cautious approach, Stanley Spencer made indoor jumps at Olympia. His older brother Percival was the first Spencer to make a jump from a balloon, also in January—but Percival performed this in India, far from the glare of English newspapers.

Charles Green Spencer involved himself deeper a few months later in April 1889. He tutored an 18-year-old student, Frank Russett of Nottingham, to make test jumps from cliffs at Derbyshire's Black Rocks. Next, Russett was taken across the English Channel to Rouen, France to make his first jump from a balloon. Finally, Charles Green seemed satisfied that Russett could appear in England, and he successfully made his first English leap at Birmingham on the last Saturday in April.[8] Following that success, Spencer entrusted Russett to the care of his future son-in-law, balloonist Auguste Gaudron, to make a tour of ascensions and parachute drops throughout Northern Europe. Charles Green Spencer did not live to see either Gaudron's marriage to his daughter Marina, or the height of parachuting activity in Great Britain; he died of an unrelated illness in April 1890.

Percival Spencer returned from his tour of Asia in June 1889 and spent the summer making jumps throughout the Midlands and in Dublin, Ireland. During that same period, brother Stanley Spencer took on his own student parachutist: Alma Beaumont. Beaumont, whose real name was Mary Brown, spun several different backstories for reporters during her performing career, starting with the assertion that she had just arrived from "Omaha, USA." Prior to trying parachuting, she appeared as a swimmer in a water act in London. Later in her career, she gave up parachuting and returned to vaudeville and music halls with a swimming and trained seal act, calling herself "Odiva," a shipwreck victim raised on the South Sea island of Mauna. As Odiva, she performed all over the world until 1930, rivaling swimmer Annette Kellerman in both her popularity and sex appeal.

Percival, Stanley, and their brother Arthur Spencer performed

Alma Beaumont during a tour of South America, likely with one of the Spencer brothers (*Vida Fluminense*, Brazil, February 1890, http://www.amigospqd.com.br/Diversos/Alma.Beaumont-1890.html).

parachute jumps throughout the 1890s, but only occasionally. Both Percival and Stanley were keenly interested in other aspects of ballooning and often made voyages with scientists to conduct experiments and to test new innovations like a water "anchor" to keep balloons at an even altitude during water crossings. Additionally, all the Spencers conducted basket ascensions with passengers, which provided better publicity and income than parachute jumps. Alma Beaumont and Jenny Dene accompanied the brothers on some of their ascensions throughout the 1890s.

Following George Higgins's first leap in 1888, the next repeat in Great Britain of Baldwin's jump was not performed by any native son, but by Baldwin's first American mimics, Charles W. Williams and Samuel C. Young. Through the winter of 1888–1889, the two vaudeville veterans arranged a deal with English agent George Ware. Williams himself arrived in London in January 1889 to further the advance work. His first jump was in early April at Barnes, in conjunction with a university boat race. Unlike Baldwin and Higgins with their gas balloons, Williams used a much larger hot-air balloon. Moreover, as with the jumps he and Young made in America, the parachute was attached directly under the balloon, rather than hung from the side. A couple of weeks later, Samuel Young arrived from America and made his first jump at Harrow on April 22.

More uneventful jumps were made by Williams and Young in May 1889, but on June 4 at Alexandra Palace, Young used a new parachute that proved too small for his weight, and he dropped too fast, striking the ground hard. He was concussed and badly bruised, but the initial reports that he had broken limbs proved incorrect.[9] The management of Alexandra Palace sent a letter of reassurance to Parliament, which had expressed concern over allowing parachute leaps. A few days later, Williams went aloft and found himself unable to cut loose the parachute from the balloon. Instead, he sank down with the cooling envelope to alight on top of a roof; he was able to get down without injury. Williams and Young returned to America in September 1889, declaring their English tour a success. Samuel Young then devoted himself to his stage act and never returned to parachuting; he died of an unrelated illness just two and a half years later. Charles W. Williams, as will be seen later, saw the parachuting craze through to its peak and beyond.

Far from the metropolitan center of Victorian England, a local amateur balloonist from Huddersfield, Yorkshire was the next Briton to be billed as a parachutist. His name was "Captain" James Whelan, a former constable and town market official, who had been going aloft since 1875. Whelan himself did not make any jumps; instead, he appears to have had a unique talent for convincing other young men and women to go in his place. On April 22, 1889, in Belfast, Northern Ireland, Whelan offered a young lad only known as "Professor Ball" the chance to make the leap, which he performed flawlessly.[10] A couple of months later, back at Huddersfield, Whelan employed a local member of the town athletic club, John Whiteley. He, too, came down in good fashion.

Whelan continued to make infrequent ascensions that featured female parachutists from 1890 to 1893. He recruited them from the ranks of music hall performers including Maude Brooks, May/Lydia Niagara, Rose Bell (aka "Belle Carlotta"), and, on one occasion, Jenny Dene, on loan from Signor Balleni. Whelan broke his pelvis in August 1893, when he fell from a balloon basket during an ascension that did not feature a parachute jump. He lingered for a week, made out his will, and then died.

In the 1890 season, a new British parachutist joined those booking appearances at fetes and fairs. He started with immediate name recognition: Baldwin. However, this was not one of the American Baldwins, but an English music hall entertainer originally from Fareham, Hampshire. Charles Baldwin was managed for a year by his outspoken brother, Richard J. Baldwin. However, in October 1891, Charles placed an ad in the *London Era* announcing he no longer was represented by his brother.[11] Not to be outdone, Richard Baldwin took over as manager for Emmie Devoy, who was available due to the death of George Higgins. Charles Baldwin continued making self-managed jumps until 1896 and later resumed his career as the leader of a music hall comedy troupe.

Joining Whelan and Balleni in the employment of multiple women parachutists was a former Royal Navy military balloonist, George Philip Lempriere. A resident of Birmingham, Lempriere competed with Whelan for ascents in the Midlands and North England. When Whelan introduced female jumpers, Lempriere hired his own, also recruiting from the ranks of music hall dancers and acrobats. His first protégé was Cecelia "Cissie Kent" Browning, a music hall actress from London who made her first jumps in the summer of 1890. After jumping for two years, Cissie Kent returned to a successful stage career. Lempriere also managed ascents for Maude Brooks after she departed company with Whelan.

Lempriere's star for the 1891 season was Marie Merton, who—like Alma Beaumont, Ada MacDonald, and others—claimed to be American, in line with a trend among acrobats and music hall performers. By 1897, Lempriere advertised parachute drops by three women aeronauts: Maude Brooks, Marie Merton, and Kitty King.[12] Lempriere's troupe continued performances a few years into the new century, but in a tragic 1902 incident, Edith Brooks, the inexperienced sister of Maude Brooks,[13] made a drop in which her parachute lines got tangled, causing her death. That signaled the end of Lempriere's parachuting performances.

Perhaps the most famous corps of women parachutists were those managed by Auguste Gaudron, the husband of one of the Spencer siblings. After the death of Charles Green Spencer in 1890, the family ballooning firm slowly dissolved, as each of the sons pursued separate careers. In 1894, Gaudron began advertising himself for parachute drops and soon enlisted as a partner Alma Beaumont. Alma made jumps for Gaudron, Percival Spencer, and Stanley Spencer throughout the mid–1890s. In 1898, she was still working with Gaudron at Alexandra Palace, despite a failed marriage to a music hall comedian, Herbert Conway.[14] At the turn of the century, Alma pursued her aquatic act in Europe and later in the United States, where she became "Odiva."

Gaudron attempted to supplement Alma Beaumont with another young woman, Louisa Maud Evans, whom Gaudron introduced as "Mlle. Albertina." Gaudron had Louisa make her first ascent at Cardiff in July 1896, but for unknown reasons, she did not jump, but came down with the balloon in Bristol Channel and drowned. It was soon discovered that she was only 14 years old and had never parachuted before—facts that Gaudron testified he did not know. There was great public outcry over Louisa's death, with calls to prohibit parachuting and to prosecute Gaudron—but neither occurred.[15]

Gaudron did lay low for a season but returned with a running engagement at Alexandra Palace in 1898. He was a fixture there for over a decade, performing parachute drops there as well as sending teams around the country. However, Guadron remained interested in scientific ballooning and navigable flight, as did several of his Spencer in-laws, as well as his good friend at Alexandra Palace, the Wild West showman Samuel F. Cody. The fact that the parachuting act center of Great Britain was also its hub for airship development will be seen in more detail in a later chapter.

In 1903, Auguste Gaudron hired Dolly Shepherd as a jumper. Dolly was working for Gaudron alongside another woman, Edith M. Cook, who went by the stage names Elsa Spencer or Viola Kavanagh (or Viola Spencer). Dolly recalled that Edith was always willing to substitute for other members of Gaudron's team, as she did for Dolly at Coventry on July 9, 1910. At the end of her descent a gust blew her onto the roof of a factory. A second gust pulled her off the roof, causing her to fall. She sustained fatal internal injuries.

Many years later, Dolly penned the only memoir published by a balloon-parachute jumper, titled *When the 'Chute Went Up*. Dolly's book remains an invaluable resource on the techniques and experiences of early parachutists, though her performances took place more

Six—The Craze Arrives in Britain

than a dozen years after it was first introduced and after the heyday of most of the other performers mentioned in this text. As Shepherd's account makes clear, the British popularity of the balloon-parachute act was largely based on the appearance and charisma of its female practitioners, even more so than in America.

TERRIBLE DESCENTE EN PARACHUTE

Death of Viola Spencer (Edith Maud Cook), employed by Auguste Gaudron (*Le Petit Journal*, July 24, 1910; author's collection).

Seven

A Global Frenzy

Following Tom Baldwin's triumphal three-month tour of Great Britain in the summer and early autumn of 1888, he resumed his year-long west-to-east world tour. From Britain, his itinerary included stops throughout Europe, South Africa, Australia, and New Zealand before a planned return to the United States in the summer of 1889. The world's show-ballooning community was aware of his plans and jealously envisioned the wealth he would accumulate. However, by the summer of 1888, there was no mystery left concerning the equipment and techniques used by Baldwin. Little wonder, then, that more than one aeronaut realized that riches could be made by eclipsing Baldwin's slow-paced tour schedule, thereby beating him to be the first to parachute in many of the nations of the world.

As mentioned in an earlier chapter, the first entrepreneur to realize this possibility was not a balloonist, but was the shrewd sporting goods magnate, Albert Spalding, who needed a complimentary act to draw audiences to his worldwide (east-to-west) professional baseball tour. Spalding arranged to have Coryell Bartholomew, the Jackson, Michigan, aeronaut who had been tutored by Edward Hogan, meet the baseball team in Honolulu, Hawaii.

Upon his arrival in Hawaii, Bartholomew made no jumps, but he told reporters that there was no reason why the balloon-parachute act could not be accomplished locally—the smoke balloons he used went straight up so quickly that they did not travel far, allowing the parachutists ample time to make a drop before encountering the danger of drifting out to sea. After the baseball all-stars arrived in Hawaii, Bartholomew joined them on the voyage to Australia, reaching Sydney in mid–December 1888.

Imagine the chagrin of Spalding and Bartholomew (not to mention balloonists around the world) to learn that a 33-year-old local watchmaker had already made Australia's first parachute jump the week before their ship arrived in Sydney. The jeweler's name was John T. Williams. He was an amateur gymnast and inventor who had been experimenting with parachutes for many months. Williams was a friend of fellow Sydney watchmaker Harry Henden. Henden, as it happened, was an amateur balloonist and had learned aeronautical skills from the early resident balloonist of London's Alexandra Palace, John Morton.[1] When Henden emigrated to Australia in 1884, he brought a balloon with him, acquired from the Balloon Society's Thomas Wright.[2] With it, Henden had made several ascents in Sydney before teaming up with John T. Williams to make a parachute jump on December 8, 1888, at the city's Ashfield recreation park.

Albert Spalding was further annoyed by the fact that Bartholomew's ascensions were often cancelled due to wind, whereas the same conditions allowed baseball to be played. When Bartholomew declared he could not go up, crowds often left in disappointment without even bothering to stay for the demonstration of the American pastime. As the tour progressed across Australia, Bartholomew made a jump at Ballarat on January 12, 1889, that resulted in a serious injury to his leg. Consequently, Bartholomew was sidelined for much of the remainder of the Spalding tour of India, Egypt, and Europe. Accounts of the 1889 baseball exhibitions, such as Mark Lamster's book *Spalding's World Tour*, portray Bartholomew as mercurial and eccentric—made into a comic foil by the baseball men due to his glass eye.

When Spalding's tour left Australia and made a brief stop in India, they discovered that Percival Spencer had already made several jumps there as demonstrations for British Army officials. On January 27, 1889, Spencer made his first descent in Mumbai (Bombay) in front of a crowd of 190,000—likely the largest audience ever to witness a balloon ascension up to that date.[3] Less than two months later, Spencer made an ascension in Kolkata (Calcutta) in front of what was reported as over 200,000 spectators. Spencer relied on gas balloons, and on this occasion, the gas available to him was barely enough to inflate the envelope. Rather than disappoint the crowd, Spencer went aloft without the added weight of the parachute, in belief that the crowd would be somewhat pleased by the ascension alone. He drifted out of sight, leaving the entire populace to wonder about his fate. He landed in a small remote village, requiring three days to return to the city. By that time, he was given up as dead and the rejoicing at his return was immense.[4]

Spencer returned to England after this short trip, realizing that he needed to conduct future tours with much better gas generating equipment. He returned to tour the Far East the next year, in 1890. This trip included jumps performed for the Japanese emperor and an audience of

Percival Spencer's parachuting demonstration at Bombay (*Scientific American*, Supplement, Volume 28 [Munn and Company, 1889]; author's collection).

thousands. A notable by-product of Spencer's Japanese visit were several startling paintings made depicting Spencer's balloon-parachute act, rendered in traditional Japanese style. They represent one of the earliest examples of Japanese enthusiasm for ephemeral elements of Western popular culture. The Spencer brothers continued to make tours throughout the globe during the 1890s.

Charles Leroux, the Connecticut gymnast whose loan of a parachute to Tom Baldwin helped kick off the parachuting craze, embarked on a foreign tour of his own in 1889. In mid–April 1889, Leroux performed at jump in Berlin from the grounds of the German Military Aeronautical Department. Leroux was said to be somewhat alarmed at the keen interest shown by the German officers. From Germany, Leroux toured through Russia and Latvia before arriving in Estonia in September. The tour had been plagued by failed ascensions and underwhelming receipts, but the residents of Tallinn, on the Gulf of Finland, were eager to see him. Leroux launched the balloon despite a stiff wind and drifted over a residential area. After clearing the buildings below, he cut loose; the wind quickly took his chute out over the Baltic Sea, where he dropped into the water and drowned. The townspeople provided him with a lavish funeral, and to this day Leroux is revered there as an aeronautical pioneer.[5] Ironically, Leroux is better known in Estonia than in his home country.

As Tom Baldwin finally reached the final stages of his 1888–1889 tour—New Zealand and Australia—he had grown used to commanding large fees for his jumps. Bartholomew had cancelled an ascension while in New Zealand, so Baldwin was the first to parachute there. In New Zealand, the promoters set high ticket prices at the gate to the ascension grounds to cover Baldwin's appearance demands. This caused a low turnout, with Baldwin's share so paltry that he lost money. Once he reached Sydney, Australia (where Williams and Bartholomew had already made jumps), the advance ticket sales were poor that they did not meet Baldwin's standard of £500, and he refused to go up. This caused his Australian backer to lose £1500. Baldwin reversed his journey and returned to Europe and England, where he was hailed as a returning hero, and then sailed home via New York.[6]

A little more than a year after his return to the United States, in November 1890, Baldwin set sail from San Francisco for a second overseas tour. He was lured by standing invitations he had received during his previous tour, as well as by the success that his British counterpart, Percival Spencer, was currently garnering on his second Asian tour.

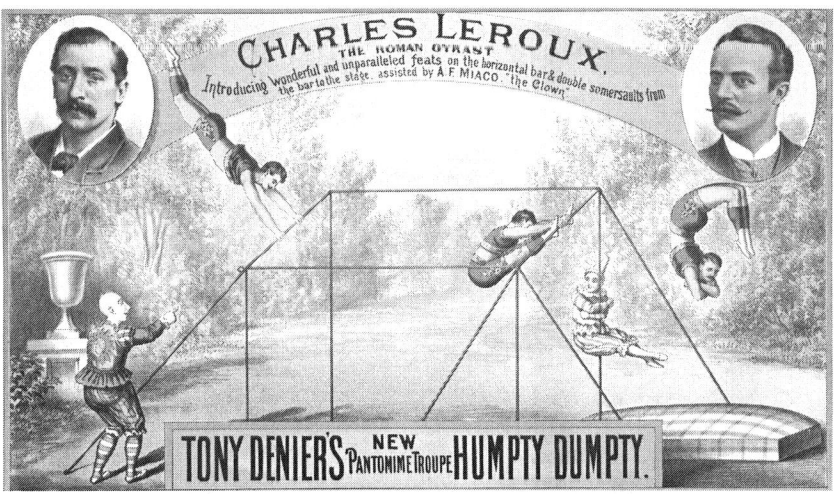

Tony Denier's new pantomime troupe Humpty Dumpty: Charles Leroux (left), the Roman gymnast. The man at right may be Al Miaco, a famous clown, but his identity is not confirmed (Jay T. Last Collection, Huntington Digital Library, priJLC_ENT_000278).

Baldwin was accompanied by his wife; brother Sam Baldwin; and William Ivy, i.e., "Ivy Baldwin," a charismatic acrobat and aeronaut who was a favorite associate of the brothers. They arrived in Japan just after Spencer completed his last performances. Despite having had its thunder stolen, the Baldwin troupe still was able to impress the Japanese with its double jumps from one balloon and with Ivy Baldwin's high-diving act.

Percival Spencer dropping flyers during an ascent in Japan before descending in a parachute. Artist: Kunisoda III ("Japanese scene with one man ascending with a balloon and another man descending in a parachute," Smithsonian National Air and Space Museum [NASM A20140967000]).

From Japan the Baldwins visited Chinese ports, Hong Kong, Vietnam, Singapore, Java, Malaysia, Burma, Calcutta, and other cities in India. A constant irritation was trying to find enclosed fields from which they could make ascensions while charging admission. In most cases they had to resort to using open fields with rope boundaries maintained by police. Their tour was cut short by Mrs. Baldwin's final trimester of pregnancy, and they returned to Quincy in late spring 1891.[7]

By the summer of 1889, Park Van Tassel—Baldwin's original partner in San Francisco—was doubtless aware of Baldwin's original letdown in the South Pacific and of the small handful of jumps made by Bartholomew and J.T. Williams in Australia. Van Tassel would have also seen how the deluge of parachuting aeronauts in the United States was driving down gate receipts in his native land. Van Tassel decided that a balloon-parachute tour of the South Pacific and East Asia still held great promise and that his experience as both a professional tour promoter and experienced balloonist might reap more success than those without that background. However, Van Tassel was no acrobat, and though his wife had jumped once in Los Angeles, neither she nor he wanted her to repeat the stunt. Van Tassel himself, though overweight, made a few jumps in California the first half of 1889, but weight often made a difference in getting a balloon to ascend at all, so he needed a more slightly built aeronaut.

Two years earlier, he had tried to employ a surrogate, "Charles Van Tassel" (Charles Oliver), who soon sought a different vocation. In the summer of 1889, Van Tassel took under his wing Joseph Lawrence of Fort Scott, Kansas, and dubbed him "Joseph Van Tassel." In October 1889, Park Van Tassel, Joseph Lawrence, and their partner Frank Frost set sail from San Francisco for Honolulu, Hawaii, the first stop in their Pacific tour. A fourth man rendezvoused with them in Hawaii: James W. Price, the Springfield, Illinois, aeronaut, travelling now as "James P. Van Tassel."

Arriving in the islands, Joseph Lawrence made his first successful jump at Kapiolani Park, near Diamond Head on November 2. On November 16, Lawrence made another ascension, rising from the Punchbowl north of the Palace in Honolulu, where he cut the parachute loose. He was carried by a stiff wind westward over the Kalihi waterfront, helpless as he drifted out 600 yards over the water and splashed into the Kalihi Channel. No boats were nearby, and it was reported that Lawrence had refused to take a life buoy with him. By the time a launch arrived on the spot where he had splashed down, there was no trace of him except a trail of blood. Most observers concluded that he had been attacked by a school of sharks. Later, a Kansas newspaper printed the last letter Joseph had sent home, which read:

I have got properly "on to" my partners. Frost is all right, but Van has been beastly drunk ever since we have been here, and has made more enemies than friends. I have not been going around with him, and he is mad about it. I told him I was not raised among bar room loafers, and would not associate with them. We are supposed to make an ascension this afternoon, but things are not ready, and Van is at home in bed, drunk, and if there is anything done he will have to do it, as I will not take any chances on my life with a drunken man. If I can get a position here of any kind I will remain in preference to going along with the party all of whom have been on a continuous toot since leaving Frisco. They have all spent the money they had. I am very nervous this morning.[8]

Frank Frost later wrote to American newspapers and denied that Van Tassel had been drunk the day that Lawrence died.

Imagined fate of Joseph Lawrence, aka Joseph Van Tassel (*Illustrated Police News* [London], December 14, 1889; author's collection).

With the death of their aeronaut, Van Tassel and Frost turned to the veteran of the balloon-parachute act, James W. Price. Price, as it may be recalled from an earlier mention, had spent the season of 1888 and 1889 with Cleveland's Oscar Hunt and his wife. In early 1889, Price's wife had died, and later that summer he split up with Hunt and headed to the western states. He hired a new female partner who employed the same stage name as his deceased wife, "Millie Viola" (this was likely done so that printed publicity material from the previous year could be used). The real name of this young woman is not known, but she did pose as Price's wife when the pair went to perform at Salt Lake City's Lake Park in June 1889. In Salt Lake at the same time was Park Van Tassel, and, though temporary rivals, the two balloonists struck up a friendship.

While performing in Salt Lake, a 14-year-old girl named Georgie Angell became infatuated with Price, and he took advantage of her, promising to wed her. Her parents found out and had Price arrested. Price consented to marrying the girl, realizing that was his only way to avoid jail. Price then left town with the girl, heading north to engagements he had made in Montana. At Butte, Georgie Angell went to the sheriff and accused Price of adultery and of encouraging her to engage in prostitution. Price was brought before a court, but Angell declined to appear against him. Upon hearing threats that he would be tarred and feathered, Price hastily left town, abandoning Georgie Angell. She was provided with means to get back to Salt Lake City.[9]

Price, now owning a foul reputation that threatened to hang around his neck like an albatross, headed west to California, where he rendezvoused with his new pal, Park Van Tassel, and made plans to join Van Tassel's Pacific tour. Price later stated that he and Joseph Lawrence both made jumps while in Hawaii. Despite the gruesome fate of Lawrence, Price, Park Van Tassel, and Frank Frost left Hawaii in early December 1889, determined to continue their tour. Their mail packet stopped first in Auckland, New Zealand, and by early January the party disembarked at Sydney, New South Wales, Australia.

Price made his first jumps at the Bondi Aquarium near Sydney in the first weeks of the new year. By the end of the month, the Van Tassel balloon ascensions were preceded by a non-balloon trapeze act performed by sisters Gladys and Valerie Freitas, who were announced as "Gladys and Valerie Van Tassel."[10] Most accounts described the group as a family, with Park and James Price as brothers and the Freitas women as sisters; however, in some cases Park Van Tassel was listed as the father of the clan. The Freitas sisters had been performing in Sydney music halls since the previous November, but newspapers failed to identify the

Van Tassel sisters as the Freitas sisters until years later, so the public believed them to all be related.

The intent of adding the Freitas sisters (both under twenty years old) to the party was to train them in the balloon-trapeze and balloon-parachute acts. Both Valerie and Gladys made their first jumps at Newcastle in February 1890. The Van Tassel troupe had a good run in the towns around Sydney in February and March, but the allegations that they spent money as soon as they made it must have been true, because they ran into a bind once they moved south to Melbourne. There, Park Van Tassel needed to take on a backer to fund the purchase new equipment. He brokered a deal with Madame Cora de Lamond, an experienced magician who had conducted her own successful international tours for years. Unknown to her, Van Tassel also made a separate deal to split profits with actor Edwin Thorne. When Madame Cora learned of Van Tassel's duplicity, she brought a legal suit against him.

Whether this legal woe was the direct cause of a split between Park Van Tassel and James Price or whether Price cut ties first and thereby caused Van Tassel to seek other partners is not known. In April 1890, Price started to make appearances under his own name, and he was accompanied not by one of the Freitas sisters but by a new female partner who adopted Price's well-worn co-star name, "Millie Viola." The real name of Price's newly incarnated partner was Ruby Hawker, one of a trio of sisters from New South Wales who would all eventually become parachutists.[11]

James Price and Ruby Hawker worked their way through south Australia, then headed south to Tasmania, and finally northwest to Western Australia, reaching Perth in February 1891. There, Price and Hawker struggled to get a balloon in good repair and inflated; they had to call off several ascensions. Ruby ("Millie Viola") and Price parted ways in June 1891, after Price determined to make his way to South Africa. Price spent the next four years in South Africa making ascensions before returning to Australia in late 1895. Meanwhile, Millie Viola stayed in Perth for several months, making solo ascensions. She then returned to New South Wales where she and her sister, Ethel ("Essie Viola") performed the balloon-parachute act for several years, as did their older sister, Lillian Hawker as "Leila Adair." In late 1895, Ruby and Ethel set sail for America, arriving there in January 1896.

At about the same time, in late 1895, James W. Price returned to Sydney from South Africa and convinced the third Hawker sister, Leila Adair, to come to America with him via a steamer bound for Hawaii and Vancouver.[12] She was, at that time, recovering from a failed romance that had produced two children and had been part of an underwhelming tour of New Zealand in 1894. Upon their arrival in Honolulu, Price opted to stay in the islands for nearly a year, performing ascensions in conjunction with Wirth's circus, managed by an old friend of his, Wilfred Burns. Burns had made a balloon tour of Western Australia in the last half of 1891, perhaps using equipment left by Price. Leila Adair did not delay in Hawaii with Price, instead continuing to America, where she settled with her sisters in San Francisco. All three sisters continued to perform as parachutists for roughly a year before pursuing marriages. Leila also made headlines in San Francisco when she tried her hand at hard-helmet sea diving.[13]

After splitting with James Price in Australia in April 1890, Park Van Tassel continued to tour with the Freitas sisters, aka Gladys and Valerie Van Tassel. Disaster struck a few weeks later in late May at Breakfast Creek, New South Wales. During inflation of the balloon, one of the two large poles used to hold it up fell into the crowd, landing with full force on the head of a young boy, who was killed instantly. Van Tassel defended himself during the resulting inquiry, maintaining that he had warned the crowd several times to stand clear. He was acquitted, but controversy followed the troupe.[14] At Townsville, Queensland, the Van Tassels performed on a Sunday in a very conservative, Christian community drawing the ire of a major local pastor—who was further incensed to see the local military unit participating in the festivities.

Perhaps aware that his tour was facing waning popularity, Park Van Tassel left Australia in late summer 1890 and headed north to Java, and from there he traveled to Sumatra, Malaysia, Shanghai, the Philippines, Penang, Burma, and India. In a letter he sent from Calcutta to a friend in San Francisco in September 1891, Van Tassel also made a claim to have performed for the Emperor of Japan (as Percival Spencer had in 1890).[15] Sometime in 1891, he lost the services of the Freitas sisters. Gladys married an estate manager from Delhi she met in Malaysia, and years later, Valerie married the son of a British army officer in Calcutta. In their place, Van Tassel trained a young woman from England named Jane Rumary, who adopted the name "Jeanette Van Tassel." In March 1892, while performing in Dhaka, Jeanette landed in the trees. Bamboo poles were extended for her to crawl down, but she fell from them directly onto her head. She died shortly afterwards.[16]

Park Van Tassel toured Asia conducting balloon-parachute ascensions from 1892 until 1901, but never revealed much detail about his travels other than that he had visited many countries, among them the Philippines, Hong Kong, Persia, Russia, Germany, France, Italy and India, where he had spent the majority of those years. More light on his activities can be found in the letters of Van Tassel's likely partner during those years, John Adelbert "Burt" Walker of Adrian, Michigan, who was very likely the mysterious aeronaut dubbed "Professor Lawrence" who worked with Van Tassel during that period.

Burt Walker had been a student of Coryell Bartholomew, the Jackson aeronaut, during 1891. Bartholomew had just completed his worldwide tour accompanying Spalding's baseball exhibitions and must have placed the idea of going abroad in Walker's head. In the fall of 1891, Walker made ascensions under Bartholomew's direction in company with a young woman, Gertrude Clausen, who went by the stage name Gertie Carmo. During one dual ascension, while in mid-air, Burt Walker asked Clausen to marry him. They agreed but settled on having the ceremony after Walker returned from his world tour. Their dreams were never realized—in August 1892 at the Detroit Exposition, Gertie struck a tower during an ascension and fell to her death. Her compact with Walker was found in her diary after her death.[17]

Walker left Adrian for the Orient in December 1891, before Gertie's accident. It is not known whether he received an invitation from Park Van Tassel before starting out; more likely, he teamed up with him after arriving in the Far East. But Walker did come back to the United States in July 1901, on the same Hong Kong steamer with Van Tassel. Upon his homecoming, the *Adrian Daily Telegram* reviewed his travels, which align with the stops mentioned by Van Tassel:

> He first visited Japan and China, in which countries he spent only about three months. He was allowed to make ascensions only at Shanghai, for it was feared that when the vast crowds assembled (he having at times an audience embracing as high as 800,000) a riot would follow, which usually occurs when so vast a multitude gets together.
> From these countries he next visited the Strait settlements, found along the straits of Malacca. He stopped enroute at the islands of Borneo, Sumatra, Java and the Dutch East Indies. Then followed his trip to Australia and Tasmania, where about eight months were spent making some 25 ascensions.
> Burt then went to India, where he spent two years, virtually traversing that great country from length to breadth. At Calcutta he made the only gas balloons, two in number, that he ever used, as gas was only obtainable there and at Bombay. A trip down the east coast of Africa was next in order, where he landed at Durban. From there he went by rail to Petermaritzburgh and Ladysmith, also to Charleston, which borders on the Transvaal. He afterwards visited Johannesburg and Pretoria, and while in Africa visited the old home of Rider Haggard, in which he wrote "She" and "Allan Quartermain." He next visited the Orange Free State and Cape Town. Having seen all the sights in this part of the world, he again sailed for India by way of Mauritius, Ceylon, and Colombo. This time he passed through India and

commenced his tour of Persia. His trip from Bombay by the way of Baghdad to Teheran was by caravan, which occupied two months. Completing the Persian trip he went to Batum, Russia, where practically all of the oil for that country is obtained. Next Odessa, also on the Black Sea, was visited, the trip being made by way of Constantinople. While in Persia he visited the governor of Tigris, who is now the shah of the entire country.

En route to Berlin, Germany he spent some time at the famous hot springs at Aachen. Then followed ascensions through Germany, France, and Italy, returning again to India. For the past three years he has made no ascensions, spending that time as one of the foremen who superintended construction of a railway from Burma through the border of China. This took him overland to the borders of Tibet.[18]

During all his travels, Burt Walker kept a diary (as his fiancée Gertie Carmo had done), collecting enough anecdotes to publish in a book. The diary, along with a fine collection of gifts he had received and artifacts he had collected, were lost during a shipwreck near Bombay in 1897. Had Walker written his book, it might have become a classic travel adventure narrative. When Walker returned to Adrian, Michigan, in 1901, he never again ventured abroad. He married (but did not have children), operated a quarry and spent the rest of his active years moving rocks and gravel. A more unfitting end to a career of youthful, romantic adventure is hard to imagine.

Eight

A Carnage of Daredevils

At the close of the year 1888, Thomas Baldwin was in the middle of his round-the-globe tour; his first English imitator had made his first drop; J.T. Williams had just made Australia's first jump; and the world tours of Bartholomew, Van Tassel, Price, and Walker had yet to conduct their first performances. At this point in time, the balloon-parachute act had been successfully executed hundreds of times by a few dozen people (perhaps 30), nearly all of whom were experienced balloonists or acrobats, or both. Their safety record was impressive: by the end of 1888, the only fatality to a performer was the drowning of Hubbard Frank Vandergrift at Columbus, Georgia—a freak accident attributed to a swift current. That illusion of manageable danger was about to change.

A few of the deaths that occurred in the years after 1888 have already been mentioned: Joseph Lawrence (Joseph Van Tassell), Jane Rumary (Jeanette Van Tassell), George Higgins, Edith Brooks, Gertie Carmo, Louisa Maud Evans (Mlle. Albertina), and William K. Perry. There is no accurate count of the number of those killed performing the balloon-parachute act. A gleaning of newspaper clippings from the period provides most of the names, but even they were often inaccurate—sometimes newspaper accounts pronounced certain deaths that later proved to be non-fatal injuries. In July of 1891, the manager of a parachuting troupe, Mortimer McKim, told the *New York Herald* that twenty-two aeronauts had died in the 1889 season; thirty-eight had died in the 1890 season; and on the Fourth of July 1891, four had died in one day in separate incidents.[1] In 1895, the *Boston Post* estimated that the average career span of a parachutist was two years before they suffered a life-ending accident.[2]

The deaths previously noted also introduce the variety of dangers that faced parachutists. Landing in water was often preferred by aeronauts as softer, but if one became entangled in the floating lines of the sodden parachute, one could easily be dragged beneath the surface (see

Eight—A Carnage of Daredevils 79

Vandergrift, Lawrence, Evans). Landing in a tree or atop a building could leave the jumper dozens of feet above the ground, with no easy way to be extricated (see Rumary). Ascents made in windy conditions, with inadequately inflated balloons could sweep a parachutist against buildings and structures, knocking them off their perch (see Higgins, Carmo). An overinflated balloon might not tear until it ascended, due to decreased air pressure, causing the fabric to burst at its seams (see Perry). Parachute lines could tangle, causing the fabric to not fully open. Trapeze bars on which one sat were held by ropes that sometimes rotted. Hot-air balloons could be sent aloft with smoldering embers from the inflation fires settling into the fabric, which could consume the balloon envelope in fire. Sadly, there were incidents where sabotaged equipment caused accidents. Even normal, seemingly safe landings were still jarring enough to gradually cause lasting damage to the spine; though these did not cause immediate injury, they might manifest as a suspiciously short lifespan.

There was a distinct dividing line between the parachuting landscape of 1888 and 1889. Writing in August 1889, in the middle of that new season, veteran balloonist Carl Myers explained the situation in a letter to the editor of the *Buffalo Express*, as that city's International Exposition was considering acts to engage:

> The success of a few pioneers in a specialty which has become known as "parachute leaping" has stimulated hundreds of reckless men to rush into "the fields of air" with hot-air projectiles, and at the extreme height of their brief ascent, cast themselves into the void below and gamble on the chances of survival. The very small expense of inflating a hot-air balloon, its simplicity of construction, and the originally large rewards offered for these spectacles, stimulated every adventurer with the prospect of sudden fortune at the risk of sudden death.
>
> Competition broke the market, and from receipts of $1,000 and upwards the price has fallen to anything you like, and at the close of last season many "jumped" for $20 a leap, and I have myself had many letters from such men, experienced and ignorant, who sought engagements at such rates, for single jumps, or for $100 or $200 per month for continual service. These low prices for a sensational spectacle are the inducements which urge many fair managers to accept the risks offered them.
>
> The hot-air balloonist's method last year was to get as much as possible, but to accept all offers, regardless of ability to fill the many engagements for the same dates. This kept competing balloonists from obtaining engagements they might have filled, while balloonists having the engagements select those paying best, and left their other would-be patrons without attention, thereby disappointing hundreds of thousands of people all over the country whose appetite for sensational spectacles and possible disaster

was whetted by the blood-curdling posters displayed by the fair societies. The frequent disappointments from the non-appearance of balloonists, added to the frequent failures when ascents were attempted, has given ballooning a character for unreliability everywhere, and I am constantly in receipt of letters from fair managers relating their woes, and even asking that a forfeit be deposited in local banks to insure an appearance.

There are, and always have been, reputable aeronauts with either years of successful experience or character for integrity, just as in other professions, but I think today the aeronautical "profession" includes more unreliable operators than any other calling in the world, and the public, or rather those who engage balloonists, are to blame for it by not scrutinizing the "goods" offered....[3]

Myers had more to say in his letter to the newspaper that will be revisited later, but these paragraphs serve to frame an event that occurred a little more than a month later, just twenty-five miles distant from Myers' home. It is likely that one of the young men that unsuccessfully approached Myers in early 1889, hoping to become one of his aeronauts, was a 22-year-old from Ilion, Herkimer County, New York, named Edward Walrath. Undiscouraged, Walrath announced he would go into business on his own and secured an engagement for his hometown's Fourth of July celebration. For this first engagement, Walrath would perform the trapeze act and not parachute.

To assist him in constructing the balloon and inflating it, Walrath called upon William Rulison, the former aeronaut-acrobat who had worked with Carl Myers. Rulison no longer performed ascensions himself, but still knew how to handle gas balloons, as he had shown when he assisted with getting Tom Baldwin's balloon ready at Potsdam in 1887. The local newspaper reported on Walrath's Fourth of July ascension:

> The men in charge insisted that a net should be suspended below the trapeze.... Walrath had objected ... but the committee insisted on a net or no ascension. So one was made from a wagon wheel rim with a rope net in the center which hung about three feet below the bar. Then Walrath removed his clothes showing a handsome suit of scarlet tights. His coat was rolled up and tied to the ring and his pants fastened to the side. A large jackknife with a hole in the handle was also tied to the ring open and ready for use in emergency. The cloth pipe which fed the gas was removed from the mouth of the balloon and the valve cord which drops down through the center of the balloon was securely tied to the ring in easy reach.
>
> The last act of the aeronaut was to take the money paid him by the committee and place it in his shoe. It was 3:40 when the plucky boy took his seat on the bar and the balloon was let go. At the same instant Walrath, unnoticed, had cut the cords holding the net below him and as he ascended shouted with a derisive laugh "Where's your net now? Where's your net?"

In another instant he had dropped backwards and was hanging by his feet from the bar. As he sailed up Walrath performed the evolutions at which in the Ilion gymnasium he had long been adept, amid the hearty cheering....[4]

Based on that success, Walrath secured an engagement to make his first parachute jump at the Otsego County fair at Cooperstown, New York, on September 24, 1889. The fairgrounds were located adjacent to the southern end of Otsego Lake, less than a mile wide, but several miles long. Walrath made a perfect ascension and cut loose from thousands of feet high. The wind drifted his parachute so that he dropped in the middle of the lake; no provisions had been made to have boats standing by. By the time that anyone could reach the spot, both Walrath and his parachute had disappeared under the surface.

Two weeks passed with no body rising to the surface. Walrath's local mentor, William Rulison, faced both the recriminations of his neighbors and his own guilty conscience. Rulison, though now in his mid-thirties and in the photography business, called in an apparatus diver and had the diver show him how to use the equipment.[5] Finally, on October 29, the divers found Walrath's badly decomposed body. William Rulison spent the next fifteen years as a salvage diver and recovered many more bodies of drowning victims. He even teamed up with his old mentor, Carl Myers, to successfully spot shipwrecks from a balloon and then dive to salvage them.[6] He was perhaps the only man in the nineteenth century to navigate both the sky and the underwater realm.[7]

Though Carl Myers was the Cassandra of American ballooning— who warned of the dubious safety of hot-air smoke balloons and inexperienced aeronauts—he was tangentially involved in another one of the most widely-publicized parachuting deaths of the era. Five years after Walrath's 1889 death, a 17-year-old woman named Ella Beatrice VanDresen fell to her death at the Franklinville, New York Fair. She ascended in a basket, and when she was at 1000 feet, spectators saw her reach out to loosen the parachute from the side of the balloon. Somehow, she lost grip of both the basket and the parachute ring and fell from that height to the ground. The impact drove her body nearly a foot into the earth and broke every bone. Her parents were among the first to reach the spot, and "their demonstrations of grief were terrible." The fair was immediately dissolved, and the fairgoers were left traumatized. It was said that grown men cried and women fainted.[8]

VanDresen had been touring with a 25-year-old hot-air balloonist from Ithaca, New York, William E. Townsend. However, her home was in Frankfort, New York—the same town where Carl Myers lived. Subsequent interviews revealed that Myers had known VanDresen and had cautioned her several times against using hot-air balloons. By implication, it appears that Myers had some hand in her training as an aeronaut, even if he did discourage her from the balloon-parachute act. In response to her death, Myers wrote letters to New York legislators begging them to enforce an 1892 act forbidding parachute exhibitions in New York State. According to Myers, the law had initially discouraged parachute performances, but because of lax enforcement of the $250 penalty, more and more exhibitors were ignoring the statute.[9] Young Townsend, whom it was rumored was VanDresen's fiancé, abandoned ballooning and lived a life abbreviated by chronic alcoholism.

The Jackson, Michigan, contingent of aeronauts suffered a constant string of fatalities, starting with the loss at sea of Edward Hogan in the summer of 1889, which will be discussed in a later chapter. Hogan's wife, Augustina, kept the balloon-parachute troupe together for the remainder of the 1889 season, assisted by Coryell Bartholomew, William W. McEwen, and the youngest Hogan brother, John. Later, in 1892, Bartholomew and Augustina married, but their years together were brief. She died of diabetes in 1896.

Bartholomew, it should be recalled, had an inauspicious start to his parachuting career in August 1888, when two boys were killed when one of his balloon's large inflation poles fell into the crowd. Between September 1888 and July 1889, the Jackson aeronauts had experienced several accidents, but none were serious. That changed with Edward Hogan's death and, in October 1889, with the death of George T. Rice. Rice was a Michigan native who had been trained by the Hogans; in the summer of 1889, Rice and William W. McEwen were traveling with the popular Wallace Circus as their aeronauts. On October 7, Rice made an ascension at Mount Vernon, Indiana, and drifted over the Ohio River. He became tangled in the parachute lines after landing in the water and drowned.[10]

The Jackson clan had a fortunate 1890 season, with no mishaps other than a few broken bones. However, on August 29, 1891, John Hogan made an ascension at the Detroit Exposition grounds. For reasons unknown, instead of sitting on the trapeze bar during the ascent, Hogan grasped it with his hands and dangled underneath. As he rose to 1,000 feet, spectators saw him trying to climb up on the bar, but he weakened and lost his grip. The *Ottawa Journal* reported: "[he] fell with frightful velocity, head downward, and struck on the River street sidewalk. The two-inch planks of the sidewalk were broken and splintered. Blood spurted 100 feet from where the corpse struck, every bone in the body was broken and the head was smashed beyond recognition. Thirty thousand people witnessed the tragedy."[11]

Eight—A Carnage of Daredevils

Exactly one year later, in August 1892, at the same venue, the Detroit Exposition grounds, parachutist Gertie Carmo (Gertrude Clausen) struck a tower while being driven by the wind during an ascension and fell to her death. She and Burt Walker were both performing jumps for Coryell Bartholomew, who now was the leader of the Jackson troupe. On the evening following Clausen's demise, Bartholomew somewhat callously requested that the exposition managers allow him to fulfill his contract with them and make more jumps. They wisely declined.

The Jackson aeronauts made frequent ascensions in Detroit, as did a new colony of aeronauts hailing from Sturgis, Michigan. The Sturgis balloonists were led by Edward E. Craig, who was inspired by and became a client of the Baldwin brothers of Quincy, Illinois. The Sturgis and Jackson contingents often crossed paths in Michigan and particularly in Detroit. It was there in 1890 that two sisters from Detroit, Louise Rehahn and Edith Rehahn, caught the parachuting craze and allied themselves with these groups. Louise became "Lulu Randall," and frequently partnered in shows with a Sturgis-trained aeronaut, Charles H. Kabrich. Edith became "Nellie Lamont" and partnered with and eventually married Jackson-based aeronaut Charles Walcott.[12]

The sisters had successful seasons from 1890 through 1894, but disaster struck both in August 1894. At Haverhill, Massachusetts, on August 2, Edith ("Nellie") ascended, but at 100 feet her parachute fell loose from the balloon. Realizing that she could not jump, she pulled the balloon's release valve to let air out, but a rip lengthened along the balloon fabric that caused it to plunge. She fell heavily, breaking her leg above the knee and suffering a concussion.[13] Then, a week later at Nashville, Tennessee, Louise ("Lulu") made an uneventful ascent and jump, but when her parachute approached earth, she drifted into a tree. Her body struck a limb and broke her grip, and she fell about 75 feet to the ground, killed instantly.

Edith expected to recover quickly and rejoin her husband Walcott on their scheduled tour, but the leg did not heal properly, causing her constant pain. She self-medicated with morphine and fell into fits of depression. After suffering in this state for eleven months, in July 1895, while home at her apartment in New York City, she overdosed on morphine and did not regain consciousness. Walcott had been away in Canada making ascensions, and upon hearing of her death, he came back to the city and canceled the rest of his season.

Within months, Walcott would experience the most excruciating parachuting accident ever recorded. Perhaps seeking to escape familiar places and faces in the wake of his wife's death (which many called suicide), in October 1895, Walcott ventured to Venezuela at the invitation

Charles H. Kabrich, one of the best known of the parachutists who descended astride a bicycle (Library of Congress, Reproduction Number LC-USZ62–24481).

of a wealthy trader he met in the United States, who, with the blessing of Venezuelan government, had invited him to perform his parachute jump exhibition at several towns—a tour that was to have culminated with celebrations on the anniversary of Simón Bolívar's death on December 17. Walcott's first stop on his tour was the inland town of Villa de Cura on October 28, 1895.

Eight—A Carnage of Daredevils

Walcott used his usual "smoke-balloon" that was inflated with the help of local volunteers. Once it was ready, Walcott took a seat on a bar suspended underneath the patched canvas globe. He issued the orders for the rope holders to let go, and his balloon ascended above a throng of celebrants standing next to a small cluster of buildings situated in a clearing, surrounded by a tropical forest. According to Walcott, he immediately felt disoriented. He did not understand the shouted Spanish words coming from the crowd below, save for several cries of "Dios Mio." He expected the air to feel heavy and humid on his skin, but instead it felt light.

Walcott was supposed to jump off his perch at an altitude of 5,000 feet and then hang by his hands from an iron hoop that was attached to the parachute lines. However, he had difficulty judging his rate of ascent and altitude. The balloon launch had been made early in the evening and Walcott expected to see more sunlight shining down below as he rose, but because the sun sets quickly at the equatorial latitude, much of the earth below him was in already in shadow. He also could not estimate his height by looking at the foliage of the treetops—the tree species were unfamiliar to him and appeared as one flat continuous plane. He could not judge the distance by the seconds he had been aloft, since the rate of ascent varied wildly from one launch to another depending on the buoyancy of the balloon and the outside air temperature. He could be rising fast or slow.

Walcott only hesitated an instant before he cut the parachute loose from the balloon and leapt off his perch. Split seconds into his free-fall jump, Walcott realized that something was very wrong. His parachute was not unfurling. Looking up he saw that some of the parachute's lines had gotten tangled and were caked with mud—likely they had been trampled by the crowd getting too close before the ascension. Moreover, he could now make out details of the ground and saw that he must have jumped much lower than 5,000 feet—perhaps just 3,500 feet—and he had already dropped a third of that distance.

Walcott frantically shook the lines, willing the chute to open. In another ten seconds he was less than 1,000 feet off the ground. Two hundred feet from earth, the parachute finally opened, but it was too late to fully arrest his plummet. He knew he was going to smash into the ground and pointed his toes down, leaning his shoulders to the left, hoping that his ankles and knees would take some of the shock to protect his vital organs. It was the way he had been taught to fall and how he had taught others. He hit the ground hard, and his legs crumpled beneath him.

His crushed and mangled body was picked up and carried to the only clinic in Villa de Cura. The local medic took one look at Walcott and knew that his injuries were beyond any of his skills. Walcott was somehow still conscious, though he was paralyzed below the waist, and both legs and one arm dangled at odd angles. When the "doctor" offered to bleed him, Walcott declined and instead asked to be taken to Caracas, where there was a hospital. The closest train station was in Cagua, about twelve miles from Villa de Cura, but Walcott would need to be carried there along mountain trails. Walcott requested that a telegram be sent to his sponsors in the Venezuelan government. Those contacts responded and in turn wired instructions to the local army garrison to provide a team of twenty soldiers to carry Walcott on a stretcher to Cagua.

The agonizing overland trek lasted from midday of the day after his crash to the following morning. He was carried up and down steep mountain paths in blistering heat, and each jostle of his stretcher produced waves of pain. Clouds of insects swarmed over his face, but he could not swat them away, so he smoked cigarettes continuously. They arrived at Cagua at 9:00 in the morning, but the only train to Caracas did not leave until 1:00 p.m. When it finally arrived, the doubtful engineers took one look at Walcott and said that the passenger cars were too crowded to accommodate the stretcher and that he would have to be moved to a freight car. Walcott was placed on the wood floor of a metal boxcar, the interior of which was as hot as an oven. The sixty-mile journey from Cagua to Caracas took about three hours. He was charged a freight fare of $125.

When the train arrived in Caracas, Walcott was carried by four policemen along the two-mile route to the hospital. Doctors there then placed him in an operating room, though they soon realized that Walcott's injuries were beyond their expertise; among his more obvious injuries, Charles Walcott had a broken spine. They told him that there was nothing they could do and that he would soon die. Walcott disagreed and asked that they let him take up a bed and keep him supplied with cigarettes. A nun was assigned to look after his needs.

After several weeks, his condition stabilized, though his legs were still paralyzed. The medical staff offered minimal treatment—they did not even try to set his bones. However, after a couple of months he could feel pinpricks in his legs and could twitch some muscles. He spent his time learning Spanish from the other patients in his ward. Walcott sent letters to newspapers back in the United States—the ones that had declared him dead—and thanked them for the free publicity. He next contacted his aeronaut friends in New York City and asked them to find the best hospital they could. Finally, after six months, the Caracas doctors deemed Walcott stable enough to be transported to a ship.

Eight—A Carnage of Daredevils

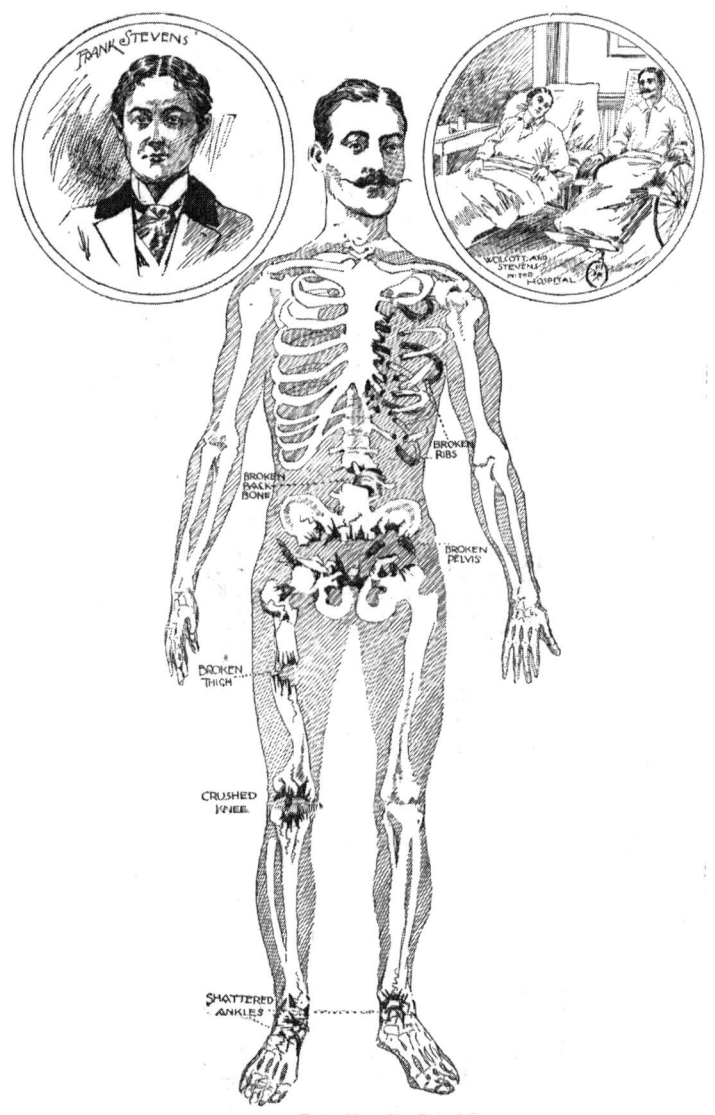

Diagram of injuries suffered in 1896 by Charles L. Wolcott (*San Francisco Examiner***, Sunday, October 18, 1896; author's collection).**

   Walcott was again carried through the streets of Caracas back to the railroad station in a torrential rain, with no cover other than the jackets that could be thrown over the cart. It took another, shorter rail trip in a freight car to get to the dock at La Guaira on the Caribbean coast. Walcott was loaded aboard a Red D line steamship bound for

New York. After a journey of a week, he was carried off onto a Brooklyn pier and then was taken by cart across the bridge to Manhattan and up to St. Luke's Hospital in Morningside Heights. Despite all his sufferings, his main complaint once installed at St. Luke's in April 1896 was that the nurses there did not keep him supplied with cigarettes, as the ones in Caracas had.

The last of the original Jackson aeronauts to lose his life to the balloon-parachute act was Edward Cole. On August 30, 1896, at Toledo, Ohio, Cole made a double-parachute ascension on one balloon with Lillian Trautwein, to whom Cole had given the performing name "Josie Carmo" in honor of the late Gertie Carmo. The balloon was underinflated and only rose a couple of hundred feet before drifting over Maumee Bay. Cole, who could not swim, told Trautwein to put on her life preserver, as they might have to wait in the water for a boat. However, Cole fumbled and dropped his own life jacket. They dropped from the balloon into the water 100 feet apart, and Trautwein could not swim over to Cole before he went under the surface.

Perhaps the saddest figure among the Jackson aeronauts was their leader (after Edward Hogan's death), Coryell Bartholomew. Bartholomew had many accidents but endured to see at least a half-dozen of his comrades die while parachuting and to see his wife, Augustina, die after four short years of marriage. Perhaps Bartholomew carried on thanks his eccentricity. As will be mentioned again later, Bartholomew built a muscle-powered airship in 1891 and piloted it from Jackson to rural Franklin Township, about 20 miles southeast. It proved unable to steer against a wind, and Bartholomew soured on the whole idea of navigable flight.[14] In April of 1892, he let it be known that he was developing a new daredevil stunt to be unveiled at the Chicago World's Fair in 1893. He proposed replacing the balloon as the means of the parachutists' ascension with five harnessed American eagles.[15] An even more ambitious endeavor was surely the most spectacular daredevil stunt ever conceived. In 1895 he proposed going over Niagara Falls suspended on a bar between two huge hydrogen-filled rubber-and-cork spheres. As the dumbbell-shaped device was swept over the cascade, Bartholomew would drop his ballast, the gas-balls would lift him clear of the basin, and he would parachute from between the floating globes.[16]

When this project collapsed as being too foolhardy, Bartholomew took the sheets of rubber he had purchased and cut them up into a medical bandage design that he patented. Though it was not mentioned in his patent application, the malady he intended the large rubber bands to correct was impotency, to be applied to male genitals. Without medical proof of the efficacy of his design, he was arrested multiple times for mail fraud. Throughout his adult years Bartholomew was never able to hold onto his money. It all came to an end on October 16, 1913, when he was 63 years old. Bartholomew was by then a recovered alcoholic; however, he had not forsaken his gambling habit. He traveled to Maryland to visit the Havre de Grace racetrack and soon lost a great deal of money. He wandered the streets afterwards, ad stopped on the bridge over the Susquehanna River, and then stepped off. It was by no means the greatest drop Bartholomew had ever taken. With his death, the aeronauts of Jackson were no more.[17]

A parachuting death that attracted more attention than any other involved a St. Louis-based aeronaut, Robert E. Scanlon. Scanlon made infrequent jumps regionally starting around 1900, having learned the business from the St. Louis balloonist, John Berry. Scanlon gained some infamy in 1902, when he refused to make an ascension at St. Louis and gave no excuse, whereupon a 14-year-old boy from the crowd volunteered to take his place. The boy, Tommy Potts, accomplished the jump without incident.

Three years later, in August 1905, at Cahokia, Illinois, Scanlon prepared for his ascension and, once the balloon was fully inflated, told the rope holders to let go. At that moment, a drunken young man, John A. Williams, who had been dared by a young woman to go up in a balloon, bolted from the crowd and grabbed hold of Scanlon's legs as he rose from the ground. Scanlon's first impulse was to try to shake off Williams so that he would fall to the ground before the balloon climbed too far. A kick and a punch in the face did not loosen the man's grip, at which point Scanlon realized they were now too high for the man to drop down. Scanlon also understood that he could not make the jump holding Williams; the parachute was not designed to take that much weight. Their only chance was to let the balloon cool and descend together without cutting the parachute loose.

That option was taken away when the balloon ripped under the strain of their weight and began leaking smoke. Scanlon realized that if he cut loose with their combined weight, the parachute would immediately collapse, and they both would die. He made the decision to dislodge Williams and attacked the man's grip on the trapeze bar. Unable to pry William's fingers, Scanlon finally brought up his knee and shoved Williams off using his leg. Scanlon then cut the parachute loose and drifted toward earth. Williams whirled downward as Scanlon watched, then Scanlon heard the sickening thud as Williams struck the ground. Scanlon was arrested that evening for manslaughter but was quickly cleared at the inquest.

Scanlon told his version of events two weeks later in an exclusive to the *St. Louis Post Dispatch*, which ran it as a full-page feature article titled "My Thrilling Fight with a Madman 1400 Feet Above the Earth," complete with an illustration of Scanlon punching at Williams. It was rewritten six years later for the *Pittsburgh Press* as "A Murder in the Sky: Aeronaut's Death Fight on a Balloon Trapeze." Scanlon had not performed as a parachutist in those intervening six years, though he still worked as a high diver. The *Pittsburgh Press* article concluded with a quote from Scanlon: "It's the nights that make me miserable," he said, buttoning and unbuttoning his coat. "I can stand the daytime pretty well, for there's people around then. But the nights! I always see something falling, falling and waving its hands."

Scanlon was not heard from again until 1916, eleven years after his deadly encounter with Williams. Scanlon's siblings believed that he had not parachuted in all that time, but for some reason he was cajoled into performing a drop in Salem, Missouri, for a meeting of the Brotherhood of American Yeomen, a fraternal organization that (like other similar organizations) provided insurance policies during the decades prior to social security. Scanlon ascended from a field and rose above the nearby treetops but cut loose at only 150 feet above the ground—too low for a normal balloon-parachute to arrest his descent. His chest and skull were crushed, and he died four hours later. All accounts suggest he simply misjudged the height, but although he had avoided balloons for eleven years, he was still an active veteran high diver, so perhaps the nightmares caught up with him.

NINE

Eldorado and the New York Balloon Company

As a response to the many public parachute descents that ended in gore and death, in January 1892 the New York State legislature passed a bill making the outfitting of a balloon with a trapeze or parachute a misdemeanor. This was a huge blow to touring show balloonists, which faced the loss of several large urban audiences as well as many popular county and town fairs. The largest and most lucrative venue was, of course, New York City, where parachute jumps had been made at Rockaway Beach for several years. Fortunately, Manhattan was situated across the Hudson River from New Jersey, where no such statute existed. The New Jersey Palisades, the cliffs overlooking Manhattan, already sported several resorts catering to visitors ferried over from the metropolis.

The most elaborate and lavish of the resorts, named Eldorado, opened atop the cliffs at Weehawken in 1891. It was the vision of Bolossy Kiralfy, one of a pair of Hungarian-born brothers that had revolutionized musical theater and outdoor stage spectacles, creating huge, elaborate historical costume dramas, like those created many years later by film director Cecil B. DeMille. Eldorado featured a large luxury hotel, an indoor theater called the Casino, and a large outdoor Roman-inspired amphitheater, seating nearly 15,000. Almost as iconic as these, however, was a trestle that stretched out over the cliffs above the shoreline below. Ferries brought visitors to the base of the trestle, where they boarded an elevator taking them to the top of the trestle, where a short track train carried them to the Eldorado entrance.

Kiralfy's epic outdoor productions of *King Solomon's Mines* and *Ancient Egypt* only lasted two years, but Eldorado remained a popular recreation center until 1898. One of the main draws during the years that Eldorado existed were regular presentations of the balloon-parachute act. From the very start, Kiralfy wanted ascensions to be made from

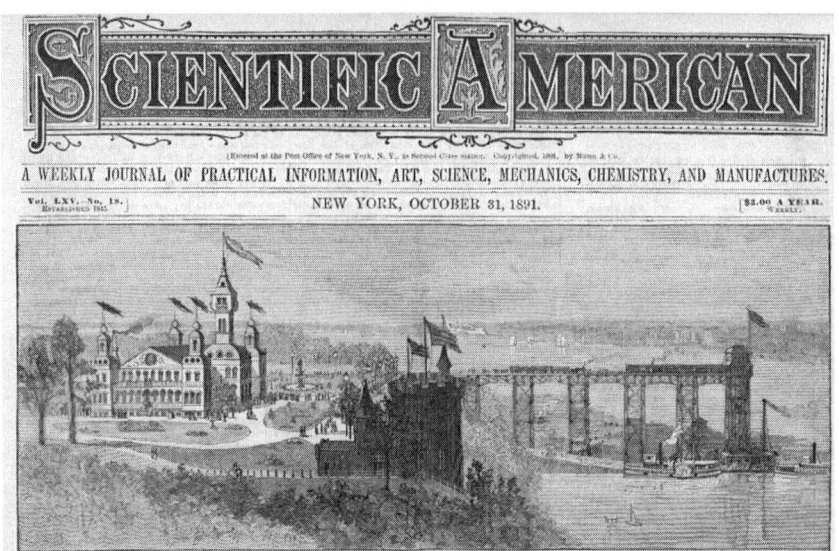

Eldorado Amusement Park, Weehawken, New Jersey. The amphitheater was located behind building on left (*Scientific American* 65, no. 18 [October 31, 1891]; author's collection).

the amphitheater during the day, reserving his theatrical productions for the evening. He engaged two young men in their twenties who had recently been performing parachute jumps at a resort near New Haven, Connecticut: W. Morton "Mortimer" McKim and Marion L. "Daring Donald" McDonald. McDonald was a New Haven resident, a clerk, who had learned parachuting from Edwin J. Northup, a one-time Quincy, Illinois, resident who in turn had been a client of the Baldwins and had migrated to Connecticut.

McKim was from Keokuk, Iowa (twenty miles from Quincy), and was an energetic, fast-talking theatrical actor and agent. In 1890–1891, his only known clients were two martial artists: Major J.A. Maguire and Helen Englehardt, both experts in a now-obscure form of sport fencing: the broadsword. Fencing contests for the championship of the broadsword were popular exhibitions in the late nineteenth century. Major Maguire was one of the best, despite his fabricated resume as a British military officer; he had both a victory and a loss to the recognized world champion, Duncan C. Ross. Englehardt also drew notice, due to her challenges to men. These facts are noted only because Ross and Englehardt figured in one of McKim's later parachuting adventures.

McDonald and McKim started their engagement at Eldorado in late July and performed several jumps per week.[1] These appearances

Nine—Eldorado and the New York Balloon Company 93

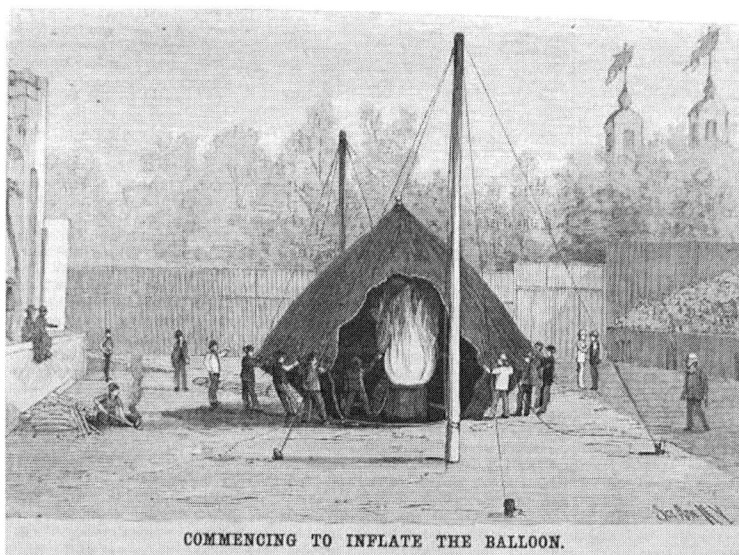

Commencing to Inflate the Balloon. Hot-Air Ballooning, Weehawken, New Jersey (*Scientific American* 65, no. 10 [September 5, 1891]; author's collection).

Generating Heat During Inflation. Hot-Air Ballooning, Weehawken, New Jersey (Scientific *American,* Sept 5, 1891, v65, n10; author's collection).

Ascent with Parachute. Hot-Air Ballooning, Weehawken, New Jersey (*Scientific American* 65, no. 10 [September 5, 1891]; author's collection).

proved immensely popular and even drew the interest of the magazine *Scientific American*, which published a feature article on their ascensions in their September 5, 1891, issue. As their engagement was ending, newspapers reported a tragedy at Eldorado. An inexperienced aeronaut named George White was sent aloft and appeared to the crowd below to be paralyzed with fear. Instead of jumping, he stayed on his trapeze seat until the balloon collapsed into the Hudson. George White never rose to the surface. Eldorado's manager, Fred Walker, told reporters that he had boats out looking for White's body and offered a reward for its recovery; he offered to pay for the expenses of his funeral.[2] The *New York World* reported the accident on the top center of page 1.

However, it turns out the incident was a hoax perpetrated by Fred Walker and the Eldorado balloonists: George White was only a dummy

Descent Over the Hudson. Hot-Air Ballooning, Weehawken, New Jersey (*Scientific American* 65, no. 10 [September 5, 1891]; author's collection).

crafted by the theatrical wardrobe staff working on Kiralfy's drama. The prank was revealed by the Eldorado staff a day later, and the newspapers that had not been taken in by the story had a field day making fun of those who had been fooled. Kiralfy himself was less amused, and no parachutists appeared at Eldorado the next season, in 1892. M.L. McDonald went back to performing at New Haven for a year and then quit the business, while Mort McKim spent the year performing minor roles in touring plays and acting as vaudeville agent for the broadswordswoman Helen Englehardt.

Ballooning came back to Eldorado in 1893, starting with a guest ascension by Emile Carton, a French scientific balloonist. However, when regular parachuting over the Palisades returned to the resort a few days later, the ascensions were made by members of a new combine.

Mort McKim, now the Eldorado manager, brought in a new team called the New York Balloon Company. The leader of this loose association of aeronauts was Charles W. Williams, the veteran Coney Island, Ohio, aeronaut. Both McKim and Williams still had one foot in the New York theatrical world, but the typical shutdown of theaters in the summer months allowed them to run a resort and a parachuting troupe. To avoid conflicts in securing theatrical engagements, Williams made a point of adopting a separate stage name for his aeronautical work: "William C. Williamson" or sometimes "C.W. Williamson."

Williams was injured making a heavy landing during an August 2, 1893, jump from Eldorado. Because of this, he relied on two other members of his troupe, A. Leo Stevens and a railroad brakeman from New Jersey, Charles Lastrange (real name Charles J. Peterson). By the end of August, just before Eldorado's parachuting season ended, a female aeronaut named Maud DeHaven had joined the company. Although her real name is unknown, she continued to make jumps arranged by the New York Balloon Company until the end of the 1897 season. Her specialty was jumping with a dog, although that drew complaints from the ASPCA on at least one occasion.

In 1894 teams from the New York Balloon Company spread out through the northeast, as well as continuing at Eldorado. In May and June of that year, Leo Stevens toured Ontario, Canada and Pennsylvania with a new female aeronaut, Nina Madison (real name Agnes Grace Stage), who was recruited from Jersey City, close to Eldorado. Charles Lastrange anchored descents at Eldorado along with Maud Dehaven and Clara Delmore. Charles Williams made jumps in Vermont, while Mort McKim teamed up with Lulu Bates and his sister, Eola Lee McKim, to appear in Connecticut and Rhode Island. Lulu Bates had moved from Cincinnati with her adopted father and mentor, Harry Gilbert. She toured the east with Gilbert in the early 1890s until his death in 1892. Charles Williams knew Bates very well from their years in Cincinnati and so invited her to join the New York Balloon Company.

After the 1894 parachuting season ended in September, several members of the New York Balloon Company continued to board in New York City, some as roommates. Flush from a successful season, they partied with New York's sporting and theatrical communities, which led to a curious series of daredevil pranks. On October 13, 1894, a man calling himself "Captain Montague Martin" arrived in Poughkeepsie accompanied by the sword experts Helen Engelhardt and Duncan C. Ross. "Captain Martin" declared himself an expert broadswordsman from England and that he had come to Poughkeepsie to make a jump off the Poughkeepsie Railway Bridge. He intended to surpass the feat of daredevil Steve Brodie, who claimed to have jumped off the Brooklyn Bridge in 1886, earning widespread publicity and acclaim. The Poughkeepsie Bridge was one of the longest and highest in America at that time—over 30 feet higher than the Brooklyn Bridge.

"Martin's" plans were frustrated by the city's police force and bridge guards, who were alerted to his intentions by the drunken behavior of his party. In the end, the pranksters had to row out in the dead of night to one of the metal piers supporting the bridge. Martin climbed the rungs of the tower to an unknown height and then jumped into the water. He later claimed that he had climbed to the top, but the consensus was that he had only ascended thirty feet above the water.[3] Captain Martin was never heard from again, but his alter ego was likely Mort McKim or Leo Stevens.

McKim and Stevens were, at that same time, dreaming up other promotional schemes. A lightweight hydrogen generator had long been sought by balloonists as a key to long-distance flights, and Stevens believed he found a solution to this. On October 31, 1894, they ascended at Bridgeport, Connecticut, after inflation with this new device and were blown southward. They reached Manhattan in about three hours, but rather than being blown out to sea, they descended in the city, landing on a tenement building on East 79th Street. Stevens and McKim considered the test a success, foiled only by a southward wind.[4] All through the winter and spring of 1895, McKim announced plans that he, Leo Stevens, and Frank "Don Carlos" Stevens would attempt a New York-to-San Francisco flight. However, it never was attempted, perhaps because an east-to-west prevailing wind that they theorized never existed at the altitudes in which they could operate.

During these same months, more bridge jumping took place. On November 27, 1894, a person naming himself as "Henry Menier"[5] proclaimed that he had jumped from the Brooklyn Bridge with a parachute and listed as his witnesses Charles Lastrange, Charles Walcott, Frank Stevens, Mort McKim, Harry Webb (boxing manager), and William E. Harding (sportswriter for the *National Police Gazette*). The name of McKim may indicate that the jumper in this case was Stevens or they could have just switched names. Despite this list of witnesses, the police denied that the jump had occurred. "Menier" maintained that he jumped for a wager made in desperation, as he was destitute, and Frank Stevens and Charles Walcott were refusing to take him on a parachuting tour to Cuba.[6]

On December 26, 1894, "Henry Menier" returned to the Poughkeepsie Railway Bridge and was unimpeded by any guards. He made a parachute jump from the span in broad daylight, in front of a boatload of newspaper representatives. One paper tracked down the broadsword champion, Duncan Ross, and asked him if "Henry Menier" was the same person as "Captain Montague Martin."[7] Ross at first responded yes, and then no, and then said he was not sure. Ross was probably thinking that any one among the band of aeronauts could have done the feat. On January 7, 1895, it was Nina Madison's turn. She made her jump from the Brooklyn Bridge, witnessed by Leo Stevens, who she said was her husband. However, without reporters on hand, her accomplishment was questioned.[8]

The parachute used in these jumps, it was said, belonged to Charles Walcott and had a much smaller diameter than a regular balloon-act parachute. The smaller size allowed it to deploy quicker but did not slow the jumper as much as a full-size canopy would have. Walcott's involvement in the bridge jumping indicates that he was now an associate member of the New York Balloon Company, though it is unclear whether he and wife Nellie Lamont were still booking their own engagements. At any rate, he seems to have brought some of the Jackson, Michigan, ill luck to New York. In June 1895, at their Manhattan apartment, Nellie Lamont fatally overdosed on morphine that she used to alleviate a leg injury. Louise "Lulu" Bates and Mort McKim spent the season making ascensions around Lake Champlain and the Finger Lakes of New York, but both suffered leg sprains from hard landings. Nina Madison sprained both her ankles at Haverstraw, Massachusetts, in July. In early August 1895, Charles W. Williams made an ascension from Eldorado, but landed on a rooftop from which he fell, knocking him out and damaging his spine. Finally, after the 1895 ballooning season in the United States had ended, word came from Venezuela about the horrific accident suffered by Charles Walcott.

Once Walcott's broken body was transported to New York City and examined at St. Luke's, they cataloged all the injuries: his ankles were broken and foot bones shattered; his right hip was dislocated and the bone broken; his right leg was broken at the knee and the knee joint torn apart; his pelvis was broken in half, lengthways; all ribs on his left side were broken cleanly; and his spine was broken, with one piece of it dislodged and suspended in the tissue of his back. He was subjected to a series of delicate operations, unprecedented in orthopedic surgery. During the months of April and May 1896, he was visited in the hospital by his two aeronaut friends, Frank Stevens and Nina Madison. They offered to take over the Walcott's 1896 summer engagements in New England and Canada that he had committed to a year earlier.

In September 1896, Frank Stevens and Nina Madison arrived late to their engagement at a fair in Huntingdon, Quebec. Stevens had to make the first ascension without thoroughly checking his equipment; he neglected to notice that several of his parachute lines had been frayed during transit. During his drop, the lines on one side of his parachute snapped, causing him to plunge, much like Walcott had. A fortunate gust of wind into the limp chute slowed his fall, but he was found splayed on the ground unconscious and immobile. A local doctor declared that his spine was broken and that he would die. However, it later resulted that his injury was limited to a spinal concussion that left a large lump below the small of his back. Nina Madison arranged for Stevens to be taken to St. Luke's and placed in a bed alongside his friend Walcott.

Both Frank Stevens and Charles Walcott were eventually able to walk again, though Walcott was left with permanent disabilities. Frank Stevens continued his storied career as an aeronaut, often accompanying his brother, A. Leo Stevens. From his bed, Charles Walcott managed the business affairs of his own troupe of jumpers in the 1896 and 1897 seasons, consisting of Lillian Temple, George W. Hibbard, and Nina Madison. Then, in 1898, Walcott resumed touring New England and Canada with his team. He continued to make balloon ascensions for the next ten years. His vocation had cost him his health and the life of his wife, but he could not set aside his fascination with "the Leap from the Clouds."

The antics and ambitions of the Eldorado comrades were not quite finished. In late 1895, Mort McKim traveled to the west coast as an actor with a touring company performing the play *Trilby*. The production fell apart in the Pacific Northwest, stranding many of its performers, including Mort McKim. He was able to make his way to St. Paul, Minnesota, before running out of money. So, he once again became "Harry Menier" and made wagers that he could jump off the Wabasha Street Bridge over the Mississippi. The leap from 125 feet was successful, though whether McKim had a parachute is not known. McKim stayed in the area, and "Harry Menier" made parachute jumps from a balloon throughout Minnesota in 1896.

In May of 1897, Leo Stevens, Frank Stevens, and Charles Lastrange attempted to cross the Atlantic Ocean by balloon (a feat not accomplished until 1978). They did not get far; a gale forced them into the water near Sandy Hook, New Jersey, where they were fortunate to be spotted by a ship and rescued. Undaunted, in August of 1897, the two Stevens brothers, Lastrange, Mort McKim and his sister Eola announced plans to balloon from New York City to Kansas City, from there to Seattle, and then northward to the Klondike gold fields. Funding for the unlikely project never materialized.

On October 20, 1897, Charles Lastrange made the group's final jump off the Brooklyn Bridge. He employed what were described as "parachute wings" designed by Leo Stevens. He had a cab stop on the middle of the span, jumped out, and leapt over the railing. Lastrange at first plummeted straight down but then straightened out and soared past the boat containing his friends. He landed in the water a full thousand feet from the bridge. He said the wings worked perfectly, and he could have flown for miles without difficulty.[9] Though the closure of Eldorado in 1898 caused the original fellowship of the New York Balloon Company to disperse,[10] Lastrange's experiment with the glider-parachute serves as an appropriate bookend. It signified the new directions that aeronautics was taking and counts as one example in which practitioners of the balloon-parachute act were anxious to participate in that progress.

Ten

Other Company Troupes

The New York Balloon Company was founded early in the 1890s by a group of experienced aeronauts, some of whom had already established a circuit of repeat engagements from year to year. As the decade progressed, fair, resort, and exposition managers grew leery of dealing with individual balloonists and sought to make contracts with reliable companies that had good track record—not only for showing up but also for successfully performing. These companies, like the New York Balloon Company, advertised in entertainment trade magazines like the *New York Clipper* and (after 1895) *Billboard* and in circulars mailed out to fair and resort managers. These troupes accounted for most of the balloon-parachute act performances of the 1890s, although a substantial number were still performed by individuals or circus employees. There were more than a dozen such companies, but in the 1890s and early 1900s, the most active were the Baldwin Brothers; the Grace Shannon Balloon Company; the Leroy Sisters; the Jewell Brothers; the Flying Allens; the Forsman Balloon Company; the Hepner Brothers Balloon Company; and the Belmont Sisters. Each has an interesting story.

The Baldwin Brothers

The Baldwin brothers, Thomas S. Baldwin and Samuel Y. Baldwin, set up their own balloon and parachute manufacturing business in Quincy in 1888, capitalizing on the fame they earned as early performers of the balloon-parachute act. They provided basic instruction on how to inflate balloons, make ascensions and perform parachute jumps, and they sometimes traveled to assist their new customers make their first ascensions. They also established their own park/resort in Quincy, Baldwin Park. However, before long, the Baldwins began to rely on a cadre of Quincy-based aeronauts to support their business, as well as to take the place of Tom or Sam in presenting a performance. These trusted aeronauts were often named as further "Baldwin Brothers": Ivy Baldwin (William Ivy); Thomas Greenleaf (who sometimes was known as a second "Tom Baldwin"); Chet Baldwin (Chester Swearingen); Charles J. Eddy; William S. Steward; and Frank Jacobs.

Eddy and Steward were friends of the Baldwins and Quincy residents prior to 1887. Eddy married Steward's sister. Both men worked with the Baldwin Brothers until the mid–1890s, during which time Eddy sometimes signed on to travel as a circus aeronaut. In the mid–1890s he branched out to start his own medicine show, first touting hair tonic and later selling spectacles. He and Steward moved from Quincy to Cincinnati, leaving ballooning behind. Frank Jacobs had a similar, but abbreviated, fate. He was trained by the Baldwins, making his first ascension in 1889, and toured with circuses for several seasons. In 1896, he had a balloon-parachute race at a Baldwin Park, the summer resort built in Quincy. Jacobs's balloon burst when 300 feet high, and he plummeted before he could cut loose and open the parachute. His wife was in the audience. His pallbearers were Tom Greenleaf, Sam Baldwin, William S. Steward, and Chet Swearingen—they placed underground the man they had often sent aloft.[1]

By the time of Jacobs's death, Chet Swearingen was a bit of a pariah in Quincy and with his fellow aeronauts. He had married briefly, but his wife left him and made headlines for her involvement with other men. In 1893, Swearingen was accused of throwing a chemical into the balloon inflation furnace of a Quincy resort that recently had reneged on paying him a bonus. The aeronaut slated to make the ascension the next day was Gene Perkins, an African American parachutist trained by Charles J. Eddy. Newspapers supposed that Swearingen's sabotage was motivated by racism, until others came forward to suggest that his real target were the resort managers that deprived him his earnings. At any rate, the evidence against Swearingen was inconclusive, and the charges were dropped.[2]

Like the other Baldwin "brothers," Swearingen traveled with circuses as their aeronaut in the late 1890s and later as an independent ascensionist after moving from Quincy to Kansas and subsequently to Texas. After his marriage in Quincy soured in the early 1890s, he was something of a lonely heart. In 1905, he placed the following classified ad in an Eau Claire, Wisconsin, newspaper: "Will young lady who sent box of flowers to Chet Baldwin in Aug. 1895, when he was making a balloon ascension parachute jump, please send her address to Chet Baldwin, Hillsboro, Texas, c/o YMCA So. Yards."[3] He was recalling a fleeting flirtation incident from ten years earlier.

Thomas Greenleaf was an old acrobat friend of the Baldwins—a tightrope walker. After spending the early 1890s helping the Baldwin Brothers as an aeronaut, Greenleaf and Sam Baldwin organized the "Flying Baldwins," a touring aerialist trapeze act. In the 1900s, Greenleaf took over management of the "Flying Baldwins" troupe, which produced several circus and vaudeville trapeze stars, including Greenleaf's own two daughters.[4]

By far the most trusted and favored associate of the Baldwin Brothers was "Ivy Baldwin." William Ivy was a tightrope walker from Texas who was performing the balloon-trapeze act in the late 1880s. He teamed up with the Baldwin Brothers in San Francisco in the spring of 1890, performing with them through California that summer and accompanying them on their Asia tour in the fall. Ivy spent little time in Quincy; he was sent by the Baldwins in 1893 to run a tethered balloon attraction in Mexico. A year later, after the Army Signal Corps expressed interest in using tethered observation balloons, Ivy Baldwin was recommended to provide instruction to the Colorado-based unit. He did so and made Denver his home for the next several decades, performing his aerial acts at Rocky Mountain resorts. Among the dozens of balloonists who offered their services to the Army during the Spanish-American War, Ivy Baldwin was one whose experience in Cuba in a balloon is documented.[5]

Noticeably absent from involvement with the Baldwin Brothers enterprises, except in the earliest years, was Thomas S. Baldwin himself. Although Sam Baldwin undoubtedly informed and consulted with his brother about the family business, Tom Baldwin wanted the freedom to pursue more serious aeronautical interests. Moreover, the tour circuit and many banquets in his honor had taken their toll on Tom Baldwin—he no longer had the physique of an acrobat and his weight made parachuting more problematic than it was for other aeronauts. The directing force behind the Baldwin Brothers enterprises was Samuel Y. Baldwin, not Thomas S. Baldwin.

The Jewell Brothers

The Jewell Brothers traced their origins to the Gomes-Jewell Balloon Party, the Springfield, Illinois, group of trapeze-act aeronauts that toured in the 1880s. When that partnership dissolved in during the 1889 season, Thomas Jewell went his own way, partnering with bartender/aeronaut Harry Gruber and employing as assistants Charles Richmond of Springfield and Edward Baltz of Buffalo, New York. Gruber adopted the identity of Thomas's imaginary brother, "Harry Jewell." The troupe had success through the 1889–1891 seasons, but in December 1891, Thomas Jewell went out drinking in Springfield, took a cab back to his home, and then argued with the cabbie over the fare. The argument led to shoving, and Jewell tripped over a low fence in his own yard. He hit his head hard and suffered a brain hemorrhage that caused his death a few days later.[6]

The Jewell Brothers continued to perform, but were now headquartered in Trenton, New Jersey, near Gruber's hometown. Edward Baltz had been elevated to a brother, "Edward Jewell," earlier in 1891. The troupe performed uneventfully until June of 1893, when Charles Richmond, who was described by one paper "as intelligent as he is daring," decided to try an experiment. Richmond had devised two fabric sails hinged together, designed to work as a glider. He announced that he would test them at Trenton's Cochran Park. Several hundred people were on hand to see the event. Richmond ascended, and at about 3000 feet, he stood up on the trapeze bar, grasped the wings, and jumped. One side filled with air, but the other did not, and Richmond fell like a stone. His body was found embedded in the mud at the bottom of a nearby pond. Harry Jewell (Gruber) later denied that Richmond had been using anything other than an ordinary parachute, and moreover, he refused to pay the funeral expenses, leaving that to the charity of the community.[7]

Gruber and Baltz continued to operate the Jewell Brothers franchise from Trenton until 1899, when Baltz returned to Buffalo, his hometown. His family had connections and through them Baltz obtained a political appointment as a customs and immigration inspector. However, within a year or two he was arrested for helping to smuggle Chinese immigrants across the border from Ontario. For this offense, Baltz was sent to jail. By the time he was released, he no longer had the support of his family. He was arrested again in 1918 for supplying narcotics to military veterans.[8]

Gruber, after Baltz left the firm, performed a light schedule each season until 1913, when he found an intrepid young teen named Walter S. Leonhauser. Leonhauser revived the fortunes of the Jewell Brothers, becoming "Walter Jewell." In 1917, he became an instructor at the Army's Balloon School in Maryland; he also had, by that time, purchased an airplane and obtained his pilot's license. Following World War I, Leonhauser resumed the balloon-parachute act and performed dozens of engagements every summer. However, in 1930, Leonhauser's luck ran out when his parachute failed to open at a jump made at Denton, Maryland. One of the spectators was his 8-year-old son.[9]

Harry Gruber was once again undeterred by the death of one of his aeronauts. He hired a new assistant, known only as "Daring Dan Jewell." Over the years, the Jewell Brothers act had been embellished: Daring Dan ascended with a lit fuse leading to a "bomb" (large firecracker) attached to the balloon. When the balloon reached 3,000 feet, the charge exploded, and Daring Dan released. To spectators, it appeared as though the balloon had burst. On the way down, Dan released three parachutes: red, white, and blue, each in succession.[10] The last known performance of the Jewell Brothers took place in Londonderry, Vermont, in 1934.

The Flying Allens

The Jewell Brothers span of over 45 years of continuous presentation of the balloon-parachute act is only exceeded by the multiple generations of the Allen family of Dansville, New York. Ira, Martin, and Comfort Allen performed jumps starting in 1888, performing at rural fairs and carnivals, mixing their balloon act with high-wire and trapeze acts. Occasionally they were joined by balloonist John J. Frisbie, who had also worked with Carl Myers. All three Allen brothers performed for decades without serious injury, and all died from natural causes at ages 80 (Comfort), 86 (Ira), and 90 (Martin).

Comfort's son, Warren "Speck" Allen, was the most active performer in the next generation, though he was joined later by his brothers Edgar "Red" and Edward "Ed," twins who were twenty years younger than Warren. Two cousins, Martin Allen's sons Stephen and William, were also second-generation balloon-parachute act performers. Stephen Allen made jumps from the late 1890s until his premature death in 1915; although a parachuting accident was not the specific cause of his death, many believed that hard falls and an exhausting experience landing in Lake Ontario might have contributed to his demise. Of this generation, Edward was the one whose career lasted the longest; he made his last jump in 1976, at age 80. However, starting in the 1930s, most of the leaps were made by Edward's son, "Eddie Jr.," and his daughters Gloria and Florence.

In September 1937, the "Flying Allens" were performing at Blackstone, Virginia, doing a simultaneous drop. During the descent, Gloria's parachute tangled in the lines of her brother Eddie Jr.'s parachute, causing her chute to tear. She fell hard on the ground, conscious but fatally injured. Her last words to her siblings were to continue the act. Edward, Eddie Jr., and Florence did soldier on, joined by "Speck's" son, Warren Jr.

Another son of Edward, Joseph Allen, was being prepared to join the act at age 15 in 1942 but was fatally injured while in a workshop preparing an explosive charge used in the act. In 1946, Edward's youngest child, daughter Arlene Allen, parachuted onto a high-tension wire and was nearly fatally electrocuted. She died of the effects in 1948.[11]

Eddie Jr., Florence, and Warren Jr. all quit the Flying Allens as their lives progressed and as they developed other careers and a family life. Edward, the last of the Flying Allens, stopped performing engagements in 1966 at age 70; he made his last jump at a balloon festival in 1976. His parachute tore and he was jolted by the landing, which put an end to his jumping. He passed away four years later at age 80, a revered figure in the ballooning community.

W.H. Leroy and the Leroy Sisters

While the Allens were a true family dynasty and the Jewell Brothers were started by Thomas Jewell, many different parachutists employed a wholly fictional moniker: Leroy. "Leroy" was a popular stage/circus name before the advent of the balloon-parachute act and remained so with several parachute acts, starting with W.H. "Harry" Leroy of Iowa. Harry Leroy, whose real name is unknown, was an itinerant tightrope walker through the 1880s, surviving by wandering from town to town conducting street performances. He was often criticized for his churlish behavior; notably, he often berated residents if they did not drop enough change into his hat. Tom Baldwin's parachute jump changed Harry's life. He hastened to Quincy and ordered a balloon, and Sam Baldwin gave him lessons. Harry's first jump took place at Quincy on April 4, 1889.

Harry Leroy made several jumps between 1889 and 1890, but he had little business acumen and did not know how to advertise or book engagements. Fortunately for him, at Fort Worth, Texas, he met a talented theatrical manager, John B. Hogan (no relation to the Hogan aeronaut family) who was left without a troupe and stranded penniless due to string of fires, train wrecks, and a smallpox outbreak. Leroy and Hogan's partnership was significant to more than one aeronaut. To enhance some of the shows, Hogan brought in another aeronaut for a balloon race against Leroy: Peter Zimmerman of Albuquerque, New Mexico. Zimmerman adopted the name "Herr Kyle, the scientific German aeronaut."[12]

After Leroy was injured at Belton, Texas, Hogan wired for another aeronaut, George W. Hibbard of Jackson, Michigan. While Leroy was injured, Hibbard performed in his place, unknown to the public. Harry Leroy recovered and continued to perform for another two years with several women aeronauts, including Helen Gaylor and Estella Graves (real name Maud Shaw). However, after a hard parachute descent in California broke both of Maud's legs in January 1894, nothing was heard from Harry Leroy or Maud again.

The above-mentioned George Hibbard, who had once substituted for Harry Leroy, expanded his act to include female aeronauts. He advertised in a Detroit newspaper for a woman to join him and hired Wilhelmina Heid, who was dubbed "Victoria Leroy." After working together for two seasons, they married. The couple moved to the bride's family home in Fremont, Ohio, where they received a cold welcome from her parents. Hibbard vowed to get a job at the local water works but nevertheless contracted to make three drops at the local fair, intending those to be his last. He was severely injured during the second ascension. While he recuperated, Wilhelmina made the third jump in his place. This caused her parents to condemn the couple, and so they left Fremont and decided to go on the road again.

Hibbard and Wilhelmina did take in new partners to expand their schedule: Charles Henry "Harry" Snyder of Dayton, Ohio, and Edith Finn of Mt. Vernon, Ohio. Edith became "Sadie Leroy," the supposed sister of "Victoria Leroy." The Leroy Sisters sometimes performed together, sometimes separately. On August 29, 1896, Hibbard and Wilhelmina were in Clayton, Missouri, where Wilhelmina—as Victoria Leroy—was to jump. As she ascended, the parachute detached from the side of her balloon, and as it fell, she reached out to grab it. She slipped off the trapeze and was left hanging to the bar by her elbow. Before the smoke-balloon could cool and descend, her arm tired, and she fell to her death. Hibbard was so distraught that he tried to grab a revolver and shoot himself but was prevented from doing so.[13]

Hibbard's grief did not deter him from touring with the Leroy Sisters for a few more seasons, though now the sisters were named as Sadie Leroy and Eva Leroy.[14] Sadie made headlines, but not due to any accident: she sued another aeronaut, Louis N. McNeal, for bigamy. McNeal went by the stage name Hi Sidney Wallace and performed high jumps and bridge jumps as well as parachute jumps. During balloon ascensions, McNeal took part in balloon marriages, where a couple would ascend in a basket with a clergyman and conduct a wedding ceremony for the audience below. This performance dated back to the early years of show ballooning and was still a staple in the 1890s. Most of the marriages were shams, performed as needed by members of a balloon troupe, but a few were genuine.

McNeal took part in more than a dozen of these sham marriages with different partners, but apparently used them as a convenient ploy to seduce his fellow performers. Edith Finn, aka Sadie Leroy, was one of those abused by McNeal, but she investigated his background and discovered he had a real wife. Edith charged McNeal with bigamy, and when the case was brought to court, the judge refused to accept McNeal's excuse that most of his marriages were shams. He was sent to the Ohio State Penitentiary for 18 months. Upon his release, he resumed his high-diving act—but also had several more recorded marriages.

Despite a serious injury to Eva Leroy (or one of the women using that stage name) in 1899, Charles H. Snyder continued to advertise the Leroy Sisters in *Billboard* through to 1912. Later in the 1890s and early 1900s, two other aeronauts employed the name Leroy, but their connections to the Hibbard/Snyder Leroys are tenuous. Frank Leroy was a French Canadian whose real name was Emile Marcotte; he told stories of the past accidents that befell the Leroy family, including Victoria and Eva, but often got his facts wrong. Frederick A. Harding of Connersville, Indiana, who performed as "Jack Leroy," married aeronaut Eva Leroy, but the two soon divorced, and the real name of this Eva was never revealed.

Just days before she suffered a serious mishap on October 4, 1899, Eva Leroy was interviewed. She had an interesting perspective on the economics of her calling:

> New novelties are constantly being invented in the balloon business, just like everything else. In order to make money at the business nowadays we must be up-to-date. You see, there are so many aeronauts these days. Take the little town of Sturgis, Mich. Why, over there alone there are fifty-nine. Every other person you meet on the street is an aeronaut. School boys go up in a balloon for a quarter in that place. That town has done more to hurt our business than all the others in the country. The competition there is so sharp that they cut prices, and that hurts business. But they can't introduce the novelties; only experts can do that.[15]

E.E. Craig and the Hepner Brothers

Eva's assessment of Sturgis, Michigan, was an exaggeration—but a slight one. Sturgis, it should be recalled, was the original hometown of the heir apparent leader of the Jackson aeronauts, Coryell Bartholomew. However, the man who can be credited with starting the aeronaut colony in Sturgis was a contemporary of Bartholomew's, Edward E. Craig. In interviews, Craig said that as a young man he had met both W.H. Donaldson and Edward Hogan. Craig made his first parachute jump on

Ten—Other Company Troupes

July 3, 1889, at Sturgis, using a balloon he had purchased from the Baldwin Brothers in Quincy. Craig's parachute hung limp from the side of the balloon, the same configuration used by the Baldwins.

Craig's success inspired several other Sturgis residents, foremost among them being the Hepner family: Fred, Frank, Christian, and Frank's wife, Gertrude. Fred and Frank originally were aeronauts, but soon moved into the balloon and parachute manufacturing business. The list of occasional aeronauts associated with Craig and the Hepners is a long one: G.W. Moore; Charles Johnson; William Kulp; Frank Robinson; Bert Young; H.L. Williams; Jerry Stackhouse; and George W. Barnhart were among the Sturgis natives who engaged in parachute jumps. None made ballooning their career and disappeared from mention after a season or two. However, Edward E. Craig stuck to it as a vocation, though it led him to ruin.

Other disciples of Edward E. Craig, dating from 1893, were two brothers from Ohio, John J. Coughlin and Felix Coughlin. The Coughlin brothers made more headlines for their non-performing careers than as balloonists; both were attendants at one of Ohio's state insane asylums and saw inmates being abused. Fearing that any internal complaint would be ignored, they took the issue to the newspapers. Their jobs were sacrificed, and asylum officials denied any wrongdoing, but their efforts put the State on notice that the institutions needed to be better managed. Their ballooning career was long and included mentoring other aeronauts. One of them, Harry Eibe, was on the team that developed the U.S. Army Type A parachute pack.

Starting in 1889, Edward E. Craig made good money for three seasons and invested it in forming a female vaudeville minstrel troupe that operated in the non-ballooning seasons. He married one of the performers, Annie Meyers, but the union did not last long. On June 26, 1893, Craig made an ascension at Celina, Ohio, but the underinflated balloon only rose a few hundred feet. Craig decided to cut loose at that low altitude, perhaps because he felt the balloon was going to descend too quickly. His parachute opened but did not prevent a hard impact with the ground. Most observers thought his injuries were fatal.

Craig recovered a few months later, as evidenced by his arrest in Indianapolis for impersonating an officer. Craig was stopped after escorting a woman to the city jail to see her lover, who was behind bars. Craig told the jailer he was a detective bringing a witness to identify a suspect. A year later in 1894, Craig himself was jailed for assaulting (and likely raping) a woman in Columbus Grove, Ohio; newspapers claimed that if he had not been jailed, he would have been lynched.[16] He must have escaped conviction, for he was known to have made parachute jumps during the next two seasons. In 1895 he suffered another serious fall in Hancock, Maryland; again, many believed his injuries would be fatal, but he was back in business the next season.

However, after the ballooning season of 1896, Craig was arrested in Maryland for robbing a shoe store. He was convicted and spent the next two years in prison. While confined, Craig hatched a plan for the ultimate daredevil stunt: he would ride a boat down the Niagara River that had a line leading up to a balloon, and just as the boat would plunge over the falls, he would cut the line and be lifted by the balloon out of danger. He did not receive permission to make the attempt.

For the next several years, Craig lived as a tramp, moving from town to town in Indiana, Ohio, Pennsylvania, West Virginia, and Maryland and eking a living as a sign painter. In 1907, a ten-year-old girl residing at a boarding house in Huntington, Indiana, accused Craig of rape. In early 1908, he was found guilty and sent to the Indiana State Prison for two to twelve years.[17] Upon his release in 1914, he tried to interest hospitals into sponsoring balloon ascensions to raise money for charity, but nothing appears to have come from this offer. Edward Craig faded into obscurity, dying in 1918 while staying near relatives in Kansas, the last relic of the original Sturgis aeronaut colony.

Peoria Rivals: Milton M. Forsman and the Hagel Brothers

When Thomas Jewell left the Gomes-Jewell Balloon Party combination, he founded a new, long-running company: the Jewell Brothers. His partner, Joseph Gomes, also inspired two companies performing the balloon-parachute act. Both operated out of the same city: Peoria, Illinois. One outfit was run by Milton M. Forsman as a "school" for aeronauts. The other was a family business, run by Fred, Harry, Frank, Charles, Lewis and Carl Hagel, i.e., the Hagel Brothers. The story of the Peoria colony of aeronauts begins with Joseph Gomes, stranded in that city without cash and in need of a temporary job to raise funds.

Gomes found a job in the warehouse of the Wheeler Paper Company, where Milton Forsman was a foreman. Gomes taught Forsman how to make ascensions and jumps, and Forsman started touring on his own in August 1889. Gomes also became friendly with the Hagels, who ran a box factory nearby the paper company. The Hagels caught the parachute enthusiasm and began touring the next year, 1890. The most frequent aeronauts among the family were Harry and his younger sister, Tillie.

Ten—Other Company Troupes

The year of 1890 was also the year when Milton Forsman decided to stop touring and instead run his school for parachutists. He was interviewed the next year and proudly mentioned his graduates:

> Yes, I train men and women to become aeronauts. In one sense of the word I am the father of many aeronauts who are now scattered over the country. My first pupil was Albert Cotterman, but he is not now in the business. Charles E. Sims was the next. He is the man who went above the clouds at Crawfordsville, Ind., and was completely lost to sight for about fifteen minutes. I thought he had fallen, but he came down safely from a height of a mile and a half. Sims was a daring fellow.
>
> Richard J. Hartman was also a student of mine. At Merrill, Wis., he made an ascension he will never forget. A very high gale was blowing, and when he was up about five hundred feet the balloon caught fire. Dick saw the flame start and cut his parachute loose, descending in safety, although the burning balloon gave him an uncomfortably close chase. Hartman in now making leaps in Iowa.
>
> Mike Reardon was probably the most fearless aeronaut I ever had. He traveled all over the South and made some wonderful leaps. He scorned to wait until the balloon flattened, but made what we call the "cold cut" or "jump." It is a leap directly from the balloon while it is yet going up. One of my balloons will hold 150,000 cubic feet of hot air, and, with an ordinary man aboard, will rise to a height of from 3,500 to 5,000 feet. Then they begin to flatten and descend. At the same time the parachute will fill, and when it is cut loose the aeronaut experiences no sensation in leaping. But in the "cold cut" one drops fully 100 feet before his parachute takes air and begins to open. You can readily see the difference. Reardon always made the "cold cut." He was never hurt but once. That was at Mendota, when he landed on a telegraph wire.
>
> Frank Kiefur [sic, Franklin Keifer], George C. Frazier, William Carroll, Dan Driscoll, and William Smith all made their first trip under my direction, and all are in the business now. James Gomes is another pupil and a good one. Last year at El Paso he was slammed against the amphitheatre on the race track, but held on. He is now riding with his brother, Joe Gomes, who was a circus balloonist for seventeen years. Frank Filey and Eugene Kiesler [sic, Keesler] are also my pupils.
>
> Some of the best riders are women. You would be surprised to know how many girls come to me and want to go up. They desire to avoid publicity if possible on the first trip, but after that, the larger the audience the better suited they are. Mamie Keifer was my first lady pupil, and she is a fearless and plucky little woman. It is a singular fact that on her thirteenth leap she should fall in the lake and almost drown. The parachute settled over her and kept her head under water. Some fishermen got her out and rolled her over an inverted boat until the water was out of her lungs. She is now at the Monmouth races making daily ascensions. She also went into the river at Newark, Ohio, May 30, 1891.

Another daring little woman is Rosa May. She came to me last summer and said she wanted to make a balloon ascension. I told her she would have to get her parents' permission. The next day she came back with an elderly lady whom she introduced as her mother, and I let her make the trip, going along with her. I have since learned that she is from the South and attends a theological school, and the person who gave the consent is not her mother at all. She avoids the crowds when she makes an ascension and no one has ever been able to identify her. Some day she will be recognized and then I will lose one of my best pupils and probably have trouble with her parents.

About a year ago my wife got an idea that she would like to make a trip to the clouds. I tried to dissuade her, but you knew when a woman makes up her mind she will go, so what was there for me to do but to quietly submit! She only weighs ninety-five pounds and rides the smallest parachute in existence. It weighs but thirty-five pounds, while the others weigh sixty pounds. Since then she has made numerous ascensions and always escaped injury. She is an expert at modeling balloons and parachutes. She modeled, cut and made her own balloon and parachute and rode it into the clouds—something, I venture say, no other woman in the world has done.

I made an ascension at Mackinaw once and was dragged through the trees. We had been afraid to send the balloon up all day on account of a violent wind. You know there is a blaze ten or twelve feet high inside a balloon all the time it is being inflated. Well, if it sways badly there is great danger of the sides catching fire. Late in the evening the committee offered me an extra purse to make the trip, and I did so As soon as the balloon arose above the trees the gale struck it and I was dashed through the forest at a terrible rate. I knew it was suicide to let go and also certain death to hang on, but chose the latter course. The stars were shining when I cut loose and dropped.

The parachute swayed terribly. There is a six-inch escape valve in the top of the parachute, and it swung so low at one time that I could distinguish the green trees through it. That was the most eventful trip I ever had. Twice coming down the parachute collapsed, and I dropped with terrible force each time. My wife was in the crowd and she fainted. I landed all right, but it was an awful trip.

I told you of the fear a man experiences the night before he makes an ascension. There are two other points in the trip. One is when he hears the man inside the balloon tell his companion to put on the cover, meaning that the bag is sufficiently inflated. A moment later you are being jerked skyward. The other point of terror is when you decide to cut loose and begin to pick out a good place to land. As a man sits there looking up into the month of the balloon forty feet above him, then at the little parachute, which may or may not work all right, be begins to get cold and, as a rule, he cuts loose right then. Otherwise, he would not have the nerve left to do it. I carefully instruct my pupils not to look at the parachute. There are little straps attached to the bar and the hands are thrust through these. This is to prevent the rider from falling if he or she should become unconscious and release their hold on the bar.

One curious feature of ballooning is that after you leave the ground you never feel a breeze. One can breathe all right, but the air seems dead. I suppose it is because one is traveling along with the current of air instead of opposing it.[18]

Forsman's aeronaut academy took a bite out of the business of the Hagel Brothers, although Harry Hagel continued to operate as a Peoria parachutist through the 1890s. Sister Tillie Hagel made jumps from 1890 to 1894. Two of the brothers, Fred and Frank, moved to Idaho in the mid–1890s and started summer balloon-parachute tours on the West Coast. They hired desperate, inexperienced young women to make jumps and billed them as "Lillie Hagel" or "Nellie Hagel." One "Nellie" was killed in San Francisco in 1893, and a second was killed near Los Angeles in 1895.

Milton Forsman, meanwhile, met his own fate in 1898. After years of risking his life and the lives of dozens of others, he stepped on a rusty nail, contracted lockjaw, and died from the infection. Forsman's death signaled the end of what some had derided as "a training school for idiots" and a "seminary for suicides." Forsman's ballooning tour engagements were taken over by a wild Peoria character named Estes Ashlock. Ashlock hailed from the ballooning city of Springfield, Illinois. His first wife died in 1885 after seven years of marriage, and Ashlock immediately remarried, taking as his wife Elenora Wing—who had just been divorced by budding balloonist James W. Price. Ashlock and Wing's union was also short-lived; she divorced him for adultery. Ashlock's new lover was Juanetta "Nettie" Stubbs. Once Ashlock and Wing's divorce was finalized, he and Stubbs married and moved to Peoria. There, Juanetta Stubbs became "Rosa May," the prize aeronaut pupil of Milton Forsman.

Ashlock mistreated Juanetta Stubbs, forcing her to run away once; they reconciled, but soon separated, and she was thrown onto the street. The local newspapers chronicled her descent from a daring aeronaut to a prostitute. Ashlock married three more times, his last wife being Dolly Stubbs, the sister of Juanetta. None of his marriages lasted long, and in his last years, Ashlock moved to Wisconsin to live with his daughter.

The Grace Shannon Balloon Company

Of all the notable balloon-parachute act companies, the most successful was one with no connections to the balloonists of Quincy,

Springfield, Cleveland, Cincinnati, or Jackson. It did not arise in the upper Midwest, but instead had its roots in Alabama, Georgia, Tennessee, and North Carolina. The Grace Shannon Balloon Company lasted from 1889 until 1917 and employed dozens of aeronauts; they were brought together and managed by Edmund R. Hutchison, the son of a Southern-born Union spy who risked his life to bring down the Confederacy. Grace Shannon herself reigned as the "Queen of the Clouds" throughout the 1890s, but her family origins and fate remain an enigma, as she doubtless intended.

Edmund R. Hutchison, as a young man, had a keen desire to break into the entertainment business. At age nineteen, with his father's support, he was named the manager of Chattanooga, Tennessee's East Lake Summer Theatre and Museum resort. His tenure lasted less than a month, with the resort's season falling into disarray and legal action taken by unpaid performers. Hutchison escaped by joining an acting company and met them in Knoxville to perform at the Bijou Theater. Sometime in the next year (1888–1889), Hutchison realized the entrepreneurial opportunity of the balloon-parachute craze; perhaps the motivation was a performance by Frank "Don Carlos" Stevens in Nashville in September 1889. By October of 1889, Hutchison was attempting ascensions in Sparta, Tennessee, located roughly in the center of a triangle formed by Nashville, Knoxville, and Chattanooga. His female partner was Grace Shannon.[19]

The most Grace Shannon ever revealed about her background was that she was born about 1872 and hailed from Indianapolis—clues, that, even if true, are insufficient to identify her. Given Edmund Hutchison's status at the time, it is likely that she was also recruited from a regional theater troupe and that "Grace Shannon" was a stage name. A few newspaper articles described Hutchison and Shannon as husband and wife, but no record of a marriage exists, and in interviews, Grace herself described Hutchison only as her manager and trainer.

In 1890, the pair conducted a series of engagements in Birmingham, Alabama, including balloon "races" against the transplanted Springfield aeronaut, Ira N. Fisk, and his female protégé, Edith Everett. Hutchison had a very bad fall in June at Knoxville—several reports said he had broken his spine and would die.[20] To fill in, Hutchison hired Nina Melvin to make ascents in his place. Grace performed solo at various cities in the Mid–Atlantic states in 1891, allowing Hutchison to add new aeronauts in 1892, Marion Francis Ezzell and his teen brother Charles, natives of Georgia. Marion adopted the name "Frank Zelno" and became a crowd favorite. During a stop in Charlotte, North Carolina, a local teen named Delia Jaquins begged to join the troupe, and with the consent of her parents, she debuted as "Dot Zelno." Also joining the Balloon Company that year were Leonidas N. O'Dell and his wife, "Leona" (Emmalou Penn), Pearl LeRoy, and Joe Hollemon. In 1893, the Grace Shannon Balloon Company fielded several crews around the country, including Hutchison and Shannon; the O'Dells; and a new manager, J. Henry Crew, and his star aeronaut, Ruby Deveau (real name Louise Schroene).

Frank Zelno and "Dot" left the Grace Shannon Company that year and organized their own balloon company based in Savannah, Georgia. Frank also performed high dives of 80–100 feet into a tank measuring 12 feet long by eight feet wide containing a depth of five feet of water. In 1895 he fractured both feet when he hit the edge of the tank. Frank married several times. In 1893, his bride was Jessie Brown, who became the aeronaut, "Jessie Zelno." He married again in 1908 and in 1916 and a final time sometime after 1916. He died in 1926 but might have been the hand behind an earlier death announcement printed in *Billboard* in 1916, just six months into one of his failing marriages. In his later years he painted scenery for theaters.

In 1898, Edmund Hutchison married his newest aeronaut star, Reta Danzelle (real name Flora Ames). At about the same time, Grace Shannon herself disappeared, though her name lived on in the name of the balloon company.[21] From the mid–1890s to 1910, the company employed an average of seven male and three female aeronauts each season. The company adopted every proven variation of the balloon-parachute act: drops with pets; night ascensions with fireworks; balloon races; double drops; drops using multiple parachutes on the same jumper; and even the giant exploding shell gimmick. The Hutchisons stopped touring around 1912 and ran operations from their balloon/awning factory in Reta's hometown of Elmira, New York.[22] There they settled in as fixtures of the community for the next forty years.

One of Hutchison's later aeronauts went on to greater fame as a daredevil: Robert "Bobby" Leach. Leach, raised in England, emigrated to the United States in the late 1890s. He first appeared as a performer with Reta Danzelle at Crescent Park in East Providence, Rhode Island. He was a frequent parachutist at that location. At Niagara Falls in 1906, Leach parachuted from the Upper Steel Arch Bridge into the Niagara River. That was a prelude to realizing his ambition: to go over Niagara Falls in a barrel. He accomplished this feat—only the second person to do so after Annie Taylor in 1901—on July 25, 1911. Not yet finished, Leach parachuted from an airplane over the Falls and landed on Canadian soil. He was 63 years old at the time.

The Belmont Sisters

A major troupe that first appeared a few years later than those mentioned above was a company billed as the Belmont Sisters. As was the case with the Leroy Sisters, there was no aeronaut among them with the real name of Belmont. The company could trace its roots to two men who briefly started out as aeronauts themselves: Clarence Earl Baldwin and William E. Carrow, both hailing from small towns in Michigan. Baldwin, born in 1872, claimed to be a nephew of Thomas S. Baldwin, but his documentable family tree suggests otherwise. The details of how Baldwin and Carrow met and became aeronauts are not known, but they likely started out as circus performers around 1896. The two struck out on their own in September 1898 and recruited others to work with them in 1899.

That summer, Carrow worked with aeronauts Eugene Sprague, "Madame Carmon" (Cora Johnson Carman) and Willard A. Thayer. Sprague and Thayer were recruited locally in Michigan, while Carmon was a veteran circus aerialist. It did not take long for disaster to strike. On July 10, at Streator, Illinois, Madame Carmon was ready to ascend when the inflation flue sent flames onto the balloon. Someone yelled to the holders to let go the guy lines, and one of the loose ropes then whipped around the aeronaut's legs, pulling her into the sky under a burning balloon, with her head facing downwards. Fortunately for her, the fire burned a hole in the balloon so that it descended quickly onto a house, and she escaped with only a few bruises.

Two weeks later at the same location, Willard Thayer had ascended only two hundred feet when the balloon turned over prematurely, expelled its smoke, and plummeted. Thayer had no chance to cut the parachute loose and the balloon soon dragged it down, along with Thayer. He landed on his back on a railroad track, breaking his back, neck, arms, and legs, and he breathed once or twice before dying. The Streator papers described him as having been a pleasant young man, but his hometown Michigan newspaper reminded readers that he had served time for larceny and had been divorced.

Less than a month later, in Racine, Wisconsin, Eugene Sprague was scheduled to perform a trick that Carrow had taught him: making an ascension while astride a bicycle. However, before Sprague even had a chance to perform, he was driving his bicycle through the city streets and swerved to avoid another bicyclist, a young woman who was the daughter of a police officer. Both cyclists fell in the path of an oncoming streetcar and were killed. The young woman's body was picked up off the street by her father. Sprague left behind in Michigan his recent bride, Dorothy Gates, pregnant with their daughter.

Ten—Other Company Troupes

That same season, Clarence Baldwin had marginally better luck with 16-year-old "Cleo Belmont" (real name unknown) and "Lillian Belmont" (real name Adela Sowards). At the Ionia County, Michigan, Fair in October 1899, against the law of averages, nearly the same accident happened to "Lillian" as had to Madame Carmon: a rope holder got tangled and was lifted into the air ten feet before dropping, while at the same time the balloon caught on fire. Aeronaut Belmont cut loose as soon as she could and was unhurt.

Despite all these mishaps, Baldwin and Carrow opened the 1900 season with replacement aeronauts, as well as a returning "Cleo Belmont" and Adela Sowards. Sowards discarded her "Lillian Belmont" name and became "Lillian LeFay," reflecting the fact that Baldwin and Carrow were now fielding two separate teams, the Belmont Sisters and the LeFay Sisters. Joining her were Alfred J. Seeley and "Mabel Belmont." That season and most of the next (1901) appeared to go well, but tragedy struck again in October 1901. Adela Sowards, as "Lillian LaFay," made an ascension over the Illinois River at La Salle, Illinois. Her spotters saw her drop and believed that she had descended on the opposite bank. They later found the balloon but could not locate Sowards or the parachute. Her body was found near the water a week later, sixteen miles downriver. The next summer, in August 1902, Alfred Seeley performed a jump at Homer, Illinois, as "Professor L.A. Sartell." He ascended and cut loose, but the parachute lines tangled, and it never opened. He broke both legs and suffered unknown internal injuries, dying the next day, but in his last moments dictated an apology to his father for not quitting the business sooner.

Following 1902, Carrow and Baldwin improved their equipment and training and suffered few serious accidents. Their stars from 1903 to 1915 were "Clara Belmont" and "Flossie Belmont." In 1905, they agreed to make some joint appearances against a long-time competing act from Michigan, the Davonda Sisters, led by Dorothy Davonda. Davonda, it happens, was none other than Dorothy Gates, the widow of one of the first Belmont aeronauts, Eugene Sprague. It is possible that she had earlier been a "Belmont Sister" before striking out on her own.

In 1913, Clarence Baldwin divorced his third wife and a few months later married Lucielle Dashiell of Fort Worth, Texas, who would become the most famous member of the troupe, Lucielle Belmont. Lucielle quickly became a star, and her signature features were to drop from a balloon using a parachute pack and to deploy two parachutes in succession. For a short time, she was joined by her sister, Gertrude Dashiell. Lucielle and Baldwin stayed together for many years and took the act to Canada and South America.

The last woman aeronaut to join the act was "Madeline Belmont," otherwise known as Madeline Davis. Like Lucielle, she used an early parachute pack, but made jumps from a seaplane as well as from a balloon. Because of her fearlessness, Madeline was invited by stunt flyer Ruth Bancroft Law to join her "Flying Circus." To convince Law that she was capable, she agreed to perform the trick of jumping from a moving car to a rope ladder dangled by an airplane passing overhead. The *New York Times* reported the attempt:

> The trio practiced for half an hour before they made the actual test. Miss Law drove the car at about 45 miles an hour back and forth along the road and the aviator, slowing down to automobile speed, flew close to the earth over the motorists several times. By this time it was late afternoon and the day was becoming dark, but Miss Davis insisted on going through with the test.
>
> The crowd held its breath as the two machines shot down the wide boulevard for the final trip, the automobile with its passengers a good distance in advance of the airplane. Miss Law bent over the wheel to hold the car in the center of the road. Miss Davis, her face determined and hands clenched on the side of the car, waited.
>
> Behind them roared the airplane, first speeding up to a short distance behind the automobile, and then slowing so that it was going only a little faster. Slowly the dangling rope crept closer to Miss Davis's grasp. She jumped and caught the bottom rung of the rope ladder. She swung to and fro a moment, but her strength was not great enough to enable her to climb up the ladder and board the plane. As she tried to climb, her hands slipped and she fell to earth.[23]

The last and most famed Belmont Sister, Lucielle Dashiell, outlived husband Clarence Baldwin and remarried in the 1930s, moving to San Diego. There, for three decades she sold flower bouquets on the street that she gathered from her garden, outliving her second husband, Harry Rutshaw, by many years. In the late 1950s she was diagnosed with cancer, which caused her health to deteriorate, to the point where she determined in 1961 to end her own life rather than endure more pain. Before she died, she had been elected as member 345 of the Early Birds, a "last man" organization of pre–1916 aviators. She left money to the Smithsonian National Air and Space Museum money for its Early Bird plaque and sent her collection of newspaper clippings there. Though of seemingly modest means, she also left a $200,000 trust fund in 1961 for the California Community Foundation, which continues to distribute money to charities and non-profits to this day.

Eleven

Notable Parachuting Performers

While circuses and balloon companies advertised nationally and toured widely, other individual performers of the balloon-parachute act established solid regional reputations. They often made their own ascensions, working with one or two assistants per season, but did not field separate teams. Since these performers frequently returned to the same venues year after year, they earned the trust and respect of annual fair managers. Because they appeared for several seasons in the same locations, they were remembered by residents of these regions even decades after their last performances. From east to west, here are brief sketches of these notable American aeronauts.

Clarence C. Bonette—New England

Clarence C. Bonette was raised and resided in northern New England, outside of St. Johnsbury, Vermont—an area not known as a ballooning center. Even so, Bonette went on to become perhaps the most prolific balloon-parachute act performer of all time. In 1943, when Bonette was 72, he was interviewed by his hometown paper, the *St. Johnsbury Caledonian Record*:

"What started you in the balloon business?" we asked.

Bonette's eyes twinkled. "I guess its just because I took the first opportunity that came along. It was in Plymouth, N.H., way back in 1893.

"Just before they let her go, the balloonist took sick and the manager was furious. The crowd was yelling 'Fake! Fake!' so I stepped forward and said 'I'll go.'

"I didn't say I had never been up in a balloon before. They strapped me in, gave me a few instructions, and the first thing I knew I was dizzily dangling every which way—1,000 feet up in the air.

"Being way up there in the sky, all alone, appealed to me. I was where I belonged, and all sense of fright left me.

"All of a sudden I heard a pistol shot coming from the ground, and then I remembered what the balloonist had told me, 'I'll keep an eye on you, young feller, and when you're high enough I'll fire this revolver. When you hear that shot, cut loose. Don't wait an instant—cut loose immediately.'

"I heard the shot, all right, and looked down. There was the Pemigewasset River right under me. I didn't know anything about air currents, or drifting, but I did know I didn't want to land in that river. Besides, I was having too much fun where I was. I kept right on, going higher and higher.

"Pretty soon I ran into some clouds and lost sight of the ground, so I screwed up my courage and cut away. By golly, I'll never forget that first jump. I must have gone down 500 feet before the 'chute opened, and what a yank.

"Soon's the 'chute opened up I saw everything was O.K., I slid off the trapeze bar and did a few tricks. That made a big hit with the crowd. I guess the other feller was jealous, 'cause he scolded me something awful."

"How many times have you jumped since then?" we asked.

Bonette reached for a well-worn diary and scanned it carefully.

"Let's see," he said. "My last jump was in Lancaster, N.H. last September [1942]. That was my 4785th jump, and before I quit I'm going to reach the 5000 mark.... I've been smashed so many times and spent so many hours in hospitals I can't keep track of it. I have had more broken bones than any other man alive today." Then he laughed.

"I have had some queer experiences. Came down in a pigpen once, right through the roof where an old sow had a litter of kids. Did she come after me? Probably because I had on a bright red suit of tights.

"'Nother time, I landed on a building right in the heart of a city. I hit a roof with slate shingles and went right through it. Those shingles skinned every rag off my body and most of the hide, too. Left me standing in a top floor dance hall—naked as the day I was born.

"Once when I went up from the fairgrounds at Bangor, the wind blew me out over the Penobscot River. My 'chute caught in the top rigging of a three-masted schooner, and there I swung. Then she let go and I went whizzing down into the water right in front of the Boston-Bangor boat. But I managed to swim to one side.

"Things that stick up in the air like the spire of a church, chimney, or radio tower are hazards.... Live wires, any wires are what we dread." He paused and said, "That's how my wife was injured, just two years after we were married. We made a double jump, over in Malone, N.Y., and she hit some wires. She grabbed on to 'em, but they broke and she crashed onto the street. It broke her back, and for 25 years she suffered as few humans ever have.

"I made her a special wheelchair-bed," he said, "and for 15 years she went with me and watched me jump. I never knew a braver woman. I promised her I would never marry again, and I've kept that promise.

"Sometimes I wonder if the public realizes what performers go through just to give them a thrill," and he asked to change the subject.[1]

Shortly before Bonette's wife Minnie died in 1921, they adopted the orphaned son of a local neighbor, Louis Lapoint. Bonette introduced Louis to the balloon-parachute act in the late 1920s, when he was 15.[2] The two of them started taking engagements outside New England, which took them to Oklahoma in May 1930. While there, the Bonettes were involved in a potboiler drama the details of which will never be fully known. Louis Lapoint and a local man assisting the Bonettes—named Earl Fairbairn—were arrested for sabotaging a balloon by putting acid onto it, which was fortunately discovered before an ascension by the senior Bonette was made. The charges against Lapoint were dropped almost immediately, and he rejoined his adopted father on tour. After many weeks, the charges against Fairbairn were also dropped for lack of evidence. At some point during these events, Fairbairn and his wife Madge, age 30, separated. Madge returned to New England with the Bonettes and in September of 1930 married the 21-year-old Louis Lapoint.

The Bonettes, Clarence and Louis, stopped touring in 1945. It is not known if Clarence Bonette made it to the 5,000 jump milestone at the time of his death in 1947 at age 75.

Karl Kilip and Karletta—Western New York State

In August 1893, a reporter happened to meet Mary "Carlotta" Myers on a hotel veranda and could not resist asking a question: is the "Karletta" currently using a hot air balloon and parachute near Buffalo trying to take her name and steal her fame? "Undoubtedly, though my name is spelled with a 'C' and is copyrighted. I am not at all jealous of the hot air balloonist. We left that business behind us as not worthy of our intellect a long time ago. Our operations are confined to gas ballooning and mostly from a scientific standpoint."[3]

Perhaps out of politeness, Mrs. Myers did not reveal that she knew "Karletta" quite well, as she had been one of the female aeronauts employed by the Myers in the 1880s to perform the balloon-trapeze act. During that earlier time, Karletta was using a different stage name, "Helene A. Thiers." Nor did Mrs. Myers need to be concerned with Karletta's growing fame: in August of 1893, she had already made her last jump and was sick with consumption (tuberculosis), which would take her life in October 1893.[4]

Karletta was born Ellen Augusta Benjamin, the daughter of a

Buffalo boat builder. It was in Buffalo that she began her career as a music hall dancer at age 14. Her talent as a dancer got her engagements in Rochester, Albany, Pittsburgh, and, finally, New York City. There she was one of the leading dancers in the production of the landmark musical extravaganza, *The Black Crook*. She remained with this company throughout its entire first run, during 1866–1867. She then retired for a few years but reemerged in the mid–1870s as an aeronaut pupil of W.H. Donaldson and Harry Gilbert. It was with Harry Gilbert in the late 1870s and early 1880s that she adopted her aeronaut stage name, Helene Thiers. "Thiers" was a modification of the name "Thayer," which she took after marrying actor Edward H. Thayer.

In the late 1880s, Thiers moved back to Buffalo with her husband, who also hailed from that city. She joined Carl Myers' team of aeronauts performing ascensions and the balloon-trapeze act. She was often paired with the ill-fated Edwin Claridge, the trapeze aeronaut who died at Olean, New York, in 1887 after hitting telegraph wires during ascension. During winter months, she and her husband acted on the stage. One season, she led her own troupe on tour, the Criterion Comedy Company.

In 1891, Thiers teamed up with W. Karl Killip, a 28-year-old Buffalo transplant from Pennsylvania. Killip, an electrician and amateur balloonist, was looking for a female aeronaut, and Thiers, who was by that time 49 years old, was looking once again for summer work. Thiers now became "Karletta," the partner of W. Karl Killip. The pair became a fixture in Western New York for the next two years and made routine jumps at Crystal Beach across the border in Ontario. One of her last jumps was on July 19, 1893, at Crystal Beach. She drifted over Lake Erie and dropped down far from shore but was kept afloat by a life belt.

After Thiers became ill, W. Karl Killip agreed to make a tour of Cuba in November and December of 1893 and planned to leave to come back to the United States on Christmas Day. On Christmas Eve he made an ascent in Havana during high winds. He was swept toward an electric light pole and then across a string of wires. He was knocked off his seat and fell 300 feet to the ground, suffering fatal injuries.[5] Karl and "Karletta" died within three months of each other. They left behind their student, Clarence G. Eckhart, who traveled the nation as a parachutist and tightrope walker from the 1890s to the 1920s.

Louis R. Bush—Ohio, Kentucky, West Virginia

When Harry Gilbert left Cincinnati in 1890 to move to Brooklyn with his last aeronaut student, Louise Bates, he left a gap in the

Eleven—Notable Parachuting Performers

ballooning scene of the Ohio city and its summer resort, Coney Island. All his other apprentices—Charles Williams, Sam Young, Helen Thiers, etc., had also moved on. The managers at Coney Island hired a series of other aeronauts, one of whom was a local shoemaker, Louis Bush. Bush was described as a "veteran aeronaut" in 1891, so it is possible, that he, too, was encouraged by Harry Gilbert. At any rate, Bush became the region's leading aeronaut for the next two decades, during which time he, like Gilbert, mentored other young aeronauts. He dropped the shoe business and spent winter months as an awning manufacturer (the preferred industry for balloonists). Bush's most noted assistant was Elmer Louis, who later became a wing-walker in Ruth Law's Flying Circus.[6]

Though some described Bush as a genial mentor, he had a callous side as well. In August 1891, a Coney Island (Ohio) female aeronaut named Frankie Lavell (real name Anna Harkes) fell from her bar while descending and dropped in full sight of thousands of spectators. Her demise was made more tragic by the inquest that revealed that she was a desperate unwed mother, rejected by her family and her lover. Bush was called to testify. He confidently stated that nothing had been wrong with the equipment and that Frankie had released her safety line and committed suicide.[7] Bush misread public sentiment about Harkes' death, which was driven by arguably the most gruesome newspaper accounts ever written about a fallen aeronaut. The *Cincinnati Enquirer* put the accident on page 1 of its August 16 edition, using one main headline and no less than eleven subheads:

> BLOODY MASS: Of Quivering, Disjointed Flesh; Without a Semblance to Human Form; All That remains of Frankie Lavell; Who Essayed a Parachute Leap at Coney Island; Her Hands Lost Their Hold and She Plunges; Headlong Against a Rough and rocky Hillside; In the Presence of Hundreds of Horrified Spectators; Her Face Crushed as a Ripe Tomato Thrown Against the Wall; While Portions of Her Skull are Scattered About; Five Hundred Feet Above the Earth She Hangs by Her Toes; The Remains Gathered in a Sheet and Placed in the Morgue.

A few years after Harkes' death, in 1895, Bush hired a man to help him during an ascension at Richie County, West Virginia. The man asked to go up with Bush, but once they had ascended several thousand feet, he climbed out the basket and up the rigging of the balloon. According to Bush, the man said he was going to kill himself and that Bush should cut loose with the parachute immediately. Bush, fearing that the man was going to sabotage the parachute, made the drop, leaving the man holding the balloon rigging. The balloon turned over and the man dropped to his death. Once again, Bush testified that the intent of the man was suicide.[8]

William H. Hanner—Ohio Valley

Another Cincinnati–based aeronaut was William H. Hanner, the former assistant of the Springfield, Illinois, balloonist, Joseph Gomes. Though Gomes had advertised Hanner as "the world's youngest aeronaut," supposedly born in 1874, Hanner was in fact born in 1860, just three years younger than Gomes. Hanner's youthful appearance became part of his identity, for throughout his career he was known as "Kid Hanner." Hanner assisted Gomes until 1890, when he struck out on his own and contracted to perform ascensions for small circus outfits. In 1893, he introduced his own balloon company, headquartered in Cincinnati, featuring a female partner, May Allison. Allison appeared under several stage names: "Louise Hanner" (a supposed sister), "Mlle. LeVoy," and "Miss America." Allison and Hanner were married in 1894.

Though a small family business, Hanner advertised widely and booked engagements all through the eastern United States. Disaster struck the Hanners on May 26, 1896, at the Fairy Grove summer resort on the Back River, seven miles from downtown Baltimore. Allison made the ascension, but her balloon cooled quickly after reaching only 2000 feet and began to descend over the river. She must have judged that it would go into the water before reaching the opposite shore, so she cut loose. She came down in the water but was not able to disengage the safety line that held her to the trapeze bar. Just as rescuers in boats neared her, she was pulled underwater by the parachute fabric. Hanner arrived minutes later and dived to the river bottom twenty times trying to locate her, without success. Her body was later recovered.[9]

Hanner remarried six months later to Jessie Packer, who assumed the role of Mlle. LeVoy for a high wire act that featured a slide from a 100-foot tower down a wire on a pulley disguised in her hair (and supported by a hidden body brace). However, it does not appear that she performed parachute drops, which Hanner alone performed. The odds of a mishap occurring caught up with Hanner in late September 1900, at a fair in Henderson, Kentucky. Hanner ascended in a stiff wind, and his balloon was dashed against a high tree. Hanner was knocked off his trapeze and fell 70 feet, suffering massive injuries. His death marked the end of the Great Hanner Balloon Company.[10]

Professors Zeno—Ohio, Georgia

Two aeronauts adopted the name "Professor Zeno," but it is unclear if the first Zeno bequeathed willingly the name to the second. The first

Zeno was an English acrobat named John Hunter Whorter. Whorter first appeared in the United States as a balloon-trapeze act acrobat with Ira Fisk's American Balloon Company. By 1890 he had struck out on his own and landed repeat engagements at various Cincinnati summer resorts. There he worked with a female aeronaut who went by the name "Mlle. Hortense." It is unproven if "Mlle. Hortense" of the 1890 season was identical to Alice Huonker, who, starting in 1891, performed with Whorter as "Madame Zeno." Whorter and Huonker were wed in Windsor, Ontario, in August 1891, though in her later years, Huonker described their relationship as "platonic," and said that Whorter treated her as a daughter.[11]

Platonic or not, Huonker left Whorter in 1893 to work for balloonist Patrick "Patsy" Trainer, who had spent the previous year managing engagements for Louise "Lulu" Bates. Trainer and Huonker spent three seasons together, often bickering, at engagements in West Virginia and Western Pennsylvania. Whorter, working without a female partner, toured extensively in Tennessee and South Carolina during the same period. Whorter migrated to Savannah, Georgia, in 1895 and spent the next year and half there, advertising himself as "Late of Crystal Palace, London." At some point in that period, Whorter met Paul Hague, a 21-year-old native of Springfield, Ohio. Hague had located to Savannah with his father, who had separated from his wife and left her in Ohio. Apparently by agreement, the 40-year-old Whorter bestowed Hague with the "Professor Zeno" identity. Whorter moved to Memphis, Tennessee, in the late 1890s, retired from performing, and opened a saloon that thrived for decades.[12]

Hague, as the new Professor Zeno, conducted balloon races in Savannah with William H. Hanner, the Cincinnati aeronaut who had come south for the winter. Hague then moved his operations back to the Ohio Valley, where he performed at local fairs for the next four years. He recruited his own "Madame Zeno," though it was not Alice Huonker. Instead, it was a 16-year-old Canadian, Mabel Overholt. Hague and Overholt married on July 10, 1901, the same day that Hague was said to have rescued Overholt from a beating delivered by a jealous boyfriend. Sadly, Hague was killed less than three months later after landing his parachute in the city reservoir at Lima, Ohio. Overholt made no effort to see Hague buried properly and did not even travel to Lima from Springfield, Ohio, explaining that she "did not like to see dead bodies."[13]

Alice Huonker, the original Madame Zeno, made parachute jumps off and on through to 1909. "When airplanes came in, they killed the balloon business," she related years later. She married a vaudeville comedian, took a stab at acting in movies, and then retired. She preferred to use the name "Alice Zeno" her entire life. "It was a good short name and fine for print, and I've always kept it."[14] She died in 1958 in Los Angeles.

William Z. Love and Cora Rolliston— Central Indiana

The circumstances of how Cora Rolliston of Cincinnati met William Z. Love of Indiana are not known, but took place before September 1890, the first date where Cora's name was printed as Love rather than Rolliston. Her family origins are murky, but it was said that she was the stepdaughter of a balloonist or balloon-maker. She made several jumps at fairs in Ohio between 1888 and 1890, some of which were done with Al Tolbert. After Cora met William Z. Love, she encouraged him to make ascensions. They resided at Spencer, Indiana, outside the city of Bloomington.[15] In 1891, W.Z. Love was a steady attraction at the Fairview Park resort of Indianapolis. After making jumps there successfully for six weeks, in late July he made an ascent and had trouble with entangling the parachute cords before cutting loose. After starting his descent, several of the parachute cords broke, and he fell rapidly to earth. He was found unconscious and sustained a serious injury to his spine. Cora performed the remainder of the season at Fairview Park.

Sometime after 1891, Cora appears to have lost interest in ballooning and in her marriage. William Z. Love performed parachute drops solo for the 1892 and 1893 seasons, and in April 1894, an Indianapolis newspaper noted that the couple had divorced and that Cora had eloped with another man. In July 1894, Love introduced a new female assistant: Lillian Cody (real name Maud Lee), the Wild West show trick shooter and estranged wife of Samuel F. Cody. Maud's tenure lasted just a few weeks in July, after which she returned to her fancy shooting act at the Indiana State Fair, the Iowa State Fair, and the Texas State Fair.[16]

Love, perhaps unable to continue due to lingering effects from his 1891 fall, handed responsibility off to an assistant, William Lewis of Springfield, Illinois. Love advised Lewis to hire a female aeronaut, as they were more popular with the public. Lewis convinced a girl he knew from Richmond, Indiana, named Tillie Price, to give it a try. Their first engagement was in Anderson, Indiana, where the pair presented themselves as "William Martin" and "Tillie Sibern" and claimed that Tillie was a veteran of dozens of ascensions. Her launch went perfectly, but something happened once she cut loose—she fell from the trapeze bar and plummeted to earth. It was found that her safety line—a worn thin rope—had broken.[17] Her death brought recriminations to William Lewis, William Z. Love, and the practice of using young women as aeronauts. Love remarried in 1895. Before succumbing in 1899 to the injuries he had received eight years earlier, Love mentored a young balloonist from Franklin, Indiana, named D. Luther Dennis.

D. Luther Dennis was an active parachutist from the late 1890s through the early 1930s, ending his long career only after local fair managers offered him dwindling pittances for his performances. Many photographs, scrapbooks, and equipment used by Luther have been preserved by the Johnson County (Indiana) Museum. One photograph from the 1920s shows a Dennis balloon with a Ku Klux Klan cross—an ugly, stark reminder of the popularity of the revived Klan of the 1920s, when it feigned the legitimacy of a community social organization.[18]

Willian Gaul and the Logansport Aeronauts— Northern Indiana

There is no better example of how entranced with parachuting the youth of a single community became in the 1890s than Logansport, Indiana—a small city located halfway between Indianapolis and the southern shores of Lake Michigan. The ringleader of the group was a young printer's assistant named William Gaul (often spelled as "Gall"). In 1892, Gaul was inspired by a touring balloonist to try to make his own balloon. He was assisted by pals Fred Landis, Frank Harrell (also a printer's assistant), Horace Fowler, and George Bush. Their first homemade balloon turned out to be too small to lift a human, so they sent aloft a goose. About that time, two traveling professional jumpers, Fred Royale of Indianapolis and T. Harry Simmons of Evansville, Indiana, came through Logansport and gave the boys some proper instruction; later they were given tips by another professional passing through, Samuel Z. Beam of Somerset, Pennsylvania.

After the gang had made several local ascensions and jumps, William Gaul and Frank Harrell decided to strike out on their own—separately—as professional jumpers, while the other youths gave up the practice. Gall spent the next twelve years as a parachutist at county fairs in Indiana and took on as assistant aeronauts Claude and Anna Ammons. Frank Harrell's career was much briefer. He started as a junior partner of Fred Royale of Indianapolis, but in September of 1895 made a jump at Peru, Indiana, that left him hanging in a tree forty feet above the ground. He tried crawling down, but the parachute slipped through the branches and pulled him down. He broke both ankles and suffered a spinal injury that left his legs paralyzed.[19]

The mentors of the Logansport gang hardly fared better. Two years after Harrel's accident, in 1897, Fred Royale attempted a 125-foot high-dive into a net from a car atop the giant Ferris Wheel left over from the Chicago World's Fair. He landed in the net but broke his spine and died.[20] T. Harry Simmons spent many years as a circus aeronaut; he was unemployed and living in a Chicago boarding house in May 1904. He got into a penny ante poker game with another resident. Upon losing a jackpot of thirty cents, Simmons accused the other man of cheating. His opponent cursed at Simmons, whereupon Simmons drew a revolver and shot the man through the heart.[21]

Logansport's Frank Harrell, though paralyzed, made the best of his fate. He had a special self-propelled wheelchair constructed, which allowed him to maintain a job as a commercial printer. He once overturned on a city sidewalk and waved off assistance, determined to climb back into his seat on his own. After moving to Indianapolis, Harrell asked to meet a prospective printing client in one of the city's suburbs. However, when Harrell attempted to get on a light-transit railroad, the conductors refused to allow him aboard. In 1899, Harrell sued the railroad company for $10,000 in damages—perhaps one of the first examples of a disabled person taking legal action for accommodation. Defending his rights as a handicapped person was just as courageous, if not more so, than his earlier parachute jumps.[22]

The Dennis-Woodall Company—Western Indiana

William Dennis of Terre Haute, Indiana, had dabbled with ballooning before Tom Baldwin's first jump in 1887. His friend John Woodall, a local saloon owner originally from Quincy, Illinois, convinced him that they must go there to see one of Sam Baldwin's first jumps in the fall of 1888. Both Dennis and Woodall were so enthused by the spectacle that they made plans to go into the balloon-parachute act business the next spring. What is more impressive is that the men were joined in the business by their wives, both of whom were already raising young children.[23] William Dennis made the first leap at Sullivan, Indiana, in May 1889.

By 1891 both Mrs. Dennis and Mrs. Woodall were featured in the act. On some occasions the two couples split up to make engagements in different towns on the same dates. They traveled as far north as Ontario, Canada, as far south as Alabama, and as far east as northeast Pennsylvania. By June 1891, they had made more jumps in that year's season than they had in the entire previous season. The two couples shared performance responsibilities until 1895. Following that, only William Dennis and Harriet "Jennie" Woodall continued to make ascents; it is not clear if after 1894 they were still working within a partnership or were now independent. None of the four suffered mishaps more serious than broken bones. In 1900, Mrs. Woodall had a notable experience landing on top of the steam locomotive of a stopped freight train, with her parachute fabric smothering the engineer's cabin.[24] The Dennis-Woodall Company stands as the only known example of couples partnering in the business.

Elizabeth C. Crawford—Missouri

In a profession full of colorful characters, Elizabeth C. Crawford stands out as unique. Though not a well-traveled or prolific jumper, she was notable for three characteristics: she was a great interview; she was contemptuous of other aeronauts and corrupt public officials; and she was leading spiritualist. In July 1892, she sat down with a reporter of the St. Louis Globe Democrat and required little prompting. Fortunately, the reporter recorded her verbatim, and the news editor wisely let it stand:

> I don't know what impelled me to become an aeronaut. Just my uncontrollable passion for adventure, I guess. It was two years ago when the desire seized me, and I haven't rid myself of it yet. Since then I have made 109 ascensions, have had three ribs broken and my spine telescoped, and I think now I am the only female balloonist and parachute leaper in this country. At Farmington, Mo., soon after I had started in the business my parachute got cranky when I cut myself loose 8,000 feet above the earth, and it was a wonder I wasn't killed. I sailed down easy enough for the first 6,000 feet, but at 2,000 feet I struck a swift counter-current of air which twisted the parachute around rapidly and plunged the top down so that I only prevented it from turning inside out with the greatest difficulty. I knew that I was in danger, but my presence of mind never left me for an instant. When about 70 feet from the ground another gust of wind overpowered me and turned the parachute completely inside out. The ropes tangled with my feet, jerked my hold loose from the bar, and I plunged downward head foremost. I saw a huge tree directly under me, and I reached my hands to catch a limb, but I missed it and struck the ground fairly upon my feet, fell over, and fainted away. When I came to, I discovered that I had received the injuries I told you about.
>
> What does it require to become an aeronaut? Well, the only thing I can think of is nerve. I have never yet had that feeling called fear. I wish I could experience it once; it would be such an entirely new sensation to me. With

nerve and a cool head, which always go together, anyone can be an aeronaut and parachute jumper. Oh no! I'm not afraid of getting killed. What if others in the business have had the life rushed out of them? That's no sign that I'll meet that fate. I've made up my mind that if I ever feel the least apprehensive of the result, I'll never go up in a balloon, no matter if a million people are gazing at me. That's the way I'll keep from getting killed. I have never made an ascension of less than 5,000 feet. Eight thousand is the average, and I've gone as high as 12,000.

Monday the balloon took me 9,000 feet before I jumped. I use only the hot-air balloon. It takes me up faster than the average train scoots along over the earth. The sensations I experience while going up are thrilling enough, but they are nothing like those I experience while coming down. I travel faster on the descent. A mile a minute is slower than I shoot down through the air. In ascending, the balloon continually whirls like a top. It's calculated to make one's head dizzy, but the scenes shift with such lightening-like-rapidity that I don't have time to allow my brain to get to spinning. As the earth recedes from me the tallest building in this city looks like a child's toy house, smokestacks have the appearance of broom straws, and the Mississippi River dwindles to the insignificance of a thread.

Up, up, up I go, each 100 feet adding perceptibly to the chilliness of the atmosphere and all objects beneath me growing smaller and smaller until in a twinkling they are lost to view. There is nothing under me now but a vast expanse of gray mist. Above me the sky is bluer than any blue you ever saw, and it seems to be bending toward me. When I lose sight of the earth, even with the aid of my telescope, I know that I am 7774 feet up. The air is crisp and chill and my ears and fingers tingle with the cold. A rose I wear at my throat is chilled and frozen now, and its petals warp, as in pity, and fall from the stem. But still my balloon is whirling me higher. The air is so thin. I breathe with difficulty. Through a dense cloud I am jerked, and come out drenched and numbed. Nine thousand feet, and the air in my balloon is chilled. A lurch downward, and a tremendous flap of the monster canvas tells me that it is time to cut the rope that binds my parachute to the balloon.

But a hurried look around warns me there is a danger. The rope is all twisted and twirled, and the parachute is tied into a knot. I am in a counter-current of air. The wind is blowing a tornado, and if I should loosen the rope now, the sides of my parachute would be slammed together so I could never open them, and I would drop to the earth like a bar of lead. I therefore cling on to the balloon until it floats through this fierce current that seems mocking me with its cruel whistle. Once past it and I am safe. Then I cut the rope and shoot downward like an arrow for several hundred feet. The swift motion accumulates sufficient air under the folds of my parachute to spread it out like an umbrella, and I have smooth though swift sailing for the rest of the way. But I go so fast that I am afraid to open my mouth for fear the wind will take my breath away. I have my teeth clamped tightly on a little stick, smaller than a pencil. Somehow this stick helps me to keep my mouth shut.[25]

I am hardly ever more than a minute coming down. When the air tells me that I am getting near the earth I open my eyes to look around. I have the parachute under perfect control, and if I see I am about to descend on a tree or a roof I direct the parachute around it. When 200 or 300 feet from the ground I swing from the crossbar by my hands in order that I may light on my feet.

I have known very few aeronauts. I have never met a woman in the business, and only hear of them when they get killed by a parachute leap. The men—"Professors" they style themselves—are mostly cheats and all cowards. It has been my observation that, give a man the least possible excuse and he will break his contract for an ascension and parachute leap. He always wants to get out of the leap. It takes a woman to exhibit the necessary nerve for so daring a feat., although we are called the weaker sex. I have never been out of Missouri, and have no particular desire to make a tour.[26]

Crawford was likely first given the opportunity to make a jump by her future husband (one of several), George W. Richards. Richards was a former circus strongman who organized his own low-budget troupe that played to cities along the Mississippi, traveling by steamer. A month after giving the above interview, Crawford was forced to defend the skies of St. Louis from an invasion by Rosa May, the star student of Milton Forsman's Peoria parachuting school. Crawford issued May a challenge (to which she did not respond) and derided her for using a safety harness, since she held on to her bar by muscles alone.[27]

Though Rosa May ignored Crawford's taunts, another of Milton Forsman's protégés took up the dare. Her performing name was "Madame Adair," but she was born as Alfretta Denton, the daughter of a Pennsylvania coal miner. She started performing in small vaudeville venues taking doing a variety of acts: boxing, bicycle trick riding, tightrope walking, and trapeze work, capitalizing on her pretty face and hourglass figure. Early in the 1895 season, she substituted for an injured aeronaut at Bloomington, Illinois, and was noticed by Milton Forsman, the Peoria parachuting manager. After Forsman provided her with further training, she eloped with a hotel worker, James Baum, who became her manager. When she read of Crawford's remarks, Alfretta gladly accepted her challenge and hastened to St. Louis. There, in front of a crowd of 50,000 at Sportsman Park, the two women competed for the parachuting "championship of the world," to be determined by who ascended highest and made the longest jump.

These balloon "races" were more a matter of proper inflation and the size/lifting power of the balloons, more so than any skills of the aeronauts. Alfretta Denton won the contest, which put an end to the boasts of Elizabeth Crawford. Alfretta remained in St. Louis to capitalize on her fame by appearing on vaudeville stages. She made headlines there by being named in a divorce suit by the wife of a factory worker. Her marriage to Baum was toxic; three times between 1897 and 1898 she attempted suicide to escape his abuse. However, once she recovered from an injury, they traveled the world with various circus companies. An uneasy truce existed until 1906, when they divorced. Alfretta remarried to Grover "Happy Doc" Holland, a popular blackface comic singer and vaudeville manager. By this time, she had given up ballooning and stuck to trapeze work, forming an act called the Alfretta Sisters. When one of her partners unexpectedly dropped out, the substitute was named as a man, Vander Clyde Broadway. Alfretta encouraged Broadway to do the act in drag, thereby launching the career of the most successful transvestite acts, "Barbette," the trapeze artist. Alfretta herself continued circus work until the 1940s.

Back in St. Louis, in 1900 Elizabeth Crawford sold her balloon equipment and devoted her talents to spiritualism, becoming a sought-after medium. Official efforts to shut her down under a fortune-teller ordinance were frustrated by her successful defense that Spiritualism was her religion and that readings were a service (donations accepted).

Joseph W. "Montz" Bozarth—Missouri, Kansas

Montz Bozarth has been mentioned earlier as a protégé of James W. Price, dating back to 1884 when both performed the balloon-trapeze act. By 1887, Bozarth was performing balloon ascensions on his own at local and county fairs in Kansas and Western Missouri. Bozarth was a former ropewalker, so he took naturally to performing acrobatics on the trapeze bar underneath his balloons. He also gave street performances as a "Hercules" strongman, bending iron bars. As the balloon-parachute act became more elaborate, Bozarth was one of the early adoptees of the variation involving being shot out of a "cannon."

After a decade performing solo, in the mid–1890s started to share responsibilities with assistants Elijah "Lige" Scudder; Ray Elder; and George Anderson. Ray Elder backed down from making one ascension after reading a fortune message in a candy wrapper: "You are treading on dangerous ground"—a warning that a more carefree man might have interpreted as the perfect excuse to go aloft.[28] George Anderson was killed in October 1896 while attempting the cannon trick at Paola, Kansas. He was ejected from the cannon with the parachute behind him, but the line to it twisted and broke, causing him to fall thousands of feet in front of 10,000 onlookers.[29] Though Anderson was replaced by other assistants, Bozarth himself continued to jump occasionally until retiring from ascensions in 1907. Despite many falls and broken bones, he lived until 1950, when he was 83 years old.

Depiction of the cannon stunt. Though ridiculous, this stunt required the parachute to be packed in the tube with the parachutist, demonstrating that packing techniques existed in the 1890s (Library of Congress, Control Number 2014635889)

Richard P. Hill—Kansas

The story of how R.P. Hill became a balloon-parachutist was recalled by his son, Ferris Hill, decades after his father's passing:

> It was back in 1890, or thereabouts, Ferris Hill says, when someone, he believes it was Ed Borton, a real estate man here in those days, went east and while he was there saw a balloon ascension. He came back to Emporia and told the Commercial club about it. A county fair was being planned and the Commercial club members decided an ascension would be a good attraction for the fair. But who would be fool enough to ride up in the air in a balloon? Mr. Hill's father, R. P. Hill, was at the meeting, and he said he'd be glad to make the ascension. They all thought he was joking, but he finally convinced them he was serious, and the plans were made to have an attraction at the fair. They sent away to the Baldwin brothers' company in Quincy, Ill., who specialized in making balloons and parachutes, and got a balloon ascending outfit.
>
> The first day of the fair, Mr. Hill made ready while the balloon was being filled.... R.P. Hill strapped himself to the trapeze attached to the bottom of the balloon and waved at the crowd as the big balloon rose into the air. When the balloon had gone up about 2,000 feet, Mr. Hill pulled the parachute loose and gently floated to earth with it. Mr. Hill made three ascensions during that fair. He was paid $150 for the first, $125 for the second, and $100 for the third. He decided it would be a fairly lucrative business, so he sold his second-hand store, bought the balloon and all the equipment, and for about 10 years spent his time making balloon ascensions all over the country.[30]

Hill added his dog, a rat terrier named Fannie, to the act, fashioning him with a harness and parachute. After many aerial trips, fifteen-year-old Fannie died a natural death of old age and was given an elaborate burial by the citizens of Emporia.[31] Hill also had an assistant, Sam Johnson of Emporia, who made many ascensions for Hill before striking out on own with an outfit he purchased. Mrs. Hill never reconciled herself to her husband's profession. She attended his second ascension, fainted, and never attended another.

William R. Gould and James L. "Jake" Gribble— Nebraska, Illinois, Connecticut, Kentucky

Although Bill Gould and Jake Gribble both started the 1890s as independent aeronauts, their careers intersected for a couple of seasons at Omaha's Courtland Beach, at the height of that summer resort's popularity. Gould and Gribble's careers also intersected with those of several other aeronauts—including Tom Baldwin—and in Gribble's case extended further developments in aviation. J.L. Gribble started out as a buggy salesman in Macomb, Illinois, not far from both Quincy and Springfield. After being caught up in the parachuting craze that started in 1887, Gribble moved to Lexington, Kentucky, and purchased his own balloon outfit. His first ascensions date to the summer of 1890.[32]

William R. Gould was born in Ohio but had migrated to western Iowa by the mid–1880s. His start as an aeronaut is not documented, but it may be that his ascents at Rock Island, Illinois, in the summer of 1891 were his first. His jumps there in July and August were assisted first by Sam Baldwin and later by Charles J. Eddy, who was employed by the Baldwins to go out and assist new aeronauts. In November 1891, Gould toured South Dakota with John Loomis, an aeronaut who later became an instructor at Milton M. Forsman's Peoria school for parachutists.

Both Gould and Gribble soon realized that they needed to spend more time managing engagements and less time making leaps themselves, especially since Gould suffered an injury in 1891. In 1891, Gribble married Estella Casteel, a female jumper who performed as "Stella" or "Belle" Gribble. In 1893, Gould and Gribble teamed up to present daily ascensions at Courtland Beach in Omaha, Nebraska, not far from Gould's former residence in western Iowa. Because of the frequency of jumps, many aeronauts were employed, including Estella Gribble, Dan Barnell, Jack Crosby, and—from Georgia—newlyweds Frank and Jessie Zelno.

After his seasons at Omaha, Jake Gribble returned to Kentucky and went into the advertising sign business, which proved to be very lucrative. In 1895, Gould moved across the country again to the Hanover Park resort near Meriden, Connecticut. He brought with him two of his Omaha jumpers, Barnell and Crosby. Crosby was nursing an injury from the 1893 season, so the jumping at Meriden in 1895 was done by Barnell, but Crosby took over in 1896.[33] Another aeronaut that Gould featured for the 1896 season at Meriden was Nina Madison, one of the former stars of the New York Balloon Company. Crosby spent several seasons at Hanover Park and earned an unsavory reputation for seducing other men's wives, drinking to excess, starting fights in saloons, and attacking policemen. He was sent to state prison for a year for the later offense, and upon his release, he went to South Africa and fought in the Boer War as a balloonist for the British, receiving an honorable discharge. He continued making jumps until 1914.

While at Hanover Park in 1896, Bill Gould and Nina Madison likely had a hand in developing a parachuting stunt on par with the cannon act or the "Human Bomb" of Leo Stevens. The performer who unveiled the trick was Oscar Norin, a Swedish high diver. Norin's signature act was to climb up on top on his 100-foot diving platform facing the water, wearing a red suit. The suit had an outer layer of paper soaked in paraffin. Before jumping, Norin would set his suit on fire and then make his high dive into the water, where the flames were extinguished. Gould and Madison worked with Norin to adapt the concept to a balloon-parachute jump. Norin kept the idea of the scarlet red suit, but now added a wide leather belt that had eight tubes sticking straight out, evenly spaced around the belt's circumference. The stunt needed to be performed at late dusk. He sat on the trapeze bar under the parachute, but also carried two identical tubes in his hands. The ascension was made over a body of water.

When Norin reached 1,000 feet, he lit fuses attached to the tubes, which were roman candles. Then he cut the parachute loose. The fireworks erupted as he descended. When the parachute was about sixty above the water, Norin jumped free from it, diving headfirst into the water, with his hands holding two erupting roman candles in front of him. The act was, according to the *Rochester Democrat and Chronicle*, "the most astonishing combination that an aeronaut has ever conceived."[34] Norin repeated the stunt at various locations between 1896 and 1897, but then retired as an aeronaut and returned to high diving. He later recruited family members into a high-diving troupe that toured the world for many years.

Warren A. Ward—Western Iowa, Minnesota, South Dakota

Bert Ward was a balloon-trapeze act performer active before Tom Baldwin's first jump. However, he did not make his first parachute leap until 1889, after moving to Kimball, Iowa, to take a position as postmaster. Ward was killed during an ascension in 1906, prompting the following *Anthon (IA) Herald* obituary that both sums up his career and relates the regard in which he was held by the community:

> This community was greatly shocked Tuesday evening on receipt of a telegram announcing the accidental death of W.A. Ward at Monroe, S. D., where he was engaged as a balloonist with a carnival company ... the parachute in the ascension caught a telephone wire, the velocity of the balloon unstapled the wire and drew it up seventy-five feet holding the parachute for a moment and then throwing him to the ground. His neck, arms and other bones were broken, death resulting instantly.
>
> Mr. [W]ard was a professional at his business, having made ascensions

in virtually every state west of the Mississippi river, and for the past twenty-five years had sailed into the clouds to the delight of thousands of people. As a usual thing he was very cautious as to his rigging, though at Lake View, Iowa, seven years ago, the bottom of the balloon tore off as ascent was being made and he was dropped to the ground, a distance of about a hundred yards, striking square upon his feet. The fall was so great that he sank into the sod to the ankles. He was very badly injured and for a time it was thought he would be a permanent cripple. Several ribs, both ankles, and knees were crushed and driven together, and his head was severely bruised. After months in bed he resumed the work.

A year later while making an ascension in a small town in South Dakota, a drunk man grabbed the ropes of the parachute as the balloon left the ground. Nothing could be done but to hope that he would hang on until the inflation would cool and the balloon alight. Within a short distance of the ground in the descent, the poor fellow could hang on no longer and he dropped to earth, killing him instantly. No blame was attached to Mr. Ward for this accident as he did all in his power to persuade the fellow to hang on until they came down.

Two years later while leaving the ground in his balloon at a Fourth of July ascension in western Nebraska, a young man who was assisting in filling the balloon got entangled in the ropes and was taken along. Ward by talking induced his unwelcome guest to hang on and they rode the big bag for several hundred feet into the air, alighting safely a mile from the starting point. At Mapleton two years ago he made an ascension and alighted in the overflowing Maple River two miles north of town. By swimming and wading for several rods, after nightfall, he managed to get ashore, the balloon going a mile farther before coming down. The last balloon he owned before going with the carnival company took fire and was burned as an ascension was about to be made in a small town in Minnesota, the first of last season.

Warren Albert Ward was born at Newtown, Ill., in September 1858 and at the age of 27 he was married to Miss Drusilla Turnbaugh, who with an only child, Miss Ollie, survive. They moved to South Dakota and conducted a store for a year, and eight years ago came to Leeds, near Sioux City, moving to Anthon five years ago and took charge of the Mondamin hotel where they still reside. Mr. Ward was a hard-working man, kindhearted and always attended strictly to his own affairs, molesting no one. His sorrow-stricken wife and child have the deepest sympathy of a multitude of friends in this locality.[35]

Jennie Leland, Emil Markeberg, George Weston Daggett, Otto Burke—Washington State, Northern California

A family story handed down about Jennie Leland's origins as a parachutist suggests that around the year 1900, while she was a single mother working in a newspaper office in Summerland, California, a man came in to pay for a classified ad for a female aeronaut. She asked him what the pay was and decided the job was better than her clerical job. However, some aspects of that anecdote are not true, because newspaper accounts show that her aeronautical career began years earlier—in 1893—and far to the north, in Tacoma, Washington. Leland had married Dewitt C. Ashmun in Michigan in 1882 and afterwards had two children before the family moved to Port Angeles, Washington. Dewitt Ashmun was assisting in the establishment of a colony of Michigan Civil War veterans on the west coast.

Jennie's first ascensions, managed by her husband, were in South Tacoma, a neighborhood then known as Edison. She used a dirty, worn, patched balloon that nevertheless did its job. Not long into her first season of 1893, she introduced a parachuting dog, Rollo, into the act.[36] In late October, Ashmun and Jennie allowed an employee of the local St. Paul and Tacoma Lumber Company to make an ascension. His name was Emil Markeberg, a recent German immigrant, and he wanted to parachute to win a wager with a co-worker.[37]

Jennie Leland's career as an aeronaut came to an apparent end in 1894—unless she continued to appear under a different name. Not long afterwards she divorced Ashmun and moved to Santa Barbara, California, with her children. From there she moved to Los Angeles with her son, spending her last decades there. However, Emil Markeberg's stunt, based on a dare, turned into a career. He spent the 1894 season touring Washington State and the western Canadian provinces. In 1895, he landed a steady engagement at the Chutes, San Francisco's new amusement park on Haight Street. In that season and the next, Markeberg shared parachute leap duties at the Chutes with Otto Burke (real name Otto Lochbaum), George Weston (George Weston Daggett), Robert J. Earlston, and—from Australia—"Essie Viola," i.e., Ethel Hawker, who was discussed in an earlier chapter.[38]

Markeberg and Daggett both were killed in separate parachuting accidents. Daggett was killed during an ascension in July 1897 at Eureka, California. His balloon drifted into some trees, which knocked Daggett off his perch, and his body fell sixty feet to the ground.[39] Emil Markeberg's act featured him being lifted at ascension by a leather strap held between his teeth. At Santa Ana, California, during a Fourth of July celebration, Markeberg ascended about 600 feet when the leather strap broke, and he plummeted to his death. A bystander had a new Kodak Brownie camera aimed at Markeberg and snapped a shocking, widely-published photograph of both the rising balloon and the falling man.[40]

Earlston led a long life but had many ignoble episodes during his early years as an aeronaut. He was the subject of scandalous stories describing his abandonment of his bride; the seduction of a 14-year-old girl; petit larcenies; domestic fights; and his role as an accessory to other crimes. For a couple of years, he operated a saloon in Reno, Nevada, but earned an unsavory reputation while there. He returned to California and finally managed to temper his worst tendencies once he ended his career as an aeronaut.

Portland Aeronauts and Hazel Keyes—Oregon, Washington State, California, Arizona

The "circus melodrama" is a literary/cinematic subgenre that contrasts the colorful spectacles that promoted wonders, dangers, crowd adulation, and physical skill with behind-the-scenes sex, deceit, emotional abuse, and violence. However, no example of this type of story can aspire to match the parade of tragedy and human foible that attended the careers of Hazel Keyes and other aeronauts which can be traced to a brief conjunction of events in Portland, Oregon. The saga begins with a veteran of the balloon-trapeze act, Phineas H. Redmond of Iowa, who began making local ascensions in Iowa in 1879 at age sixteen. Redmond made ballooning his summer vocation for the next decade. He married in 1882 but divorced six years later. Following his divorce he moved with his farming parents to Columbia County, Oregon, outside of Portland.

Once established in Oregon, Redmond began to conduct ascensions and parachute jumps in September 1889—the first ever made in Oregon. Within a week, an accident occurred that made headlines around the world: a 13-year-old boy, Edward N. "Eddie" Hall, assisted in one of Redmond's ascensions as a rope holder. Just as Redmond shouted "Let go" to the holders, one of the ropes leading from the balloon to his trapeze bar wrapped around Hall's neck and lifted him with the balloon and began to strangle him. Redmond jumped from the bar to the ground, realizing that it was his weight that would choke the boy. From the ground he shouted up to Hall to hold onto the ring under the balloon; the balloon would soon cool and descend. Spectators believed the boy was doomed, but his strength allowed him to maintain his grip until the balloon reached ground about two miles from where it had started. Eddie Hall was excited by the experience, but realized he had to get home before his parents found out.[41]

Redmond opened the 1890 season in March with more ascensions in Portland and then signed with a small circus, McMahan's United

Shows, traveling through the Pacific Northwest. Joining Redmond as an aeronaut in that circus was Mrs. Bertha Cosgrove, who performed under the name "Bertha Onzola." Bertha's husband, Arthur Cosgrove, was a theater manager, and it is likely that Bertha had performed on variety stages before taking to balloon work. They had a young son, Arthur Jr., born in 1888. Arthur Cosgrove suspected that Bertha and Redmond were having an affair, but if true, it was short-lived. On May 30, 1890, Redmond's balloon drifted into a stand of tall trees on ascension. He struck them and was thrown 200 feet to the ground, dying instantly.[42]

Redmond was replaced in the McMahon circus by aeronaut James J. Romig, who had left his home in Berks County, Pennsylvania, years earlier. Arthur Cosgrove's mind was not put at ease by Redmond's death. His wife's infidelity gnawed at his senses. One day in mid–August 1890, when Romig took ill and could not make his performance, Cosgrove volunteered to go in his place. To steel himself for the ascension, he drank excessively just prior to launch. It was discovered later that he had also not attached his safety line to the trapeze. The ascent and drop were accomplished perfectly, but as Cosgrove drifted downward to within 200 feet of the ground, he slipped off the bar and plummeted to earth. Those that knew him and had talked with him had no doubt that he committed suicide, caused by his marital problems.[43]

Bertha Onzola joined a different circus, Leon Brothers, for the 1891 season. In San Francisco, she was involved in a saloon fight between two men vying for her affection: Walter Denby, a trapeze performer, and John McNamara, a clown. Denby taunted and then stabbed McNamara, sending him to the hospital with two deep wounds. Bertha performed for two more seasons, managed by an abusive theatrical prop man from Los Angeles, Fred Getzler. In 1896 she and Arthur Jr., were found residing in Bakersfield, California. While there, Arthur Jr., eight years old, went swimming in a pool with a friend and drowned. Bertha then married a wealthy ranch-manager of Bakersfield, William Borgward; however, the marriage was short-lived, and Bertha's fate from that point is unknown.

It should be recalled that 13-year-old Eddie Hall was the boy who was carried away and nearly strangled by P.H. Redmond's balloon in September 1889. Two years later, in 1891, Eddie Hall joined two barnstorming aeronauts touring the Pacific Northwest. One was John E. Parker, who claimed to be from Quincy, Illinois (proof of this is lacking). The other was William Woodall, a theater carpenter from Seattle. In August of 1891 at Tacoma, Washington, Parker's parachute did not fill properly, and he fell hard from about 75 feet above the ground at Tacoma, Washington. One of his feet required amputation, and his other was badly fractured.⁴⁴ The injuries to Parker motivated the men to hire Eddie Hall, who was re-christened "Gus Woodall," as well as Woodall's wife Bertha, who made ascensions as "Nellie Woodall."

Barnstorming entailed moving from town to town, with one member of the company acting as an advance man to secure engagements for the trailing aeronauts. It was a risky business strategy, often resulting in abandoned unpaid room and board bills or in securing dates that were never fulfilled. Parker and Woodall soon earned a reputation as fakirs and split up. Eddie Hall traveled with Woodall for a few months, then gave up ballooning. In 1894 Woodall tried touring in Minnesota, the home state of his wife, but it was not a success, and Woodall was arrested for shoplifting at a drug store. The couple retreated to the Seattle area, where Woodall made infrequent ascensions until 1899. John Parker hired new inexperienced aeronauts for the 1892 and 1893 seasons to tour Montana: Rodney Darnell and boxer John Sweeney, but that enterprise ended with Sweeney under suspicion of being a member of a counterfeiting ring.⁴⁵ Most barnstorming aeronauts had brief careers, caused by injury or economics.

One further branch of the Portland parachutists follows the path of James J. Romig, the circus aeronaut who replaced Phineas H. Redmond. Romig worked the summer of 1890 with Bertha Onzola as his partner, but after her husband Cosgrove fell to his death, she left the circus. Her replacement was Mrs. Martha "Hazel" Keyes, in the middle of the breakup of her marriage to Joseph Keyes. Hazel Keyes quickly became the most popular aeronaut on the West Coast. In November of 1890, the *San Francisco Call* quoted a spectator who witnessed one of Hazel's ascensions, in which she was clad in red tights and landed in a cabbage patch: "She looked like a cardinal Venus descending into a sea of emerald."⁴⁶

By the 1893 season, Hazel and Romig were working independently of any circus, and Romig was as now frequently mentioned as her husband; their union must have been official since they later formally divorced. They added a twist to Hazel's jumps: she was accompanied aloft by her pet monkey, "Jennie Yan-Yan," obtained from a sailor in San Francisco. The monkey descended in its own parachute, released by Hazel prior to cutting herself loose. As was the case with other animals used in parachuting acts, local Humane Societies strenuously objected to using the monkey in these performances. The *San Francisco Examiner* of June 5, 1893, was on the side of those who objected:

> Thousands of people who stood along the waterfront at Sausalito and on the hills above the town at 3 o'clock yesterday afternoon witnessed an act of

revolting cruelty. The victim was a poor, dumb brute, a frightened, shivering little monkey. The helpless little animal was tortured and its life all but sacrificed to add novelty to a balloon ascension. The thousands of people who stood by and watched the preparations were inclined to be gay and jocular, but when the real cruelty of the affair was shown before their very eyes the merriment hushed and exclamations of horror and words of condemnation were heard from many lips—from all, in fact, save a few who belong to that class which always gloats over and enjoys the most horrid acts of cruelty.[47]

On this occasion, Hazel and the monkey brushed against telegraph wires while ascending, but the balloon pushed them free. They drifted out over Richardson Bay. Hazel first cut the monkey loose, then herself. Jennie Yan-Yan landed in the water, while Hazel struck the upper masts of a schooner and was hung up by her cords, swearing at the sailors below. A launch that rushed out to help her in fact ran over the monkey by mistake, but the animal surfaced and was pulled out of the bay. Hazel was brought down from the mast and soon was reunited with Romig and Jennie Yan-Yan.

Romig stopped making ascensions in the mid–1890s for health reasons. Hazel continued her ascensions with Jennie Yan-Yan, but also worked with a succession of male aeronauts, among them "Prof. Lee" and John Deering. Newspaper articles mentioned she had three children, but only once was a child mentioned as being present during her tours: in September 1895, while in Nogales, Arizona, Hazel was stabbed a drunken, jealous man who had crept into her room. Her injuries were slight, but the attacker, George Thompson, was so distraught over his own actions that he tried to cut his own throat. A son was said to have been in the room and gave the alarm.[48]

Hazel continued making jumps until 1901, and Jennie Yan-Yan was mentioned as accompanying her until 1898. She and Romig were officially divorced in 1902, though they remained close for the final decades of their lives. Hazel retired to Vernon, a neighborhood of Los Angeles, and ran a chicken farm. She lived next to an old widower and well-off hog farmer named De Turk. Two of Hazel's children, Joseph A. Keyes and Edward S. Keyes, met ignoble if not horrific ends. Joseph reentered Hazel's life in 1909, visiting from San Francisco, and promptly stole some money from his mother, whereupon she turned him in. Months later, he was involved in the robbery of an Oakland cigar store. A year later, her son Edward tried to take a pistol from the household, but was stopped by a watchman, and in the struggle, Edward shot the man. In both cases, Hazel pleaded for clemency for her sons by sending them to work on the digging of the Panama Canal.

Hazel Keyes, sitting in a studio with "Jennie Yan-Yan" (courtesy Oregon Historical Society).

Upon his return from Panama, Hazel's son Joseph was found dead in a Sacramento rail yard, his body crushed by a freight car. It was never determined whether his death was accident or suicide. Edward S. Keyes's fate was even darker: in 1914 he was sent to San Quentin for an "infamous crime against nature," i.e., the rape of a boy. Three years later, he was arrested for the rape and death of another young boy. He was convicted and sentenced to be hanged, but Hazel put up a fierce defense, arguing her son had long been insane from a head injury as a child. He was given a stay of execution for a further appeal, which was lost, but Edward died of consumption before the sentence could be carried out.[49] Joshua De Turk, Hazel's elderly husband, had died in 1914 and cut her out of his will. She sued the estate and had to fend off developers anxious to get her real estate holdings. The newspapers hailed her as "The Sand Lot Queen" without realizing she had once been called "The Queen of the Clouds."[50] James Romig married another woman for a few years in 1914, but by 1920, Hazel and Romig were once again living together and stayed so until their deaths in the mid–1930s.

Twelve

The Balloon-Parachute Act and Society

Parachuting and Race

The era of popularity of the balloon-parachute act coincided with the most brazenly racist period of United States history. It was a period that included more lynchings per year than any other. Ugly, anti-black stereotypes could be found in nearly every vaudeville performance; in popular song; and in newspapers, popular literature, advertising, etc. Misinterpretations and quack conjecture derived from the science of genetics and the theory of evolution were offered as proofs of racial superiority. In most areas of the country, non-white spectators at outdoor events were either segregated or discouraged from attending. The balloon-parachute act itself presented aeronauts as models representing the ideals of human athleticism, courage, fearlessness, physical attractiveness, and skill—all of which were contrary to the bigoted views many whites had of non-whites.

While the points above would argue against the existence of African American aeronauts, there were in fact several, but their careers likely had just as much to do with the economics of segregation and oppression than with equality of opportunity. During this period, in both the northern and southern states, there were African American fairs and fetes, offering the same thrills and enticements found at county fairs and other venues where non-whites were not welcome. Moreover, by the mid–1890s, the competition among show balloonists had become so intense that even bigoted fair managers were willing to hold out for low bidders, i.e., aeronauts willing to risk their lives for a few dollars per jump. With limited job opportunities, recruits came from the bottom of the economic ladder.

One of the first black show balloonists was John Byrd of Davenport,

Iowa. He obtained a gas balloon from Carl Myers of Mohawk, New York, in 1883 and performed ascensions locally for the next five years, before moving to Chicago. Little is known about Byrd other than that he was born around 1861 and worked as a railroad passenger car waiter in his off-seasons.[1] One reference exists from 1893 that implies he did the balloon-parachute act, but for the most part he was a dedicated gas balloonist who was loath to let his balloon fall on its own. The last known ascension by Byrd was made in Chicago in 1900.

Eugene "Gene" Perkins was a Quincy native who was instructed in making ascensions by Charles J. Eddy of the Baldwin Brothers. Perkins had one artificial leg, which may have made his parachute landings difficult. He performed at Quincy's Highland Park in the 1893 season, but it is not known whether he traveled elsewhere to make jumps.[2] Perkins may have been the target of an attempted balloon sabotage by Baldwin-trained Chet Swearingen, though Swearingen's motives have conflicting explanations.

Another black aeronaut who followed the heritage of early show balloonists was Fred Pate of Battle Creek, Michigan. Mary Butler, writing in *Scene Magazine*, summarized Pate's career:

> A popular figure on the Michigan circuit, Pate was a Battle Creek resident. He had learned his trade from Edward Hogan, traveling as his assistant for three years before making his first solo ascension in 1889. For the next six years he toured the Midwest and New York state, making almost 200 solo appearances. He performed locally several times, including a night ascension over Goguac Lake in 1892, which may have been Battle Creek's first "balloon allume."
>
> Pate had many narrow escapes from disaster, including becoming entangled in a "network of telegraph wires." He told of one experience in Ohio when his balloon caught on fire while he was performing. After cutting loose from the flaming silk, he discovered that his parachute was also burning. Descending rapidly from 150 feet above the ground, Pate remembered that he "struck a tree, which broke my fall and bounded me off like a ball. I struck a large stone and was knocked insensible. ... I was unconscious for two days."
>
> But more frequently Pate made dramatically beautiful ascensions, like this one on June 10, 1895, at the dedication of the new, expanded Driving Park. Pate's performance was the highlight of the program, which also included bicycle and horse races, a Germania band concert, a carrier pigeon release and a fox chase (with a real fox and dogs). "The air was clear and still, and the balloon ascended into azure space for a mile, ... drifting northwest. So high was it that the drop was distinctly discernable from all parts of the city, and it was, by far, the best ascension ever made here."
>
> Just two days later, Pate made his final flight, at a racing meet in Marcellus, Michigan. The erratic winds made the initial ascension tricky, and Pate

ran into difficulty when he was only 300 feet up in the air. Blown toward a grove of trees, Pate tried to escape the floundering balloon by grabbing a large tree limb. As he "released himself from the [trapeze] bar, the balloon shot upward and went out of sight." The tree limb broke, Pate fell to the ground, breaking four ribs which punctured a lung. He died two hours later. Pate was a popular local celebrity and his funeral at Mt. Zion A.M.E. Church was "largely attended" before he was buried in Oak Hill Cemetery.[3]

Perhaps the most widely known African American aeronaut was William J. Rogers of Adams County, Ohio. Rogers was active from about 1899 to 1916 and toured from the Great Lakes to the Gulf Coast. Rogers billed himself as the "Black King of the Air" and the "Black Demon of Seaman [Ohio]."[4] In 1912 it was reported that he had been invited to the Wright training grounds in Dayton to learn how to fly an airplane, but there were no follow-up reports.[5]

Daring as he was in the air, Rogers likely faced greater peril on the ground. In 1902, several major Ohio newspapers reported that he had eloped with "a petite and pretty white girl," sixteen years old, and that her father was hunting for the pair in Cincinnati. Instead, Rogers and Ocie Miller headed to Dayton, where they got married.[6] The union produced several children, but, according to one source, fell apart due to Rogers's dissolute habits. The same causes were given for his early death at age 49, though he also suffered from tuberculosis.

There were more than a dozen other African American aeronauts, but mentions of them in news accounts were so limited that little is known about them other than their names, years of activity, and locales where they performed: James Armstrong, circa 1900, Alabama State Fair; Louis B. Blake, circa 1906, Fairyland Park, Paterson, New Jersey; "Professor Phillips," 1898–99, Indiana; C.O. Smith, 1895–96, Wilkes Barre/Scranton, Pennsylvania; E.L. Radford, circa 1911, Escanaba, Michigan, etc.; Fred L. Bradford of Chicago; and U.S. Grant Watkins of Indianapolis sometimes worked together in the early 1910s. Watkins was a vaudeville performer in Indianapolis for many years and introduced the only known African American woman parachutist, Cora Buckner.

Crowds and Mob Behavior

Balloon ascensions, though often billed as main attractions, were never guaranteed to occur. Even when weather was good enough for crowds to gather outside, winds could cancel inflation attempts. This was particularly true of hot air "smoke" balloons, which employed a flue that directed the hot air, smoke, and sparks directly upward. If winds blew the envelope over the fire, it could easily catch fire, as happened on many occasions. Seams sometimes split, making inflation impossible. Sometimes the kerosene needed to generate a hot fire was forgotten. Gas balloons that used locally produced coal gas relied on the gas companies to provide a supply of adequate quality and quantity—a promise they sometimes were unable to deliver. A few novice aeronauts lost their nerve or did not appear on the grounds due to illness or injury.

In some cases, spectators were asked to stand by for hours while the inflation attempt was made. If an ascension was cancelled after such a delay, a crowd of spectators could turn into an angry mob, regardless of the reputation of the event managers or the aeronaut. This occurred not only in the United States, but also in England, Russia, Australia, and other countries. For example, on May 22, 1888, Edward D. Hogan made a balloon ascension at Passaic Falls, New Jersey, before a crowd that had paid for admittance. The envelope rose just one hundred feet before gas escaped and it fell: "as he rushed for the cottage on the cliff an angry crowd followed him, pelting him with hoops, stones, and sticks. If it had not been for the interference of the police the professor might have been roughly handled."[7]

It appeared to make little difference to enraged ticketholders whether the aeronaut was male or female. At Gloucester, England in August 1894, Marie Merton was scheduled to make a parachute drop, but the supply of gas needed to fully inflate was insufficient. "The crowd thereupon became unruly, hooting and stone throwing followed, and despite the efforts of the police a rush was made for the aeronaut, the manager, and the balloon. Several pieces were cut out of the balloon, but Miss Merton and her manager were escorted from the ground in safety."[8] Perhaps the worst example occurred on August 6, 1890, in Ishpeming, Michigan, at a performance of Rough's Circus. When the balloon-parachute act was cancelled, a mob "tore the circus-tent to ribbons, destroyed the balloon and parachute, broke open the trunks, and half-killed the circus employees. The police were powerless, and the mob, numbering nearly 5,000, wrecked everything in sight."[9]

However, despite factors that made balloon ascensions prone to unexpected cancellations, mob violence appeared to be little more prevalent at these performances than at political rallies and sporting events. It should be noted that this era was also the height of lynch mobs in the United States, when crowds, driven by rumor and racial bias, took the administration of justice into their own hands. Given this context, there does not appear to be any special correlation between the type of crowds attending performances of the balloon-parachute act (or other daredevil acts) and the potential for violence.

Laws Against Parachuting

The balloon-parachute act was a variant of daredevil acts that became popular in the mid-nineteenth century, in which performers risked their lives in front of large audiences. Wire-walking, circus trapeze acts, and the balloon-trapeze act preceded parachute jumping. In Britain, the United States, and elsewhere, no laws had been developed that prohibited these performances, where the only danger was to the willing and trained performer. That changed not long after Tom Baldwin re-introduced parachutes. During his first tour of Great Britain, several commentators begged the Government to forbid parachute jumping. The Home Secretary declined, citing the lack of any relevant law.

In the United States in 1892, mounting casualty numbers caused the New York State legislature to enact a law prohibiting parachute jumping. The penalty was a $250 fine, which proved ineffectual. The same year the Ontario, Canada, provincial legislature took up a similar motion, and again the result was a failure to stop the performances. Throughout the 1890s, many newspaper editors and letters sent to editors suggested that the act should be outlawed, but there was no groundswell of support for a state or national law. Instead, local municipalities were able to limit parachuting performances through the licensing of fairs and resorts and with public safety laws in urban areas.

Use of Animals in Parachuting

The standards for what was recognized as "animal cruelty" were only beginning to change in the late nineteenth century. The use of trained animals in performances had been in existence for centuries. The 1800s saw the formation of the first humane societies. However, frequent abuse of work animals and performing animals, as well as the existence of blood sports such as rat-killing, dog fighting, and cock fighting continued despite their efforts. This treatment was bolstered by the common conception that animals were subject to man, without possessing souls or rights—or even feeling pain in the same sense as humans.

Many of the first attempts to test parachutes were made using animals placed in baskets—usually dogs or domesticated fowls. Small arboreal monkeys were trained to make repeat descents, such as the one used by Emil Leandro Melville in San Francisco in 1886. Indeed, it could be said that the first imitator of Tom Baldwin in England was not a human being, but "the Monkey Baldwin," who was widely advertised to make regular descents at English music halls.[10] The most famous parachuting monkey was Hazel Keyes's Jennie Yan-Yan (who may have been a succession of animals given the same name). Keyes appeared to be genuinely fond of her monkey partner, as Maud DeHaven and Richard P. Hill were of their parachuting dogs. However, their attachment to their animals did not stop criticism from humane societies.

Most animals have an instinctive fear of heights, so there is little doubt that any untrained creature would experience extreme distress at falling from a great height, compounded by being enclosed in a tight space or tied in a harness. Their lives were risked to the same degree as human aeronauts, but they had no choice in the matter. These objections were made by people during the heyday of the balloon-parachute act but failed to stop more than a few performances. The use of animals in daredevil acts abated in the twentieth century,[11] and (thankfully) has all but disappeared today.

The Balloon-Parachute Act in Popular Culture

Despite the popularity of the balloon-parachute act, parachutists were infrequently portrayed in novels, short stories, songs, or dramas, as compared to balloonists and circus acrobats. However, they were a popular subject for writers fond of doggerel and for joke writers and graphic comic artists. One of the best examples appeared early in the craze, and the mention of the "derelict car" suggests a performer making the leap from a basket:

The Parachutist

The statesmen who work for the nation,
No longer are loved by the throng;
The actor, too, lacks approbation,
And meditates much on his wrong;
The poets, from loudest to mutest,
Are scorned by the popular crowds;—
Their hero's the great parachutist—
Bold cleaver of cloud!

He's the man of the hour, this cool cruiser
At heights that are hardly discreet;
Why, ev'n the belligerent bruiser
Perforce now must take a back seat;
The city man's fame's down at zero;
And there, we opine, it will stop—
For we worship the dauntless young hero
Who takes "the long drop."

> Ah, grand are his gallant gyrations,
> And daringly played is his part;
> His skill is beyond calculations,
> A literal work of *high art.*
> A lyrical tribute to render
> Is the object for which we now seek,
> For he *rises* each moment in splendor.
> Though *falling* each week.
>
> Behold him—an object of wonder—
> Rise rapidly out of our view,
> Then deftly, with never a blunder,
> He drops like a bolt from the blue;
> The parachute offers resistance,
> And falls like a sharp shooting star,—
> While floating away in the distance
> The derelict car!
>
> Those wights who in classical story,
> Fixed wings to their shoulders and flew,
> Are eclipsed by this latter day glory,
> We've paid them far more than their due;
> Icarus and Daedalus, 'cutest
> That lived in the days of Apollo,
> Compared with our new parachutist
> Are beaten quite hollow!
> —"Judy," circa 1889[12]

The *Pall Mall Gazette* inserted the following ode to Tom Baldwin in 1888, combining parachuting with previous craze imported from America, Buffalo Bill and his cowboys:

> **Song of the Parachute**
> I can sit on a broncho's hurricane deck
> When he kicks as high as the moon,
> But darn my skin if you'll get me in
> To an untamed Yankee balloon,
> That goes like a Winchester rifle shot
> Up toward Heaven's back garden plot.
>
> I have run some risks on the wild frontier,
> When the Reds war about in the land,
> But to jump in the air from away up thar
> Would exhaust my supply of sand;
> You bet I'd hang on to that old balloon
> If she bumped her side against the moon.
>
> Suppose that overgrown parasol
> Should happen to make a kick

> An' fail to do as he wanted it to,
> He'd drop to earth too quick,
> And would sink so deep that his friends, no doubt,
> Would go to China to dig him out.
>
> I'm kinder glad that the old balloon
> Refused to straddle the cloud;
> When he cut her away he meant to stay,
> Tho' he landed to fill a shroud;
> And soon or late, you hear me toot,
> He'll break his neck from that parachute.
>
> And if I'm around when the corpse comes back,
> And is laid in the last low bed,
> And the soft winds sigh a sweet lullaby
> O'er the poor balloonist's head,
> I hardly think it'll be amiss
> To write him an epitaph just like this:
> "Here lies the body of one who flew
> Like a meteor up toward heaven's blue.
> And then with a reckless sort of grace,
> Flew just as fast toward the other place.
> Sometimes t'ward heaven, sometimes t'ward—well,
> He changed so often 'tis hard to tell
> Whether upon his final scoot
> He works a balloon or a papachute."[13]

The jokes published about parachutists were frequently puns and low humor typical of publications of the era. Examples:

> "What killed Highflyer, the parachutist?"
> "He took a drop too much."[14]

"Recently a parachutist gave several demonstrations of his skill at Glasgow. One afternoon a strong wind carried his balloon rapidly away, and it was some time before he could make a descent. He touched mother earth at a moorland spot near a farmhouse, and an old man stood close by staring in blank amazement. He had seen the gaudily dressed being drop down from the clouds. 'What place is this?' asked the parachutist in an authoritative tone. The old man reverently knelt down and clasped his hands together, and his voice trembled with fervent emotion as he answered: 'Good Lord, this is the parish o' Carnwath.'"[15]

It may be that the limited, ephemeral portrayals of parachutists in popular media was a major factor in how quickly the collective memory of the balloon-parachute act faded over the decades. Unlike balloonists, there was no classic song like "Up in a Balloon," or novel like *Around the World in Eighty Days* to immortalize parachutists.

Thirteen

Kites, Gliders and Airships

The puzzle of practical aerial navigation remained unsolved for more than a century after the Montgolfiers' first balloon flight. Early in the nineteenth century, several designs were suggested for lighter-than-air craft that employed an elongated spindle- (cigar-) shaped gas envelope with a catwalk platform hanging underneath. Few of these ideas progressed beyond drawings and small-scale models, for the missing component was an engine powerful enough to move a craft against even slight winds. Human muscle (pedal-driven propellers) was a power source used in several designs. At about the same time, interest was revived in the centuries-old dream of human winged flight, using airfoils (lifting surfaces). Research in these focused on tethered kite designs and gliders launched from heights or downhill tracks. The hope was that determining the most efficient airfoil might lead to muscle- or engine-powered heavier-than-air craft.

These efforts preceded Tom Baldwin's first parachute jump, but greatly accelerated after 1887. Moreover, performers and promoters of the balloon-parachute act were often involved in this experimentation. While parachuting may not have been the direct source of heightened research into navigating the air, in the public consciousness this new breed of aeronauts heralded a coming age in which humans could defy and control gravity. From a more practical perspective, airship and glider designers had good reason to recruit parachutists to pilot their frail devices: they were typically young, light in weight, athletic, fearless, and comfortable in the air.

When Tom Baldwin returned to New York from his first world tour in the summer of 1889, he told reporters: "You have never heard of a kite taking a man up to the clouds, I'll wager. I propose to go up on one of my own kites some day before I die. I intend to build a kite that will so comply with the law of aerial balance and force as to easily carry objects weighing several hundred pounds. Already I have made several satisfactory models. With favorable winds I am confident that I can show a new order of aerial evolution that will astonish people."[1] Little more is known about Baldwin's experiments with kites, other than that he said he was inspired by kites flown in Japan and China (which Baldwin would not visit until the next year). He did not mention the subject in public again. This mention appears to predate Australian Lawrence Hargrave's first tests of box kites, which proved to be greatly influential. Hargrave was very open about sharing his results with others interested in aeronautics.

Kites had been in existence for centuries and represented a form of heavier-than-air flight—although requiring a tether to the ground. In the late nineteenth century, several researchers began testing the limits of large-scale kites of different designs. In the United States, the focal point of such testing was the Blue Hill Observatory, a weather research facility located outside of Boston. Testing of kites there began in the early 1890s, conducted by the Boston Aeronautical Society. Soon, amateur researcher William Abner Eddy of Bayonne, New Jersey, began demonstrations of a chain of his large, diamond shaped "Eddy" kites at Blue Hill. Eddy and others at Blue Hill also corresponded with Lawrence Hargrave in Australia, who had lifted himself sixteen feet off the ground with a kite-train in November 1894. Hargrave's work inspired another amateur, Charles H. Lamson of Portland, Maine, to build kite-gliders based on the box kite design. Lawson flew his glider at Portland in 1896 using a dummy to prove it could lift a man. The next year, 1897, he found a willing aeronaut: Frederick W. Bickford.[2] Bickford was a Portland teen who, at the time, was also performing the balloon-parachute act for Joseph Laroux, a former circus parachutist. Lamson went on to experiment with untethered gliders, working with Octave Chanute. In October 1902, Augustus Herring flew in a Chanute design (built by Lamson) at Kill Devil Hills, North Carolina—the Wright Brothers were there testing their glider at the same time.

Concurrently, a similar interest in large-scale kites surfaced in England. In the mid–1890s, Captain Baden Baden-Powell developed a large hexagon kite design he called the Levitor, with which he was able to lift a man to 100 feet in June 1894. Though Baden-Powell's research was interrupted by the Boer War, kite experimentation in Britain was taken up by the flamboyant Wild West performer Samuel F. Cody. Cody was not an aeronaut himself but had intimate connections to two who were: his first wife, Maud Lee, estranged from Cody in the early 1890s, worked as a jumper with William Z. Love in Indiana in the summer of 1894. A more direct source of Cody's interest was Auguste Gaudron of the Spencer family. In the late 1890s, Gaudron was operating a parachute

Lamson's Air Ship Kite ascending with pilot Frederick W. Bickford (Library of Congress, Reproduction number: LC-USZ62-7248).

jumping concession from Alexandra Palace in London, where Cody also staged his shooting and riding shows, and the two became great friends. After years of building increasingly larger hybrid-Hargrave kite designs and combining trains of kites, between 1904 and 1908 Cody was awarded British Army contracts and set records for the heights to which humans could be lifted by kite. At the same time, he realized that the natural progression was toward gliders and powered airplanes that employed lifting surfaces like his large kites. In 1905 he demonstrated a tethered, manned glider that could release its line and make a controlled descent.[3]

In the fall of 1904, California inventor and physicist John J. Montgomery conducted tests of a balloon-launched glider, which had originally been conceived during a partnership earlier in that same year with Thomas Baldwin. However, Baldwin was more focused on his airship work at that time and instead employed the propeller research he and Montgomery had conducted on his airship. Upset with Baldwin, Montgomery sought other partners, including a veteran balloon-parachutist, Daniel J. Maloney, who had made his first jumps at San Francisco's Glen Park in 1899. Maloney had learned the skill from Charles T. Conlon, an Oakland parachutist who had worked at local resorts for three years. Maloney successfully piloted Montgomery's glider several times in March 1905 and made a public exhibition on April 29, 1905, gliding freely from over 4,000 feet. Maloney and Montgomery believed that their experiments were more impressive than the flights that had been made by the Wrights. Maloney wrote:

> I was actually flying and believe that I am the first man on earth who has actually and successfully had that experience. Often I had been up in balloons, and I am a parachute jumper by profession; but never before did I feel such a remarkable sensation as comes over me when guiding this aeroplane through the air. The wings are so small and so fragile that it is like being up on a silken kite ... the feeling that came over me when I moved about in the air at will is difficult to describe, and it was not like the sensations in ballooning and parachute jumping. I was able to steer and turn and go up or down, and I think I felt just about like a bird feels. There was an intense thrill in the thought of actually flying, and I shall be glad to experience the pleasure again whenever I can.[4]

Less than three months after writing this, Maloney was killed while piloting Montgomery's glider because of damage caused when the release rope hit one of the control surfaces of the frame. The San Francisco earthquake of 1906 limited Montgomery from further experimentation until 1911. On October 31, 1911, while piloting his own glider, Montgomery was killed after the craft stalled during a landing.

A New York lawyer, Israel Ludlow, followed the reasoning of Lamson and Montgomery by designing a tethered glider, launched from the ground by an automobile or at sea by a fast-moving ship. Ludlow's first tests were made in 1905 from the cliffs of Riverside Drive, in upper Manhattan, but for a manned test, he leased the "Boer War" spectacle grounds at Brighton Beach, Coney Island. Charles K. Hamilton of Connecticut was hired to pilot the craft. Brief flights were made there and on the West Side of Manhattan, near Ludlow's home. The results impressed Ludlow, but few others.

Ludlow's ambitions resurfaced at the August 1907 Jamestown Exposition. There, he convinced the Navy Department to provide a tug to lift the glider into the air. If the first test proved successful, an engine was to be installed that would propel the craft once towed aloft. This time, one of the three pilots Ludlow called upon was James C. "Bud" Mars, a 32-year-old experienced balloon-parachute aeronaut. Mars, whose real name was James Cairn McBride, had already had a long career as a performer, starting in the early 1890s. He ran away from home at 16 to become a circus acrobat, which landed him a job with Sam Baldwin's "Flying Baldwins" acrobatic troupe.

Daniel J. Maloney being lifted by balloon for controlled glider flight in John J. Montgomery tandem wing aircraft, May 21, 1905 (https://content.scu.edu/digital/collection/montgomery/id/46/rec/29, Archives & Special Collections, University Library, Santa Clara University).

Mars learned ballooning (undoubtedly in Quincy from Thomas Greenleaf or Sam Baldwin) and added the balloon-parachute act to his repertoire. By 1903, he was alternating that with a high-diving act, jumping from 90 feet into a shallow tank. Within the next two years, he chose to concentrate on balloon work and moreover introduced a descent in a paraglider he called the "Fool Killer."[5] No images exist of the "Fool Killer," but it appears to closely match the descriptions of the paraglider that was used a decade earlier in the October 1897 leap by Charles Lastrange off the Brooklyn Bridge. That leap employed "parachute wings" designed by Leo Stevens. However, there were no independent witnesses, and Stevens and Lastrange never unveiled or mentioned this innovation again, perhaps suggesting that other tests did not prove successful. A similar device might have caused the death of Charles Richmond in 1893.

Leo Stevens, Tom Baldwin, and other veterans of the balloon-parachute act believed that steerable airships showed more promise than powered gliders in solving the problem of aerial navigation. Designs for lighter-than-air vehicles with propulsion had been drawn throughout the nineteenth century, with the vast majority following the form of a spindle-shaped gas bag with a carriage suspended underneath, upon which there were propellers. Power was supplied either by human muscle or engines, although no adequate lightweight motors existed until the last decade of the century. The scale of these airship designs varied from a small, one-person craft to ones capable of carrying dozens of passengers (none of which were ever built).

Prior to the advent of the balloon-parachute act in 1887, several airship projects met with limited success—and many more never materialized.

- In 1852, French engineer Henri Giffard piloted his steam-powered dirigible over 16 miles and was able to execute turns and circles, though it was unable to resist a strong wind.
- In 1859, German-American John H. Steiner, a veteran of Thaddeus Lowe's Civil War balloon corps, proposed a giant 300-foot-long dirigible. After the war, while Steiner was conducting tethered balloon demonstrations in Minneapolis, he discussed his ideas with a visiting German officer, Ferdinand von Zeppelin. Steiner's airship never materialized, but Zeppelin later took up the idea and created the most successful dirigibles in history.
- In San Francisco in 1869, Frederick Marriott, an assistant to the disappointing powered-glider efforts of England's John Stringfellow and William S. Henson, devised a small-scale airship, powered by a steam engine. An unmanned scale model, the *Avitor Hermes, Jr.,* successfully flew many times, but a stock market crash prevented further development by Marriott.
- In 1875, another veteran of the Union balloon corps, Frederic W. Schroeder, began building the first of several models of a

steerable dirigible. One under construction in Baltimore was wrecked by bad weather after workmen removed a protective lumber barrier due to a contract dispute. Schroeder was not heard from after 1878 and eventually migrated to England.
- In the summer of 1878, inventor Charles F. Ritchel oversaw successful, but limited flights of his pedal-powered airship at Boston, Philadelphia, and Hartford. Ritchel employed very lightweight pilots, May V. Hunter ("Mabel Harrington") and Mark Quinlan. Ritchel's plans to construct a much larger vessel were never realized.
- Through the 1880s, German publisher Friedrich Hermann Wölfert developed airship designs drawn by Georg Baumgarten. All were muscle-powered, but in 1888, Wölfert was offered a new lightweight gas motor built by Gottlieb Daimler. The powered airship made several successful flights until 1897, when Wölfert and his mechanic died in a crash when their carriage separated and fell from the envelope.
- Starting in 1885, balloonist Carl Myers constructed a series of pedal-driven oblong balloons, which came to be known as "Skycycles." The pilot (often Myers' wife, "Carlotta") supplied power to fabric-covered fan blades and steered via a rear rudder and forward vanes. The Skycycles were an improvement over Charles Ritchel's basic design but required practice and skill by the operator to properly maneuver. Myers presented them as a feature of his show ballooning engagements. He was sanguine about scaling his "Skycycles" larger, believing that no sufficient engines existed.

A Brooklyn watchmaker named Peter C. Campbell became obsessed with the possibilities of airships, and in 1888 he formed a company backed by some wealthy supporters to build a working fleet. Campbell called upon Carl Myers for his practical experience in fabricating the balloon and in the design of the steering mechanisms. During 1888, several models were constructed, increasing in size. Campbell and Myers originally envisioned that Myers' wife, Carlotta, would be the pilot, but they later called in James K. Allen,[6] son of a prominent balloonist.

By December, Campbell had built a model that was 60 feet long and 42 feet wide. A keel was fitted underneath the envelope, upon which a propeller was fitted for forward motion. Four smaller propellers were set on the fore and aft sides to provide steering, while a large downward-facing fan was used to help control altitude. Originally, power was intended to be provided by Edison electric motors, but for the initial flights, muscle power alone (from both arms and feet) was used.

From Coney Island, pilot Allen coaxed the airship to ascend to 500 feet and landed it less than a mile away in Sheepshead Bay. The test was deemed a success to the public, but no more announcements were forthcoming in the next few months. When the enterprise resurfaced in April 1889 with the announcement that Edward Hogan, the Jackson, Michigan, parachutist, would pilot the next demonstration, the names of James K. Allen and Carl Myers were conspicuously absent. Campbell had met Hogan was Hogan was making parachute jumps at Rockaway Beach in the summer of 1888. James K. Allen, it was rumored, had said that he could not control the craft, and Myers later said that significant changes to the design had been made over his objections: the removal of the envelope webbing and the top safety valve, i.e., the fail-safe feature needed to descend quickly.

After more delays, Ed Hogan ascended in the Campbell Airship from the Nassau Gas Works yard in Williamsburg, Brooklyn on July 16, 1889. After performing some maneuvers over Brooklyn, the altitude-control propeller located in the center of the pilot's catwalk was seen to fall apart. Hogan was observed walking calmly back and forth along the catwalk, trying to compensate. For unknown reasons, he released ballast to climb and was last seen headed towards Flushing. However, it was later learned that winds blew him far to the south, past the shores of Long Island and out over the Atlantic. Hogan was never heard from again. A ship pilot reported seeing the abandoned airship nearly two hundred miles to the southeast.[7]

Hogan's awful fate did not deter his protégé, Coryell Bartholomew, from building his own muscle-powered airship in 1891. He took it on a test flight on July 17, taking off from near his shop in Jackson, Michigan. Bartholomew ascended over 7,000 feet, was carried by a brisk wind, and only momentarily was able to use his foot-pedal steering controls. To avoid landing in a lake, he had to drop the steering framework and cling to the gas bag.[8] Although he exhibited his airship inside the main building of the Detroit International Fair in August, nothing more was heard about this device. During an early 1892 interview, Bartholomew's female aeronaut, Gertie Carmo (Gertrude Clausen), hinted that she was planning to pilot an airship; however, her death in August while making a parachute ascension may have ended those plans. Years later, in 1905, Bartholomew still maintained no airship would prove any more successful against winds than his.[9]

The remainder of the 1890s saw little progress in the design of American airships beyond small muscle-powered craft. Inventor

The Campbell Dirigible Air Ship piloted by Edward D. Hogan—lost at sea (*Scientific American* 61, no. 04 [July 1889]; author's collection).

Edward J. Pennington made headlines in 1891–1892 for his plans to construct a large, aluminum-frame dirigible, but nothing more than a small-scale model was ever produced. In 1897, Arthur Barnard of Nashville, Tennessee, made headlines for several weeks after some extended voyages in his muscle-powered airship. However, it was later revealed that he had purchased one of Carl Myers's Skycycles and had made few modifications to it—a detail he failed to mention to reporters. He quickly disappeared from public notice after this was revealed. The American public certainly wanted to see airships plying the skies, so much so that the mid–1890s saw a flurry of airship hoaxes attributed to unmanned balloons launched by pranksters.

More serious work on airship navigation took place in Europe, where lightweight internal combustion engines were being pioneered. In Germany, Friedrich Hermann Wölfert (see above) was active until his death in 1897. Ferdinand von Zeppelin had drawn up plans for his first monster dirigible in the early 1890s and finally found funding and began construction in 1899. The *LZ1* made its first flight in 1900. Starting in 1898, wealthy Brazilian sportsman Alberto Santos-Dumont began building a series of small dirigibles using automobile engines and improved his maneuverability with each model. The world's military powers, who had long anticipated employing airships, took notice. The successes of Zeppelin and Santos-Dumont sparked a new round of airship development which involved several veterans of show ballooning and parachuting.

In the summer of 1902, Santos-Dumont accepted an invitation to come to New York to attempt an airship flight at Brighton Beach, next to Coney Island. There, Santos-Dumont found a kindred spirit in Edward C. Boyce, a Brooklyn-based real estate and amusement park developer. Like Santos-Dumont, Boyce was an automobile enthusiast, with wealth to pursue expensive hobbies. Santos-Dumont arrived with his No. 6 dirigible but needed hydrogen to fill it. He had anticipated on being able to obtain hydrogen from Carl Myers, but that summer Myers was immersed in producing eleven balloons for the U.S. Signal Corps. Santos-Dumont waited weeks, but finally departed for Europe and sold the airship to Boyce.

That same summer of 1902, at Manhattan Beach, just yards away from the Santos-Dumont hangar, Leo Stevens was preparing his airship, *Pegasus*, which he had announced was in progress as early as 1900. Stevens, unlike Santos-Dumont, had more fame than wealth and struggled to build his craft in between his performing engagements. However, on September 30, both the Santos-Dumont craft, piloted by Edward Boyce, and the *Pegasus*, piloted by Leo Stevens, were able to make flights over the Brooklyn coastline.[10] For Boyce, this proved to be a one-time adventure; he quickly returned to expanding his amusement park empire, which crumbled a few years later when one of his parks in Cleveland, Ohio, burned to the ground, leaving Boyce bankrupt. Leo Stevens realized the faults of his underpowered *Pegasus* and made plans to build a new, bigger airship at a new facility in Niagara Falls, New York. However, the investors he needed to back that effort did not materialize.

In that same autumn of 1902, Thomas S. "Tom" Baldwin was in Northern California, where he was contracted to build an envelope for an airship designed by physician-inventor Dr. August Greth.[11] Greth was a promoter of grand ideals, who had earlier written a book on how to eradicate poverty through government work programs. Greth believed that mastery of aerial navigation would usher in an era of universal peace, once nations realized they could rain death down on each other. While assisting Greth over the next year, Baldwin took the opportunity to meet with glider designer John T. Montgomery to discuss the idea of launching a powered glider from a balloon.

Baldwin made notes about some conclusions that the physicist Montgomery had come to about propulsion methods. In retrospect it appears that while fulfilling his contract for Greth and discussing a balloon-glider concept with Montgomery, Baldwin simultaneously cultivated plans to build an airship of his own. He might have been spurred by an announcement made in 1902 that the 1904 St. Louis World's Fair (aka Louisiana Purchase Exposition) would hold an airship competition, with the prize to be at least $100,000. After several delays, Dr. Greth flew his airship, dubbed the *California Eagle*, in October 1903. However, the engine could not produce more than 6 hp, proving inadequate.[12] Flights were also made in 1904 but were truncated by mechanical problems.

As his contract with Greth neared completion, Baldwin rushed to build his own airship, the *California Arrow*, to submit as a last-minute entry to the World's Fair. Realizing that a good engine was crucial, Baldwin sought out the young motorcycle builder, Glenn Curtiss of Hammondsport, New York, and acquired a motor—and at the same time piqued the interest of Curtiss in aircraft. Baldwin made one test flight in Oakland in August 1904, then brought the craft to the St. Louis World's Fair. As the ship was being reassembled there, Baldwin sought a pilot who weighed far less than he did. On the fairgrounds, Baldwin found A. Roy Knabenshue operating a tethered balloon concession—a business that Knabenshue had been running in Toledo, Ohio, for a couple of years. Of all nineteen airship prize applicants only a few (including France's Hyppolite Louis Malecot) tried to ascend at the World's Fair, and of those, only Knabenshue was able to navigate over a 30-foot wall and complete a circular course, instantly becoming a national sensation. Baldwin took the *California Arrow* on a tour of cities following the World's Fair. At Portland, Oregon, he employed one of his young workmen, Lincoln Beachey, to pilot the ship. Over the next several years, both Knabenshue and Beachey worked together and with other airship builders, establishing navigable dirigibles as practical craft.

During the same period, airship development in England was likewise spurred by the successes of Santos-Dumont and Zeppelin—as much a matter of military fears as of national pride. As in America, those involved were several veterans of the balloon-parachute act: the Spencer brothers (Henry, Stanley, and Percival) and their brother-in-law, Auguste Gaudron. Stanley Spencer demonstrated England's first working dirigible in September 1902, by making flights over London, remaining stationary and moving in circles at will. The next month, Spencer

Tom Baldwin's *California Arrow* airship with aeronaut Roy Knabenshue in its successful flight at the 1904 World's Fair, St. Louis (Library of Congress, Control Number 2002721524).

flew over 30 miles around the Blackpool region—the longest dirigible flight on record at that time. The Spencer brothers immediately made plans for a larger craft, capable of flying from London to Paris. However, after a few hesitant trials in late 1903, it was found that the framework was not strong enough. This precipitated lawsuits between the Spencers and Gaudron on one side and the frame contractors on the other, which in 1904 was settled against the Spencers.

Despite this setback, Henry Spencer and August Gaudron assisted Dr. Francis Barton in the construction of his airship, using their shared facilities at Alexandra Palace in London. Gaudron and Spencer went aloft with Barton for the ship's maiden flight in July 1905, but the result was disappointment: the craft was carried away by a stiff breeze, unable to maneuver against it. It landed at a garden in Essex but sustained a great deal of damage. Barton did not make another airship attempt, having lately been intrigued by heavier-than-air flight.

The gauntlet was taken up by the British War Office, who charged Colonel John Capper of the Royal Engineers with producing a serviceable dirigible. Capper enlisted the aid of August Gaudron's friend, the kite experimenter Samuel F. Cody. Cody, during his years as a Wild West show marksman, had been on the same bill with several parachutists, dating back to 1889. His first wife, Maud Lee, had made several jumps in Indiana with William Z. Love. On October 5, 1907, Capper and Cody flew British Army Dirigible No. 1 from Farnborough to London, covering 50 miles. Informally named *Nulli Secundus*, the airship was dismantled over the winter to build a new version, the *Nulli Secundus II*. The newer model made just two flights in 1908 before being salvaged for parts for the first British airplane.

Leo Stevens reentered the airship business by arranging a contract between himself, a Brighton Beach amusement company, and Tom Baldwin to take Baldwin's *California Arrow* and use it to draw crowds to Manhattan Beach and other eastern resorts. Stevens garnered much

British Army airship *Nulli Secundus* (Krainik Ballooning Collection, Acc. 1990–0009, ref1710, National Air and Space Museum, Smithsonian Institution).

publicity with these flights, along with sham race challenges from Roy Knabenshue, and was able to build and sell copies of his own airship in 1906.

The airship craze also reached into America's marginalized communities. Boxing gambler George "J. P." Parks and ragtime performer-producer Ernest Hogan, both African Americans, financed the construction of the airship *Wolverine* in 1907. It was flown at Irvington, New Jersey's Olympic Park amusement center by Archie Griffin, a parachutist who was mentored by Charles Lastrange.[13]

Others who were associated with the balloon-parachute act also ventured into designing airships. Amateur St. Louis balloonist John Berry (father of balloon-parachutist Bert B. Berry) designed a unique saucer-shaped airship in 1907.[14] The same year, teenager Cromwell Dixon built a small dirigible, bolstered by advice from Roy Knabenshue and Carl Myers. Dixon appeared at fairs and exhibitions before thousands of people between 1907 and 1910, when he switched to airplanes. Horace B. Wild, a former balloon-parachute performer, piloted airships for others (including ex-aeronaut and parachutist Jake Gribble) and built several of his own.

In 1905, following the splash that Roy Knabenshue made at the World's Fair, Toledo baseball magnate Charles J. Stroebel envisioned

A. Leo Stevens, wire-walker, acrobat, parachutist, balloonist, airship pilot, inventor (Library of Congress, Control Number 2014680932).

becoming an airship impresario and hired the hometown hero, Knabenshue, to exhibit airships that he would assemble. By June of 1906, both Knabenshue and Lincoln Beachey were touring for Stroebel, though Knabenshue would strike out on his own after a year. Knabenshue took with him Charles K. Hamilton (the veteran pilot of the disappointing Ludlow glider) and another Stroebel airship pilot, Frank W. Goodale.[15] Hamilton piloted Knabenshue's airship in September 1906, at Omaha Nebraska. Observing the event were a trio of inventor brothers: Otto, Gus, and Charles Baysdorfer. They were so impressed that the next year, 1907, they built their own airship, the *Comet*. To pilot it, they hired "Bud" Mars and Horace B. Wild.

Many of those mentioned above (Berry, Dixon, Wild, Beachey, Dallas)—along with Tom Baldwin—met at the 1907 St. Louis International Airship Races. The prize was won by Stroebel's two entries, piloted by Beachey and Jack Dallas,[16] with Baldwin a distant third. However, the 1907 races can be viewed as the pinnacle of public excitement over airship development—and for the role of former balloon-parachute performers in the vanguard of aeronautics. However, dirigibles continued to be popular draws at exhibitions and were viewed by the militaries of the world as more reliable than airplanes. For example, Tom Baldwin built Signal Corps Dirigible No. 1 for the United States Army in 1908. Though the United States and Europe were rushing ahead with airplane development, much of the rest of the world had never been exposed to airships. To that end, in 1909, the well-traveled show balloonist and parachutist James W. Price returned to San Jose, California, and built a dirigible *Messenger* which he then took on a tour of East Asia, partnering with Ivy Baldwin.

Fourteen

Case Study of a Parachute Aeronaut: L. Guy Mecklem

While the involvement of some famed parachutists in "Early Bird" aviation is well-known, there are likely many more forgotten aeronauts who tried their hand at the new means of aerial navigation. No better example can be found than the experiences described in the autobiographical writings of Llewellyn Guy Mecklem of Seattle, Washington.[1] Mecklem became a balloon jumper as a school-dropout teen, made it a career as a Los Angeles Chutes Park parachutist, assisted Tom Baldwin in launches of his *California Arrow* airship, built his own airship and toured with it, flew Louis Paulhan's airplane, and bought his own airplane and toured with it in the Pacific Northwest. There was a consistent theme through Mecklem's career transitions: none of his endeavors paid very well. Mecklem married in 1910, gave up aeronautics, and worked as a sawyer and berry farmer for many years, passing away in 1973 at age 90. Mecklem's aerial career began in the late 1890s, when he was in his mid-teens:

> One day there was to be a balloon ascension and at the very last minute the aeronaut was badly burned while throwing gasoline into the furnace used to inflate the bag with the hot air that carried it aloft. There was a call for a volunteer rider and I asked for the job as I had always envied the man with the pink tights who soared aloft performing on the trapeze that dangled far below the huge cotton bag and parachute, while the band played and the crowds applauded, and then cut loose the parachute that lowered him gently to earth again—only sometimes he lit in the water instead of on the ground.
>
> On this, my very first ride, the cutoff line got fouled up with some of the shrouds and I was unable to detach the chute from the balloon, and, though I had made a beautiful take-off and ascension, I floated ignominiously

Fourteen—Case Study of a Parachute Aeronaut 169

down with the balloon into the middle of Lake Washington, where there was a launch waiting for me. In spite of a rather drab first ride, I liked it very much and decided to make balloon riding my career, little knowing how little money and how much work there was attached to it. The owner of the outfit was confined to the hospital a long time with his burns and I made ascensions three times a week, weather permitting, for five months. This was only about a mile from where my parents lived and they often saw the balloon in the air, but did not know that I was riding it until the end of the season. I was always afraid that they might learn of it and put a stop to it. I received $2.50 for each ride and at the end of the contract the owner gave me $10.00 extra and tried to get me to promise to work for him the next summer.

After taking other jobs, including operating a boathouse, Mecklem took a job in Seattle hauling grocery items onto wagons. It was heavy work for a rail-thin teen who weighed 100 pounds:

I stuck it out till late spring and then decided to build a balloon and go into business for myself, giving exhibitions at fairs, carnivals, festivals, or any place that an attraction of this kind would be desired. So I quit my job on the grocery wagon and bought a huge quantity of cotton cloth and a sewing machine and went to work, soon finding out that I should have stayed in school a little longer as there were many problems in higher mathematics involved in the laying out and the construction of a bag of this size. I went to night school for a time and was soon able to construct a model of the balloon, and from this was able to lay out and cut the gores which, when sewed together with what seemed miles of seams and hundreds of spools of thread, eventually merged into a huge bag some thirty-five feet high and twenty feet through at the greatest diameter.

I got the plans for a parachute from an aeronaut in New York through an advertisement in *Billboard*. The chutes of those times were not the packed silken or nylon affairs with which most of us are familiar today but were generally made of the same cotton or muslin used to construct the bag and were a large canopy affair twenty-two or twenty-four feet across with a hole or vent in the center. The size of this vent could be changed by a drawstring arrangement allowing the operator to open it for a more direct and quicker descent over a good landing place, or to close it for a slower and partially guided descent. The guiding was done by pulling in the shrouds or ropes on one side and side-slipping toward favorable terrain. The aeronaut or rider generally was not fastened to the chute in any way but rode on a trapeze some twenty feet below the chute and did various stunts on this bar while in flight as an added thrill for the spectators.

To detach the parachute from the balloon, a cut-off block was used. This consisted of a block of wood about four inches square and eighteen inches long. One end of this block was attached to the balloon shrouds and the chute was fastened from its top to a small rope which ran through a small hole in the lower end of the block. This rope could be cut by a razor-sharp blade pivoted or hinged in a slot in the block. When the top or ceiling of the ascent had been made, the rider would give a sharp tug on the cutoff rope and gently float away from the bag, which would then turn over from the weight of another block of wood or small sandbag attached to its top by a short rope. This allowed the smoke or hot air to escape quickly and the bag would generally beat the parachute back to earth, whereas, if it did not turn over, it might continue to rise and float miles away before coming back to earth, entailing a long search and a long haul back to the scene of operations. The softest place a parachutist could land was in the water, but it was always messy and sometimes cold, and the operator had to give up part of his take to a boatman to pick him up. Then there was the problem of drying out the bag and chute.

Finally, I got all the equipment together and advertised for a job and got one right away, making Sunday rides at Hillman City near the south end of Lake Washington for C.D. Hillman, real estate operator extraordinary, who wished to attract crowds to his newest development. I took this job at $150.00 per ride for four Sundays, hired a helper and set up the gin-poles used to suspend the balloon over the inflating chimney which consisted of a barrel at the end of a tunnel that extended horizontally to a point ten or twelve feet outside or away from the balloon. At the outside end of this tunnel was the fire pit where the smoke and hot air was made that was used to fill the bag.

A new balloon made of cotton cloth has very little lifting power the first few times that it is inflated, as the cloth is so porous it allows most of the smoke and heat to escape. Even though we had smoked this one all day Saturday, to get the pores of the cloth impregnated with soot, I could not get it to lift me on Sunday even though we used fifteen gallons of gasoline. I forgot to say that during inflation it is necessary for one man to stay inside the balloon all the time to watch for sparks and to shout out how high the flames are going when the gasoline is thrown into the fire. It is thrown into the fire with a dipper, and it is very dangerous work.

There were many disappointed people that Sunday and Hillman said that I had better make it be good the next Sunday, or else. By smoking that bag all the next week and turning it black in the process, I was able to make a low ascension of ten or twelve hundred feet the next week and made up for the poor showing of the week before by doing acrobatics on the trapeze and hanging head down by one foot (safely fastened in a loop at one end of the bar which could not be seen by the crowd). I finished that engagement and by that time was established as an "Aerial Daredevil" and plenty of engagements were offered. Hillman paid one half the promised fee. I took a job at Spokane and twice narrowly missed landing in the river so was glad when that job was completed.

I met another balloonist. He was a dapper little fellow by the name of Sylvon from Victoria, B.C.[2] He had his two upper gold front teeth set with a good-sized diamond in each and he wore very, very sporty clothes that he said he had tailored in London where he had come from a year or two

Fourteen—Case Study of a Parachute Aeronaut 171

earlier. He was working with a carnival show both as a balloonist and escape artist. His carnival showed in Tacoma at the same time that I had a contract there with some local improvement association; so, we timed it so that we were both in the air at the same time. The Great Sylvon made his ascent securely locked with leg irons and handcuffs by a committee from the crowd and escaped from them in time to cut off the parachute. He even went up once in a straight-jacket and chained to the trapeze. To offset this added attraction and showmanship on his part, I had to do extra acrobatic stunts and I also set off several dynamite blasts high in the air using five sticks of forty-or sixty-percent dynamite for each shot. The sticks were bound together, and a one-minute fuse attached and were attached to a reel with about fifty feet of line on it. The free end of the line was attached to the trapeze and, after lighting the fuse, the reel and dynamite were dropped to the length of the line, generally about fifty feet, where it exploded with a terrific crash that sometimes gave me quite a jar. I never saw The Great Sylvon, as he called himself, again; heard that he had failed to unlock or escape from the handcuffs at Calgary or Lethbridge and had been dragged by his parachute and badly injured.

My balloon was getting old and rotten and had many patches on it, so I bought one from a man by the name of Frank Woods who said that he had been working his balloon in Alabama and the South. He had bought a store in Renton and was giving up the balloon racket. I had a couple of jumps to make at Portland and on the very first bomb explosion that balloon that I had just bought opened up a tear horizontally right across the middle about twenty feet long, from the concussion. However, the parachute dropped free from the crippled bag, but I had to get rid of the other five sticks of dynamite, so had to explode it in a hurry. I landed in a swamp and the bag came down in a lady's chicken yard. She said that I could not take it away until I paid her for all the setting eggs that had been ruined by the balloon scaring her setting hens. I was so disgusted losing the next day's job, as the bag could not have been repaired in time, and being covered with mud from the swamp, and being gypped into buying an old bag that was not as good as the one I had discarded, that I took the train back to Seattle and left the whole outfit right where it lay. I often wondered, tough, how Woods had ever gotten that old bag so clean and white that he fooled me into believing that it was almost new.

For several years during his young manhood, Mecklem suffered from a crippling case of rheumatic fever and sought different cures along the West Coast, even at a clinic in Mexico. Around 1904, he found some relief through fasting and a vegetarian diet at a Bernarr Macfadden health club in Los Angeles:

> One day a friend of mine came to me and said, "Say, you used to ride balloons, didn't you? Well, there's a guy over at Chutes Park that has a great monster balloon and he's afraid to ride it and wants to hire somebody to go up with it. I told him about you, and he wants me to bring you over to talk

to him." Chutes Park was an amusement park and zoo at about Twelfth and Main, in what is now metropolitan Los Angeles. They had a Chute, from which the park derived its name, a roller coaster, funny house and some shoes and many concessions and games, also a few mangy animals and some ostriches.

This man who had the balloon was a bartender who had always wanted to be a balloon rider. He had signed a contract with the management of the park to make tri-weekly rides and parachute drops, and now he had a very bad case of cold feet. He said that he would give me a half of what he got if I would ride it. I went over to look at the bag, which was already suspended between the gin-poles and over the furnace. The size of it nearly took my breath away. It was advertised as being seventy-five feet high and the top like a skyrocket and said that was to make it go up faster and higher, though I could not see how that shape could make it go any higher. The chute was a monster twenty-nine-footer (and made of silk). This was on Saturday and the first ascent was booked for the next day (Sunday). I had no time to have tights made so he said that I should use his, which he had paid $75.00 for. They were of green plush silk with white trim, and he was very proud of that outfit. Well, he weighed over two hundred pounds and had a big beer belly, while I weighed at the time just a little over a hundred, so there was quite a little slack in the suit to be taken up. This was done in the back and fastened with safety pins.

The time finally arrived to take off and this great monster was tugging at her ropes when I gave the signal to Let Her GO! I was whisked off the ground like an autumn leaf in a tornado and then got the surprise of my life for, instead of ascending straight up, the peculiar and unorthodox shape of this monster caused it to shoot off first to one side and then to the other and the effect on me was like being the cracker on the end of a whip. It finally took its last dive and was lying there fairly quiet when I heard the pistol shot that the bartender fired as a signal for me to cut loose and start down. The canopy or chute was so big that it took longer to get down than it had taken to go up and as my weight was not enough to keep a chute of this size steady, it oscillated wildly, and I had little control and was unable to choose a landing place. A little square cottage with a sloping roof and chimney sprouting out of the center seemed to act as a magnet for that huge parachute. As it was a very quiet day, I found that I would land only a few blocks from the park and the crowd had gathered long before I got there. Sure enough, I landed near the top of the gently pitched roof, but it was just steep enough to keep me from being able to hang on and I found myself slowly sliding toward the edge. The bartender was there and gave me the big horse laugh and said that I was a h—l of a parachute rider when I couldn't even miss a house. Just about then I slid over the edge and his beautiful green tights caught on a protruding shingle nail and were torn from the sitting contact area right up to the neck. This was not so funny to him and it was my turn to laugh, though I did have to drape the parachute over my back to kind of cover up on the way back to the park.

Fourteen—Case Study of a Parachute Aeronaut

As this balloon became seasoned or sooted up so that it retained the hot air better, it went higher and higher but still with that original erratic flight that it had on its first trip. I made about sixty rides there at Chutes Park that season making several hazardous landings, once on the telephone wires between two telephone poles and it took the fire department to get me down; once in the water in Westlake Park, and several times fifteen or twenty miles out in the country.[3] In the evenings I did another act called "the Human Meteor." It consisted of riding a heavily weighted bicycle down the chutes and taking a header into the water. The gimmick consisted of an asbestos pad on my back which was soaked with a pint of gasoline and ignited just as the ride started. It made a flame about twenty feet long and a big roar and was a real thriller. For me it was much more dangerous than a balloon ride, as there was always danger of the bike slipping on the wet chutes and spilling me off and my getting burned, though there were always a couple of men posted along the route with fire extinguishers. I enjoyed my season at the park—the excitement, crowds and the balloon rides, especially as I had no worries about getting the bag back to the park, and the inflating and a thousand other details. All I had to do was grab the trapeze and soar aloft and then descend via that amazing parachute. It was so large in proportion to my weight that several times it would ride on an updraft and actually ascend hundreds of feet higher than the balloon had taken us.

After the park season we got a few balloon jobs at several small towns and real estate developments, one at Venice on the day of the grand opening[4]; also at Playa del Rey and Santa Monica. These were all beach towns and there was always the danger of alighting in Santa Monica Bay where there was generally a strong undertow and it was a really dangerous piece of water for a parachutist to fall into. Sometimes an offshore wind would blow the balloon far out over the water and then, at a higher altitude, another current of air from off the ocean would blow it back over the land again and it was always a gamble as to whether or not we would land in the water or on land.

One day at Santa Monica I was making a descent into the residential area had a pretty good breeze was blowing. Suddenly I found myself landing on the top of a huge pepper tree at the edge of a backyard that had a small greenhouse in the center of it. A lady came running out of the house and said, "Don't you dare come down on my greenhouse!" But just then the wind caught the chute and slid me right off the top of the three and I landed ankle deep in the flower beds inside the greenhouse and broke many panes of glass in doing so. The lady was very indignant and said, "I told you not to light on it!" She would not let us remove the chute until we had paid her her rather high estimate of the damages.

Always looking for new thrills both for myself and the spectators, I hit upon the bright idea—and maybe it was not so bright—of making an ascension hanging by my teeth. I had seen performers in circuses hanging by their teeth and it did not look too hard. I had a mouth-piece made of leather and started in practicing at the gym which I still attended, soon learned that it was not as easy as it looked and had to set about developing the neck muscles, finally felt that I was ready. I attached the mouth-piece to the trapeze with a swivel in between to allow me to spin, this adding to the attractiveness of the act. This swivel pretty near proved my undoing as I got so dizzy that I was almost unable to pull myself back up on the bar when it was time to cut loose. My neck and jaws were so stiff and sore that I had difficulty eating and could not turn my head at all. The next ride I left the swivel off and it was not quite so bad. The act was a real thriller and got me a lot of headlines and good publicity. However, it wasn't much fun for me and, after a few more rides, I gave it up with a view of living longer.

A man came to Los Angeles by the name of Baldwin, obtained a contract with The Chutes to exhibit and make flights with a small dirigible balloon that was to be rowed with a pair of oars like a boat.[5] I was much interested in this machine, which consisted of a silk gas-bag about thirty-eight feet long and fifteen feet in diameter, with a light bamboo framework suspended beneath and a pair of bamboo oars with silk blades on the ends. The bag was full and blunt at the front end and tapered off to a point at the read. This point was really the neck of the bag and was the inlet for the hydrogen gas which was to lift it. After inflation the neck or end was folded over and held with a large rubber band. In case of over-expansion, which might occur in a hot sun, the band was supposed to fly off and release some of the gas, thus acting as a safety valve.

Baldwin was an old balloonist and was a large man. He had overestimated the lifting capacity of the bag and it would not lift him, so I was offered the job of flying it. It would lift me and about ten pounds of sand ballast carried in a canvas bag tied to the frame near the seat. The theory was to balance the balloon or gas-bag with the addition or removal of sand until it would carry me and neither rise nor fall. The take-off day arrived, and I climbed into the flimsy framework and attempted to manipulate it. The sun got hotter, and the hydrogen expanded and it started slowly up and nothing I could do with the oars would stop it. It went up higher and higher and the safety valve did not work. I tried to row it back down after it stopped going up, but one of the oars broke and there I was stranded a couple of thousand feet in the air. The machine drifted slowly inland across the Puente Hills and, when the sun went down and the gas contracted, we landed gently in an orange grove at Pomona. The next day we rigged up a wire between two posts about three hundred feet apart and attached the balloon to the wire by means of a light line and a ring that slid backward or forward along the wire. I then practiced rowing for two solid weeks before attempting another free flight. On a real calm day, we could put on a pretty good show, ascending a few hundred feet, throwing my hat or handkerchief overboard and paddling down and retrieving it; or rowing the nose of the bag right at some pretty girl seated in the grandstand and then, when she dodged, back away quickly again. Sometimes we would bomb the audience with bags of peanuts or popcorn. If there was any breeze at all the thing was unmanageable and I now carried a reel of light line with a weight on the end of the line so that if it got out of control, I could drop a line to the ground and get assistance in landing. One night after all the customers had left the park and there was no one there except the caretaker or watchman, the gas bag exploded with a roar. We never learned what set it off.

...in the fall of 1906, I decided to do something that I had been wanting to do for a number of years and that was to build and fly a dirigible of my own design; so I cast about for a place to build it and a remunerative contract for exhibiting and flying it. I rented a hall in South Seattle from Mr. Fred Newell, a mill owner for whom I had once time worked for as a chauffeur, in which to construct the machine. I made a contract with Mr. A. Loof [Looff], owner and operator of Luna Park at Duwamish Head, West Seattle, for exhibitions the following season. My brother Ray, who at the time was working as storekeeper on a ship operating between Seattle and the Orient, was commissioned to purchase 360 yards of Japanese silk, and a Mr. Frank Jacobs, who operated a trading schooner to the Society Islands, promised to bring me some pure para gum from the island of Morea. At that time this was the finest gum obtainable. It was to be used, cut with naphtha, as a coating or covering of the silk gas-bag to close the pores in the silk and make it tight enough to hold the hydrogen gas with which it was to be inflated.

In due time the materials arrived and, with the help of two seamstresses and their sewing machines, the huge silken bag began slowly to take shape. I had expected to make the bag sixty feet long but for some reason or other when it was completed, it was only fifty-eight feet in length, even though it was built exactly in proportion to the paper scale model that it had taken me many hours to design and build. After several months and hundreds of spools of thread and hundreds of feet of seams the bag was completed. A relief valve of my own design and an inflation neck were attached, and the first layer of dope applied and allowed to dry. After several layers of dope, the bag was inflated with air by means of a blacksmith's forge blower and then, as the silk was somewhat transparent, the places where not enough of the dope or para gum had been applied could be seen and more put on. This applying or painting on the dope was a very tedious and somewhat dangerous job as the gum and naphtha had to be heated and, although this was done in a double boiler, there was always danger of the fumes becoming ignited from a spark from the wood stove or from a spark of static electricity from friction of almost anything against the silk.

After the bag or envelope had been treated with seven coats of the dope, it was ready to have the netting fitted. The netting completely covered the bag and was used to attach the framework that carried the motor and operator. The framework was of an entirely original design and was made of spruce. It was triangular in shape with a car in the center for the motor and operator. All other frames up to this time had the motor at the forward end and the operator straddled the frame at the rear end. Although thirty-six feet long it weighed only thirty-eight pounds. I built four or five frames before getting one strong enough to carry the engine and yet light enough to be lifted by the gas bag. In testing them I would suspend them from the ceiling by the same number if cords that would support them when attached to the bag; then I would climb aboard and start the motor and in a few minutes the vibration would show up the weak places. I was trying to make the complete outfit so that it could be packed into small packing cases for easy transportation, as I intended to go on a barnstorming tour if the machine was a success.

The frame telescoped into one package about eight feet long, and the little car or box carrying the motor and clutch was about two by three feet. The whole thing was braced by 200-pound-test piano wire and one-sixteenth-inch turn buckles. The motor was purchased from the Curtiss Manufacturing Company and was an air-cooled V-shaped two-cylinder with a large diameter lightweight fly wheel. The bore and stroke was 3½ × 3⅝ and it weighed 51 pounds. All the bearings were roller bearings and it turned up about 1,400. The propeller was another innovation, being 4½ feet in diameter and could be used either as a broad two-blade or a narrow four-blade. There was a friction cone clutch built for me by Mr. Joe Anderson (Seattle Automobile Company mechanic) between the engine and propeller, something that no other dirigible outside of a Zeppelin had used up to this time. The bag, netting, and empty sandbags were packed into a box about 28 inches square and weighed a little over two hundred pounds and the frame and car and motor weighed, crated, a couple of hundred more.

Finally, summer came and the whole outfit was moved to Luna Park where a canvas hangar seventy feet long, thirty feet wide and thirty feet high, was provided. The gas plant was set up and preparations made for the first inflation. The gas or hydrogen generating plant consisted of two four-hundred-gallon wine casks which were lined with carbon, one fifty-gallon ice barrel for cooling the hot gas from the generating casks, and one twenty-five-gallon barrel full of unslaked lime to remove or absorb any excess acid or impurities from the hydrogen gas which, if allowed to enter the silk gas bag, would soon eat it full of tiny pin holes. After the outfit was all set up and ready, I ordered two 1,600 pound drums of sulfuric acid from The Stuart & Holmes Drug Company in Seattle and it was sent over to Luna Park by means of a horse-drawn dray belonging to the Eyres Transfer Company, and which went to West Seattle on the ferry and thence to Luna Park, an amusement park built on piling out over the water, which had the very usual collection of concessions and rides and shows.

When the dray arrived with the drums of acid, the driver and his swamper did not bother to put up a plank to roll them own onto the deck but adopted the easier method of simply rolling them off the back end of the dray and allowing them to drop. Although it was only about eighteen inches, they happened to land on the planks midway between two stringers and their great weight (the drums were lead-lines) broke the planks and deposited them both in the mud of the tide flats beneath. It took four days and over a hundred dollars to get them back up again and involved a messy job with chain blocks and a couple of hundred railroad ties that I borrowed from The Northern Pacific. This and several other unforseen expenses used up all of my capital, so I went to Joe Anderson, the mechanic, and asked him to lend me four or five hundred dollars. He pulled open a drawer in his workbench and took out twenty twenty-dollar gold pieces and said, "Here, if this ain't enough come back." There was no note, no security, no nothing.

I had estimated that to generate 7,500 cubic feet of hydrogen would require about 2,000 pounds of sulphuric acid, 2,500 pounds of clean cast-iron shavings, 300 pounds of ice and a barre of lime and would require from forty-eight to sixty hours. I had a young fellow by the name of Uker working for me. We got the stuff all assembled and put in a charge, and then the fun began, Uker went back to Seattle on the last ferry and I had a cot in one end of the hangar, I was awakened by a terrific thumping noise about midnight, and it came from the generators which were synchronizing or tramping. First one would make a big bubble of gas and a few seconds later the other would do the same. They were in perfect rhythm and going so strong that they were fairly dancing up and down.

There was a wooden safety plug in the top of each one that was supposed to blow out in the case of too much pressure. I was afraid the casks were going to burst so I got a hammer and knocked the plugs out and was immediately covered with hot acid which shot high into the air. I ran for the end of the dock and drove into the bay. Luckily the tide was in. The salt water was not at all soothing to the burns that I had received on the head and shoulders. I swam around in the dark until I found a ladder, climbed up onto the dock where several of the performers and ride operators had been attracted by the noise. Someone smeared me over with vaseline. I continued generating gas but used only one generator.

After a few days the bag was filled and we tested it for lift and found that the lift was ample to lift me and about twenty pounds of ballast in the form of sand in a canvas bag. A trial trip was advertised for June 27. A large crowd was there when we took the trim little dirigible from the hangar. This was the first airship ever seen north of San Francisco and was different from all others in this way: it was sharp at both ends, or a true spindle in shape and the idea was that it would enter the air easier and would have little drag behind it, which should make for more speed and easier operation and maneuverability. After balancing the ship so that it would neither rise nor sink by the removal of sand ballast, and making a few minor adjustments, I climbed into the little car, started the engine, and told the men that were holding it to "LET HER GO!" They did, and the ship took off beautifully. It responded to the rudder and circled the park several times and then I headed in the direction of Seattle.

By this time it had gone up to about two thousand feet, according to the aneroid barometer in the car, and began to experience a little carburetor trouble, probably due to the difference in barometric pressure at the higher level. While trying to adjust the carburetor, the hot sun was getting in its licks and was heating up the gas bag, causing the hydrogen to expand

and, before I could valve out some and relieve it, the bag burst open along the seam in the bottom and right over and only a few feet above the motor, which was shooting out flames from the exhaust. I grabbed both sides of the tear in my hands to keep it from tearing farther and at the same time pushed the switch off with my foot and stopped the motor. Why the gas had not ignited at this time I will never know as I could feel it on my head and body. The only explanation possible is that it must have turned upward within inches of the exhaust and thus missed igniting.

I climbed up on the framework and was very busy for a few minutes jabbing holes through the silk with my jackknife and tying the rent together with cords cut from the rigging, I hit the water pretty well over towards Queen Anne Hill. The bag still contained enough gas to keep the frame on top of the water, and I only got my feet wet though the frame had hit hard enough to pull some of the bolts right through the wood and required quite a bit of fixing up. A tugboat that I had hired to stand by, just in case, picked up me and the ship and took us back to Luna Park.

I hired a couple of girls, one of whom became my wife, to sew up the tear in the gas bag. This, of course, was a hand-sewing job and one of the girls got sick from the gas. However, it was finally finished and Uker and I patched up the car and framework and made ready for a flight to be made on the Fourth of July which was being advertised as the first race ever to be run between an airship and an automobile. The automobile was to be driven by H.P. Grant, the pioneer automobile dealer of Seattle, and Dr. F.A. Bryant as passenger. The race was to be from Luna Park to The Meadows, a racetrack about eight or ten miles distant. We got off to a good start. The carburetor functioned perfectly, and I kept the ship at a low level, about five hundred feet up. When crossing the valley south of Seattle, the airship at one time was directly above the automobile, so I shut off the engine and talked with them for a while, then started again and, by taking a few shortcuts that the auto could not take, easily beat them to the racetrack, where we landed and caused a near riot both among the racehorses and the spectators.

That night we tied the ship to the top of a launch and started down the river for the bay and thence back to the amusement park. This was one of the most dangerous trips I ever made. It was Fourth of July night and many places along the river, skyrockets narrowly missed the big bag full of hydrogen. Once a ball from a Roman candle made a direct hit but to our great relief bounced harmlessly off. The drawbridge tender had gone home for the night, but a nurse from a hospital up on the hill saw us and rushed down and opened the bridge just in time.

After exhibiting the 58-foot dirigible in Washington, Idaho, Montana, Oregon and Utah, I headed for Texas where I had a contract to appear at the Texas State Fair. The open ranges of Texas were the feeding grounds for great herds of cattle. The strange craft with its noisy 10 HP Curtiss motor was an awesome experience and caused many a steer to stampede in terror. Texas cattlemen didn't seem to care much for having their cattle

Fourteen—Case Study of a Parachute Aeronaut 179

frightened. Anyway, that is how I interpreted the meaning of the potshots that were taken at me and the airship. I decided that I was no longer wanted in Texas, so I deflated the gas bag and headed for Los Angeles [after] learning that there was to be an air show at Los Angeles, advertised as the "First Air Meet Ever to be Held in the United States." There were to be captive balloons, free balloons, dirigibles and airplanes. I decided to go there as a spectator.

The San Domingo Airfield was just a sandy piece of desert with a grandstand on one side and was located about where Compton is now. Upon arriving and making myself known to the management I was immediately signed up to give exhibitions and enter a race with the other two dirigibles which were twice the size of mine. On my first attempted ride and before a very large crowd, the wind drove my ship into the top of a flagpole on the grandstand. The flagpole punctured the envelope, allowing all the gas to escape and leaving me hanging onto the framework and dangling some twenty feet above the grandstand. Some ladders were secured, and I made an ignominious descent, much to the joy and ill-concealed satisfaction of the other aeronauts and pilots. Uker and I packed the debris and shipped it to Seattle.

I was deeply interested in the four airplanes that were exhibited, three of which would fly. The one that we had seen in Texas was here and, although it was the best-looking plane on the field, it still refused to take off. Of the three other dirigibles, one had engine trouble, one had a porous bag and could not be inflated, while the other made some beautiful flights. Of the planes, the most interesting was a Farman biplane, from France that looked a little like a huge box kite. It was of the pusher type and had a five-cylinder rotary two-cycle Gnome motor. It was quite unique in that the cylinders revolved around the crankshaft, which was stationary. The crankshaft was hollow and the carburetor was attached to the front end. The two propeller blades were attached directly to the revolving cylinders. It was lubricated with pure castor oil and would leave a trail of stinking white smoke several miles behind it. The pilot sat in a little seat just in front of the landing edge of the lower wing. The rudder was operated by a rudder bar on which the pilot's feet rested. The elevator out in front was operated by one lever by the left hand and the flaps used for banking were operated by another lever by the right hand, and the throttle was beneath the seat. This may all seem very complicated, but the plane was very easy to fly. This machine took off at about thirty-five miles per hour, had a top speed of about forty-five, would stay in the air at thirty and land at twenty-five, and I know of no present-day plane that can land that slowly. It was very stable and could be flown with both hands off the controls.

The pilot was a little Frenchman by the name of Paulhan who was an ex-waiter. In order to become better acquainted and this learn more about his plane, I moved into the Rockwood Hotel where he was staying, and, by slipping the head waiter five bucks, got placed at the same table in the dining room. When the headwaiter introduced us, Paulhan said, "Oh yes, you are ze pilot what make like a bird and land on top ze flagpole. Ve-e-e-e-re, ve-e-e-e-re fonney, ve-e-e-e-re fonny—ha-ha-ha-ha-ha!" Both Paulhan and his manager, a New Yorker by the name of Voight, were giving me the horse laugh and plenty until I told Paulhan, it wasn't nearly as funny as when that girl slapped his face yesterday morning in the lobby of the hotel. He said, "She wanted one hundred dollars just for sleeping with me—pouf—she should pay me!" Then he stuck out his hand and said, "Meckie, you are all right. Let us be friends," After all, that is what I had been working for when I had moved into the Rockwood and paid the waiter five bucks to place me at Paulhan's table.

I practically became a member of Paulhan's staff, (without pay) and was allowed to help gas up and also give it its daily dose of castor oil. He seemed delighted to learn that I knew a little about gasoline motors and never seemed to tire of explaining the Gnome motor and the controls of his ship. I wanted desperately to take a ride in it, but I knew that it would not carry double, and it was too much to ask to be allowed to take it up alone. One evening after a late dinner in the Rockwood dining room and while the orchestra were getting their dinner, Paulhan walked over to the piano and started playing "The Merry Widow Waltz." I picked up the violin from the top of the piano and played with him. Then Mr. Voight came over and started in on the cello. We played several other pieces and, by that time, quite a crowd had gathered and one of the regular orchestra members took a plate from a table and placed it on the platform and dropped a quarter in it. (I think this may have been subtle sarcasm.) At any rate the crowd took the cue and there was soon quite a collection in the plate. Paulhan was delighted and said, "Now we shall have a party," and invited everyone present, including the waters, and he personally took the orders for the drink, showing us how he had done when he had worked as a waiter in Paris not long before. I ordered a milkshake, Mr. Voight a glass of milk, and Paulhan drank a lemonade which he loudly proclaimed was an insult to his "What do you call it?—bellee?" But his contract with Voight allowed him to drink no liquor. We were the only ones who did not drink cocktails or champagne.

One morning just two days before the close of the air meet, Paulhan did not show up at the breakfast table. His manager said that he was very sick, with a temperature of 105, and they were both much worried about being unable to make their flights at the air show. As the big Farman plane and Paulhan were really the whole show, it was quite serious. At noon Paulhan was no better and Mr. Voight said they had been discussing the possibility of my being able to take the ship up. Paulhan had been against it but finally agreed, providing I did not go more than three feet off the ground the first time. There was a big crowd that day, and they were disappointed when they learned that Paulhan was not going to fly. However, when Mr. Voight explained that they had been fortunate in securing the services of a famous Scotch auto racer and who could also fly and that he would make a flight only a few feet off the ground which was the most dangerous kind of flying, they responded with applause.

Fourteen—Case Study of a Parachute Aeronaut

We took the machine to the end of the field, and I went over all of the controls, turnbuckles and wires—revved up the motor several times, motioned for the men who were holding the plane to let her go, and I started off on a course that paralleled the grandstand. It was even easier than I expected, and it really took off by itself. I found it easy to hold the plane close to the ground as the elevator way out in front was very effective. I went in front of the grandstand with the wheel barely off the ground, turned at the end of the field and came back the same way. The second flight was made at about two hundred feet elevation and returning I flew with both hands off the controls the same as Paulhan did. This flew on just as steady as a boxcar.

Of course, this was not nearly the show that Paulhan put on, but it pleased the crowd, and the management was satisfied. That night when we returned to the hotel was the first and only time that I ever got kissed by a man. Paulhan was overjoyed and felt much better, but the doctor would not let him fly the next day, so I finished the engagement. This excitable little Frenchman was a precision flyer if there ever was one. He could fly past the grandstand, throw out his handkerchief and on the return pass, pick it off the ground with a wire hook attached to the end of the lower wing. He could go up to four or five hundred feet, cut the ignition, then stall the plane, allowing it to start down tail-first. After gaining speed, he would elevate the tail and stall again and start forward, repeating the maneuvers until making a dead-stick landing in front of the crowd. At the close of the air meet at Los Angeles, Paulhan and Voight wanted me to return to New York with them and possibly go on to Paris. However, it did not appeal to me.

One of the men who had a dirigible at Los Angeles and who had been able to make only a few flights was disgusted with it and offered it to me at a ridiculously low price, so I bought it. Uker and I took it to Santa Barbara to fulfill an engagement that the former owner had secured. Santa Barbara, being surrounded by mountains and the prevailing winds at that time of year being from the ocean, was a bad place to try to operate a dirigible. We were able to make only one flight, and the ship proved to be very unmanageable and the motor very temperamental. The only thing good about the whole thing was the hydrogen generator which was much better and had a much greater capacity than mine. I lost money on this job, as it was on a no-fly-no-pay basis. We packed up and went to San Francisco. Being unable to secure a favorable contract there and being more-or-less afraid of the unwieldy ship, I decided to get rid of it. I advertised it in the papers and sold it to a man that claimed he had operated a dirigible in the East. He took it to Fresno, California, inflated it and was just taking off when it exploded just a few feet above the heads of the crowd, killing him and burning many of the spectators, some of whom died later.

We returned to Seattle, where I paid Joe Anderson $400 that I still owed him. I patched up my old ship and sold it to a man who used it as a captive balloon on a rope, carrying huge advertising signs on its sides. He used coal gas to inflate it and had the mistaken idea that he could smoke cigars while inflating it. He struck a match to light his cigar one day and puff! No more airship. Fire had always been one thing that I had been afraid of when exhibiting the dirigible and, when we were allowing people to see it up close inside the hangar, we always insisted that they throw away their cigar or cigarette if they happened to be smoking, before allowing them to enter.

Back in Seattle again, I wangled a half interest in a Hamilton biplane with an anemic motor with what little money I had left. Every flight we made in this machine ended in a crackup. [But] Finally I had a plane of my own and went on to give exhibitions or barn storming in the Northwest and British Columbia, where my plane was seized for infringing on some alleged Canadian patents.

Frustrated by the expense of his aviation endeavors, Mecklem stopped flying and settled down to calmer pursuits, including work as a deep-sea diver. The same pattern could be found in countless other "Early Bird" aviators: they invested everything in one or two aircraft, but then could not recover enough in income without the support of a manufacturer to continue with newer, more sophisticated designs.

Fifteen

Airplanes and Skydiving

As the first decade of the twentieth century unfolded, public interest in airships and airplanes skyrocketed, rendering the balloon-parachute act a tamer, low-budget staple of rural fairs and fetes. Though its popularity faltered, the public was still fascinated by the sight of a balloon ascension and parachute descent, perhaps gaining in nostalgia what it lost in thrill and novelty. It could be found being performed up to the end of the twentieth century, kept alive by ballooning pros such as Claude Shafer and Peter Kreig. It has not been publicly presented since that time, although sport skydivers using modern equipment still jump from balloons, as do high-altitude researchers and record-seekers such as Joseph Kittinger, Felix Baumgartner and Alan Eustace.

Perhaps as many as a score of performers of the balloon-parachute act attempted to build and fly airplanes. Unsurprisingly, the earliest and most influential example was Thomas S. "Tom" Baldwin. In 1910, he built the first of a series of biplanes and monoplane models using the common name *Red Devil*. His first public flight was over the Mineola, Long Island airfield in June of that year. He made many flights during the summer, often trying his skill against pilots Charles Hamilton and Clifford Harmon, a wealthy former sport balloonist. Baldwin, Hamilton, and Harmon were all working with Glenn Curtiss to test his new engines.

Over the next year, Baldwin participated in several flying exhibitions on Long Island, Pittsburgh, St. Louis, Kansas City, and Iowa City, sometimes working with notable pilots such as Glenn Curtiss and J.C. "Bud" Mars. In the Spring of 1911, Baldwin took the *Red Devil* on a tour of China, Korea and Japan with Bud Mars and Tod Shriver. Baldwin sold copies of the *Red Devil* and continued to tour for the next two years, sometimes leaving the flying to his hired pilots. When war broke out in Europe, Baldwin returned to serve his country first as a dirigible

Tom Baldwin piloting the *Red Devil* (Library of Congress, Control Number 2014689410).

designer and later, after the war, as Chief of Army Balloon Inspection and Production. In the early 1920s, he joined the Goodyear Tire Company as an airship designer. Baldwin died in 1923 at age 65, having won wide acclaim for his contributions to aviation.

Other former parachutists only had brief experience with airplanes, finding them more difficult to get in the air and expensive to build and repair. Baldwin's one-time rival and long-time friend, Charles W. Williams, met Baldwin in September 1906 at the Chemung County (NY) Fair, where Baldwin was exhibiting his *California Arrow* airship. An Elmira newspaper claimed that Williams had assisted with testing and building Baldwin's dirigibles, but corroboration is lacking. Williams later designed and built his own airplane in 1908, employing compound sets of wings—but it never rose more than a few feet off the ground. Williams died in 1912 at age 48.

One of the last alumni of the Grace Shannon Balloon Company was aviator Hugh Robinson, who built his own Blériot-style airplane in 1909 and went on to work with Glenn Curtiss. Robinson was a trained mechanical engineer, and he built his own automobile, glider, and dirigible. Robinson worked with Curtiss during World War I on the engine of the Curtiss JN-4, the "Jenny." In his final years he acted as a consulting engineer for National Scientific Laboratories in Washington, D.C.

Clarence C. Bonette, New England's longtime parachutist, built his own airplane in 1910, dubbed *Vermont No. 1*. He made his first successful flight of the Curtiss designed craft in August, near his home in northern Vermont. Reports of Bonette's flights appeared for about a year, but it appears that breakdowns caused him to give up airplanes. He continued to perform the balloon-parachute act with his adopted son into the 1940s. Another balloon-parachute veteran, B.C. McClellan of Spokane, Washington, built his own Curtiss airplane and opened a flying school in 1912. John W. Vandiver, who went by the stage name Walter Ralston when he was a parachutist, became an airplane mechanic and died in an air crash in 1919. Ivy Baldwin (William Ivy) built a Curtiss plane in 1910 and flew it for about a year, before returning to balloon work. In England, Wild West showman and actor Samuel F. Cody—who helped build and fly the first British military airship—surprised many by building and flying the first airplane in Great Britain. Though there is no record that Cody used a parachute, he did fly in his man-lifting kites, inspired by his friend, balloon-parachute impresario Auguste Gaudron (and also, perhaps, by Cody's ex-wife, Maud Lee).

Parachutist John J. Frisbie, who had performed with Carl Myers and with the Allen brothers, spent the summer of 1910 ballooning and flying airplanes with the likes of Tom Baldwin, Charles K. Hamilton,[1] Clifford B. Harmon, Glenn Curtiss, and others. By the end of the summer, he had purchased a Curtiss plane and was giving exhibitions at most scheduled meets. By 1911, Frisbie was flying with the best aviators in the world and was among the first two dozen pilots to be licensed by the Aero Club of America. He was recruited to be an exhibition flyer for Moisant and then for Curtiss and won several prizes through the summer of 1911. On September 1, 1911, he was scheduled to fly at the Norton, Kansas County Fair, but it was announced that he had engine problems. The fairgoers jeered and shouted "fakir," which spurred Frisbie to try. He rose a hundred feet into the air on takeoff, banked to make a turn, and lost control. The plane crashed, with the engine crushing his body, killing him.

Several of the greatest pilots of the "Early Bird" era got their start as parachutists or as assistants to the balloon-parachute veterans who made dirigibles. Roy Knabenshue and Lincoln Beachey were recruited by Tom Baldwin. Horace B. Wild started his career as a balloon-parachute act performer, tested Chanute gliders, then piloted airships, and ultimately became a daring airplane pilot. Cromwell Dixon, who was advised by Knabenshue and Carl Myers, also graduated from small dirigibles to an airplane, in which he died at a tragically young age. James C. "Bud" Mars, the acrobat-glider pilot-parachutist-airship pilot, transitioned to airplanes in 1910, learning from Glenn Curtiss. Mars went on to become one of the most famous and daring of the early flyers.

These examples show that while the balloon-parachute act brought minimal practical application to aeronautics, those who performed it had a great impact on the development of aviation. Parachuting itself remained only an entertainment until it could be used from the new future of aviation, the airplane. Jumping from an airplane required a mechanism to store and deploy the parachute: the parachute pack. The lineage of the parachute pack is not a direct line; variations of the idea were tried at different times in different countries. As was the case with airships, balloon-parachute performers made important contributions to the development of the parachute pack.

As early as 1893, Montz Bozarth and other parachutists learned that the parachute could be folded before deployment—and did so to perform the illusion of being shot out of a cannon, emerging from the tube with the parachute trailing behind. This idea was adapted in early March 1912 at St. Louis, Missouri, by Bert B. Berry, who fitted a metal cone in the undercarriage of an airplane plane in which a parachute was folded. With Tony Jannus piloting the Benoist aircraft, Berry crouched in the undercarriage until they were high over the Jefferson Army Barracks and then jumped. He fell freely for 500 feet before the parachute opened, landing successfully. Parachutist William "Grant" Morton repeated the feat with pilot Phil Parmalee at Venice, California, the next month.

Later, some claimed that Morton's jump had pre-dated Berry's but the proof of this lacking. Neither Berry nor Morton were admirable specimens of humanity. Berry, in the decades since, has often been named as "Captain Albert Berry of the U.S. Army," which is quite wrong. Bertram B. Berry was from Elmira, New York. His parents divorced when he was ten years old, because his mother objected to the fact that his father, amateur balloonist John Berry, took him aloft too often. Fatherless, Bert Berry drifted into crime and was sent to the Elmira Reformatory. He was released, got into trouble again, and did a stretch at Auburn Prison. In 1905–1910, he became a balloon-parachute performer. While performing in Pennsylvania in 1908, he was arrested for being at the center of a racist lynch mob (Berry, and all other suspects, were acquitted). Bert's long-lost father John Berry read about his troubles and invited him to St. Louis. Bert Berry stayed in St. Louis long enough to make the parachute jump with Tony Jannus. However, his whereabouts after 1913 aren't known—not a good sign, given his troublesome past.

As for William Morton, several years prior to his notable jump he

Pilot Tony Jannus and Bert Berry with the Benoist-built biplane they used when Berry became the first person to parachute from an airplane on March 1, 1912 (courtesy Missouri History Museum).

was performing the balloon-parachute act at Chutes Park in Los Angeles. At that time, he was accused of trying to strangle his wife on a sidewalk in broad daylight. She was a vaudeville dancer who made the mistake of taking jobs without his approval. Although she did not press charges, their marriage was short-lived. About a year after his 1912 airplane jump, Morton was arrested for "lewd behavior" with two teen girls, one being 16. Like Berry, Morton faded quickly from public notice.

Both Berry and Morton relied on a specially-rigged parachute located underneath the airplane carriage—an arrangement of little practical use to those in an airplane needing to ditch a crippled craft. Even before their jumps, others had been working on a better solution. In 1910, Katharina "Käthe" Paulus, Germany's most famous balloon-parachute performer, devised a parachute pack that used a breakaway cord to separate the parachute from the pack attached to her balloon. Earlier, Paulus had lost her aeronaut husband in a fall from a balloon. Later, during World War II, she produced over 7,000 parachutes, saving the lives of many airmen in the balloon service. In 1917,

Otto Heinicke adapted the idea to a cushion pack for use in balloons and airships.

Like Paulus, Russian actor Gleb Kotelnikov was motivated to invention by a tragedy. Kotelinikov witnessed the death of Captain Leo Matsievich during an air show in 1910. He devised a backpack for the

Studio portrait depicting Käthe Paulus parachuting off a balloon (Wikimedia Commons).

parachute, opened via a cord attached to the plane or manually by the wearer. Though it was tested successfully, Kotelnikov failed to impress his country's government. He tried marketing it later in Europe, but by that time other variants were available. In 1913, French inventor Frédéric Bonnet invented a parachute pack successfully tested by pilot Adolphe Pégoud, who intentionally ditched the Bleriot airplane he was flying. However, an earlier tragic death by an amateur who jumped from the Eiffel Tower with a competing design muted Bonnet's success.

As early as 1902, parachutists introduced a new wrinkle to their act: jumping from the balloon and opening one parachute, then dropping from that to open a second, hidden parachute.[2] The crown of the second parachute is pulled by a cord leading from the first parachute, which unfurls the folded length of the second parachute before breaking. The concept likely developed from the unfurling used in the trick of emerging from a cannon suspended by a balloon. In 1908, an itinerant balloon-parachute performer, Charles Broadwick (real name John Henry Murray), introduced double and triple parachute jumps made by his partner Georgia "Tiny" Thompson. "Tiny" was Broadwick's fourth female aeronaut—and perhaps his fourth wife. In 1902, he had gone on the road with his wife Jeanette, but she divorced him in 1904 for cruelty and drunkenness. Broadwick then married a woman named Maud, who was caught in the ropes of his ascending balloon and fell to her death in November 1905.

To avoid the bad publicity that Maud's death had entailed, Broadwick started the 1906 season as "Prof. Lola," and his female aeronaut was billed as "Mlle. Theresa." Little is known about "Theresa" other than that she was from Pennsylvania and had married Broadwick in Valdosta, Georgia, just weeks after Maud's death. After a harrowing accident in November 1907, in which she nearly drowned, the role of "Mlle. Theresa" was assumed by a different young woman, Tiny Broadwick, who was 15 years old in 1908, small, and very lightweight. Over the next two years, she performed under the "Mlle. Theresa" name and sometimes under the name Broadwick and was described in newspapers as Charles Broadwick's niece or daughter. Despite her age, Georgia was already recovering from a failed marriage and already had a child of her own. Georgia and Charles Broadwick toured together for five years and in the 1910 census were listed as husband and wife, though this may have just been a marriage of convenience for travel.

The Broadwicks moved to Southern California, where a new teen-aged assistant, Leslie Leroy Irvin, was hired to make balloon jumps. On January 23, 1912, Tiny Broadwick performed at Dominguez Field in Los Angeles during the International Air Meet, her act sandwiched between airplane demonstrations by many of the greatest airmen of that era. Aircraft builder Glenn Martin was deeply impressed by her double parachute jump and wondered if the packing of the second parachute could be adapted for use in making a leap from an airplane. Martin approached Charles Broadwick to help develop a "coatpack" mechanism using a static line to the airplane. In June 1913, Tiny Broadwick made a public demonstration of the device by jumping from Martin's plane over Griffith Park in Los Angeles. The next season, Leslie Irvin took her place and made his first jump from an airplane. That same year, 1914, Glenn Martin applied for a patent of his "Martin's Life-Vest," leaving Broadwick's role virtually forgotten. However, the extent of Broadwick's contribution is unclear, since other balloon-parachutists had previously performed the double-parachute routine using a folded parachute. Later, in a 1927 deposition, Charles Broadwick claimed the lion's share of the credit for the invention of the parachute backpack.

Another strong claim belongs to the most daring parachutist of his era, Albert Leo Stevens. The longtime daredevil, as unconventional as ever, tested his new "Stevens Safety Pack" by employing other daredevils in a series of spectacular stunts. Since the early 1890s, Stevens had been experimenting with smaller, more easily deployed parachutes for short drops and to add new wrinkles to the parachuting act. The Eldorado aeronauts of the mid–1890s, with Stevens as their ringleader, had made several jumps from bridges, and Stevens' pal Mort McKim made it his feature act. One of Stevens' signature acts in the early 1900s was the "Human Bomb," which was a metal shell with Stevens and a folded parachute inside, surrounded by a second wicker covering that was exploded by charges, after which Stevens would open his protective case and drop with the parachute.

According to some accounts, Stevens began in earnest to make designs for encasing the parachute in a backpack in 1908. According to secondary sources, it was in 1908 that Stevens provided the parachute used by daredevil Bobby Leach in his jump from the Steel Arch Bridge over the churning Niagara River—such a stunt would have intrigued Stevens. He publicly announced that he was working on the parachute pack project in 1911 and soon found a willing subject to test his ideas. Frederick Rodman Law, an idle steeplejack, claimed that he approached Stevens looking for a parachute to pull off a high dive stunt for photographers and movie cameramen. The tower that Law chose to make his jump from was the raised torch arm of the Statue of Liberty—though it is equally plausible that the idea originated with Stevens. On February 3, 1912, Stevens and Law went to Liberty Island and presented an authorization paper from the War Department that Stevens had conjured. They proceeded to the top of the stature and went up inside the arm, emerging at the balcony around the torch. The wind was blowing a stiff 20 m.p.h. The *New York Daily Star* described the scene: "'It looks a little risky, Fred,' remarked Stevens, peering over the edge of the torch rim to the base of the statue, 200 feet below." F. Rodman Law took a puff from Stevens' cigar, and then jumped off Lady Liberty's balcony, pulled the ripcord of the prototype parachute pack, and drifted to the ground. The result was headlines in newspapers around the world.

After another jump later that month from the Brooklyn Bridge, Stevens made plans with Law to make a jump with the pack from an airplane, but pilots were wary, fearing the sudden drop of weight from their frail craft might cause a crash. Finally, they convinced Phillips W. Page, who flew a hydroplane, to take Law aloft on April 13, 1912. Law and the parachute pack performed perfectly over Marblehead Harbor, making him the second person to parachute

Pain's human bomb, Leo Stevens (not Louis), who descends by parachute (Library of Congress, Control Number 2012646025).

from an airplane, following Bert B. Berry (and before William "Grant" Morton). On June 26, 1912, Rodman Law repeated the feat from Harry B. Brown's airplane over a Long Island airfield.

Over the next year Stevens recruited two others in addition to Law to make jumps with the pack at air meets: Weehawken, New Jersey, milkman Arthur Lapham and balloon-parachute performer Edward Boland. Lapham's first jump on May 31, 1913, was inauspicious: the airplane had engine problems and could not climb beyond 200 feet, but Lapham decided to jump anyway; the chute did not open, and he plunged feet first into the low-tide mud flats around Staten Island. He had to be dragged out but was relatively unharmed.

A month earlier, in April 1913, Rodman Law had his own mishap attempting to test the parachute pack—but not from an airplane, balloon, building, bridge, cliff, or statue. Leo Stevens had Law step up to the top of an aluminum cylinder and crawl inside, separated from a huge charge of black powder in the lower portion; in other words, Law was to be launched skyward on a solid-fuel rocket. The idea was that at the apogee, Law would spring out and deploy the chute. Stevens had received advice on constructing the rocket from Pain's Fireworks employees, with whom Stevens had a long-time relationship dating back to his "Human Bomb" days. When the charge was lit, the bottom of the rocket exploded, throwing Law no more than a dozen feet into the air.[3] Apparently, there was a bit more to the rocket science business than they had anticipated.[4]

The onset of World War I, with a host of countries rushing military aircraft and spotter balloons into service, should have sparked a new round of development of the parachute pack. However, airplane pilots distrusted them, believing that releasing the plane's controls to make a jump was dangerous, and military commanders believed that parachutes might cause pilots to ditch costly craft that might be able to land and be repaired. Consequently, little use was made of parachutes until the closing months of the war, and little had been done by the Allies to improve their design.[5] Even so, by the end of the war, the U.S. Army recognized that a more efficient, reliable parachute pack needed to be developed, especially since aircraft had recently been built that could carry a crew—or troops.

At Dayton's McCook field, Major Edward L. Hoffman gathered a panel to review existing parachute pack features. The board included Floyd Smith, a former acrobat and mechanic for Glenn Martin; Guy Ball, another California mechanic; Harry Eibe, a balloon-parachutist from Greenville, Ohio, close to Dayton; Sgt. Ralph Bottreil, an experienced jumper; and engineers James J. Higgins and James M. Russell.

Hoffman's team examined all existing parachute pack features, including those used by the Broadwicks; Leo Stevens's Safety Pack; the German Otto Heinicke; Floyd Smith's modifications to the Broadwick/Martin pack; and, similarly, the modification that Leslie Irvin made to the Broadwick pack he had used. Hoffman's panel arrived at a combination of the best features of each and identified it as the "U.S. Army Air Service Type A Parachute."

Initially, Hoffman wanted the Type A to be used on static line (i.e., tethered to the plane) drops only. However, Floyd Smith and Leslie Irvin lobbied to include a ripcord option, to be used in a free-fall. Leslie Irvin volunteered to test the new ripcord pack on April 28, 1919, jumping from a de Havilland biplane piloted by Floyd Smith. Once the Type A design proved successful, Smith, Irvin, and other parachute makers submitted patents for their variants.[6] Some of the competing patent claims were contested.

Two of Hoffman's advisors—Leslie Irvin and Harry Eibe—had deep roots in the balloon-parachute act community. Eibe had learned parachute jumping from brothers John J. and Felix Coughlin. The Coughlins had been tutored by Edward E. Craig of Sturgis, Michigan, who claimed the have known Ed Hogan and W.H. Donaldson. Leslie Irvin's heritage was no less impressive: in 1912, he and his older brother Arthur were assistants to balloonist Edward Unger. Unger had been an assistant to Edward E. Leonhardt, an Oakland, California, government clerk who had once been an assistant to Park Van Tassel. In 1909, the balloon that Leonhardt and Unger made ascensions with had been purchased from Van Tassel. Following a stint with Unger, Leslie Irvin assisted Charles and Tiny Broadwick in making parachute jumps.

The parachute pack designs developed by Hoffman's team became the foundation for all modern military and sport parachutes developed since that time. Much of the lineage of airships and dirigibles built in America can also be traced back practitioners of the balloon-parachute act. Early Bird pilots with parachuting and airship work in their background helped to expand the technological limits of airplanes between 1908 and the First World War. These are the tangible effects on material progress that can be attributed to a forgotten generation of daredevil performers, those who made the "leap from the clouds."

Appendix: Notable Balloon-Parachute Era Aeronauts

Bold entries indicate died while performing.

Name	Career Region	Residence(s)	Born	Died
Acker, Isabelle real name of Elsie Vandell	USA	Cleveland OH		
Adair, Alfretta stage name of Alfretta Denton (Baum)	USA	Peoria IL	1872	1957
Adair, Leila stage name shared by Hawker sisters (including Lillian Mary)	Australia, USA, New Zealand			
Aiken, James	USA	Jackson MI		
Albertina, Mlle. Stage name of Louisa Maude Evans	**England**	**London ENG**	**1882**	**1896**
Allen, Arlene	USA	Batavia NY	1929	1948
Allen, Comfort	USA	Dansville NY	1850	1930
Allen, Edgar	USA	Dansville NY	1896	1989
Allen, Edward	USA	Dansville NY	1896	1984
Allen, Edward, Jr.	USA	Batavia NY	1917	2012
Allen, Florence	USA	Batavia NY	1922	2008
Allen, Gloria	USA	Batavia NY	1920	1937
Allen, Ira	USA	Dansville NY	1846	1932
Allen, Martin	USA	Dansville NY	1850	1940
Allen, Stephen	USA	Batavia NY	1878	1915
Allen, Warren "Speck"	USA	Dansville NY	1876	1955
Allen, Warren, Jr.	USA	Dansville NY	1904	1946

Appendix: Notable Balloon-Parachute Era Aeronauts

Name	Career Region	Residence(s)	Born	Died
Allen, William	USA	Dansville NY	1878	1940
Allison, May real name of Louise Hanner/Miss America/Mlle. Le Voy	USA	Cincinnati OH	**1874**	**1896**
Ames, Flora real name of Reta Danzelle	USA	Elmira NY	1880	1961
Ammons, Claude	USA	Logansport IN	1870	1919
Ashlock, Nettie married name of Juanetta Stobbs, aka Rosa May	USA	Peoria IL	1872	
Ashmon, Mrs. Dewitt C. married name of Jennie Leland	USA	Tacoma WA	1865	1947
Baldwin, Charles	England			
Baldwin, Clarence Earl	USA	Otsego MI	1872	1938
Baldwin, Ivy stage name of William Ivy	USA	Alameda CA	1866	1953
Baldwin, Samuel	USA	Quincy IL	1852	1923
Baldwin, Thomas S.	USA	Quincy IL	1857	1923
Balleni, Henri stage name of Henry Newbold	England	Lamington ENG	1841	
Baltz, Edward real name of Edward Jewell	USA	Buffalo NY	1865	1928
Barnell, Daniel A.	USA	Hartford CT	1874	1928
Barnhart, George W.	USA	Sturgis MI	1879	1904
Bartholomew, Coryell	USA, Australia, Orient	St Joseph MI	1854	1913
Bates, Louise	USA	Cincinnati OH	1865	
Bassett, Adelaide stage name of Ann Amelia Chaplin Bassett	**England**	**Bromley in Bow ENG**	**1863**	**1895**
Baum, Alfretta married name of Alfretta Denton	USA	Peoria IL	1872	1957
Beam, Samuel Zimmerman	USA	Derry PA	1874	1961
Beaumont, Alma stage name of Mary Brown	England	London; Brooklyn	1877	
Belmont, Lillian stage name of Adela Sowards	USA	MI	1880	1901
Belmont, Lucielle stage name of Lucielle Dashiell	USA	Ft Worth TX	1887	1961
Belmont, Madeline stage name of Madeline Davis	USA	**Fort Pierce FL**	**1898**	**1922**
Benjamin, Ellen Augusta real name of Helene Thiers aka Karletta	USA	Buffalo NY	1842	1893

Appendix: Notable Balloon-Parachute Era Aeronauts

Name	Career Region	Residence(s)	Born	Died
Berry, Bertram "Bert"	USA	Elmira NY	1875	
Berry, John A.	USA	St. Louis MO	1849	1931
Bickford, Frederick W.	USA	Portland ME	1879	1968
Biggerstaff, John Wesley real name of Harry Warner	USA	New Orleans LA	**1855**	**1897**
Black, Samuel	USA	**Quincy IL**	**1872**	**1890**
Bonette, Clarence C.	USA	St Johnsbury VT	1871	1947
Bonette, Louis, also known as Louis Lapoint	USA	NH	1908	1969
Bonham, Harriet S. maiden name of Woodall, Harriet "Jennie"	USA	Terre Haute IN	1868	1945
Bozarth, Ida real name of Mlle. "Millie" Viola	USA	Clinton MO	1867	1889
Bozarth, Joseph W. "Montz"	USA	Clinton MO	1867	1950
Bradford, Fred L.	USA	Chicago IL	1878	1915
Brady, Owen aka Owen Bready	USA	Westfield MA; Cleveland OH	1864	1936
Bready, Owen aka Owen Brady	USA	Westfield MA; Cleveland OH	1864	1936
Broadwick, Charles stage name of John Henry Murray	USA	CA	1874	1943
Broadwick, Tiny stage name of Georgia Anne Thompson	USA	CA	1893	1978
Brown, Jessie real name of Jessie Zelno	USA	Marietta GA	Abt. 1875	
Brown, Mary real name of Alma Beaumont	England	London ENG; Brooklyn NY	1877	
Browning, Cecelia C. real name of Cissie Kent	England	London ENG	1868	1943
Buckingham, James real name of Prof. De Ive	USA (born Manchester Eng.)			**1891**
Buckner, Cora	USA	Indianapolis IN	1892	1946
Burke, King stage name of John Henry Stokes	USA	Cleveland OH	1867	1932
Burke, Otto real name of Otto Lochbaum	USA	San Francisco CA	1874	1936
Burns, Wilfrid James	USA, Australia, SE Asia	Olympia WA	1869	1916

Appendix: Notable Balloon-Parachute Era Aeronauts

Name	Career Region	Residence(s)	Born	Died
Burson, Guy F.	USA	Schoolcraft MI	1873	1896
Busch, Louis R. aka Louis Bush	USA	Cincinnati OH	1869	1942
Bush, Louis R. aka Louis Busch	USA	Cincinnati OH	1869	1942
Campbell, James Neil	England, Australia	London ENG	1862	1926
Carlotta, stage name of Mary Breed Hawley, aka Mrs. Carl Myers	USA	Herkimer NY	1850	1932
Carlton, August aka Eddie Hall	USA	Portland OR	1877	
Carmo, Gertie stage name of Gertrude Clausen	USA	**Jackson MI**		**1892**
Carmo, Josie stage name of Lillian Trautwein	USA	Toledo OH	1877	
Carmon, Madame stage name of Cora Etta Johnson	USA	Livingston IL	1880	1919
Carrow, William E.	USA	Reed City MI	1871	1922
Casteel, Estella Belle maiden name of Stella Gribble	USA	Louisville KY	1877	1968
Claridge, Edwin F.	USA	**Los Angeles CA**	1854	1887
Clark, Elizabeth J. real name of Mrs. Oscar Hunt, Lottie Leon, Lottie Hunt	USA	Cleveland OH	1850	1923
Clausen, Gertrude real name of Gertie Carmo	USA	**Jackson MI**		**1892**
Cody, Lillian stage name of Maud Lee	USA	Norristown PA	1862	1946
Cody, Louise stage or married name of Louise Schroene aka Ruby Deveau	USA	Missoula MT	1881	1966
Colby, Charles E.	USA	Boston MA	1867	
Cole, Edward R.	USA	**Jackson MI**	**1867**	**1896**
Conlon, Charles T.	USA	Oakland CA	1876	1926
Cook, Edith M. real name of Viola Spencer	England	Ipswich ENG	1878	1910
Cosgrove, Mrs. Arthur married name of Bertha Onzalo	USA	Bakersfield CA	1872	
Coughlin, Felix J.	USA	Versailles OH	1868	1940
Coughlin, John J.	USA	Versailles OH	1881	1951
Coykendall, Clara maiden name of Mrs. Park Van Tassel	USA	San Jose CA	1861	

Appendix: Notable Balloon-Parachute Era Aeronauts

Name	Career Region	Residence(s)	Born	Died
Craig, Edward E.	USA	Sturgis MI	1864	1918
Crawford, Elizabeth C.	USA	St Louis MO	1862	
Crew, John Henry	USA	VA	Abt. 1872	
Crockett, Jennie C. real name of Nellie Wheeler	USA	**Boston MA**	**1857**	**1891**
Daggett, George Weston real name of George Weston	USA	San Francisco CA	1871	1897
Dallas, Jack stage name of Benjamin Parker	USA	Rochester NY	1879	1940
Danzelle, Reta stage name of Flora Ames	USA	Elmira NY	1880	1961
Dare, Del stage name of William Wilson	USA	Toledo OH		
Dare, Leon stage name of Tracey Tisdell	USA	Brooklyn NY	1866	1938
Dare, Leona stage name of Adaline Stuart	USA	New York City NY	1854	1922
Daring Donald, stage name of Marion L. Macdonald	USA	New Haven CT	1862	
Dashiell, Lucielle real name of Lucielle Belmont	USA	Ft Worth TX	1887	1961
Davis, Madeline real name of Madeline Belmont	USA	**Fort Pierce FL**	**1898**	**1922**
Davonda, Dorothy stage name of Dorothy Gates	USA	Sparta MI	1881	1943
De Ive, Prof., stage name of James Buckingham	USA (born Manchester Eng.)			
DeHaven, Maud	USA	New York City NY		
Dene, Jenny	USA			
Dennis, David Luther	USA	Franklin IN	1875	1948
Dennis, William "Willet" Philip	USA	Terre Haute IN	1852	1920
Denton, Alfretta real name of Alfretta Adair	USA	Peoria IL	1872	1957
Deveau, Ruby stage name of Louise Cody Schroene	USA	Missoula MT	1881	1966
Devoy, Emily stage name of Emma Louisa Dovey	England	London ENG	1869	

Appendix: Notable Balloon-Parachute Era Aeronauts

Name	Career Region	Residence(s)	Born	Died
Dovey, Emma real name of Emily Devoy	England	London ENG	1869	
Driscoll, Lewis Henry	USA	Sabina OH	1860	1933
Dwyer, Frank A.	USA	Decorah IA	1868	1930
Earlston, Robert J.	USA	Los Angeles CA	1875	1962
Eckhart, Clarence G.	USA	Buffalo NY	1866	1949
Eddy, Charles J.	USA	Quincy IL	1867	1914
Eibe, Harry Andrus	USA	Greenville OH	1886	1921
Elser, Ray	**USA**	**Omaha NE**	**1874**	**1893**
Evans, Louisa Maude real name of Mlle. Albertina	England	London ENG	1882	1896
Ezzell, Marion Francis real name of Frank Zelno	USA	IL	1872	1926
Farini, stage name of William Leonard Hunt	England	Ontario CAN	1838	1929
Finn, Edith stage name of Sadie Leroy	USA	Mt Vernon OH	1881	1841
Fisk, Ira N.	USA	Springfield IL	1858	1928
Forsman, Milton M.	USA	Peoria IL	1855	1898
Freitas, Gladys	Australia	Sydney NSW		
Freitas, Valerie Grace	Australia	Sydney NSW		
Frisbie, John J.	USA	Oswego NY	1869	1911
Gall, William H. aka William Gaul	USA	Logansport IN	1871	1944
Gates, Dorothy real name of Dorothy Davonda	USA	Sparta MI	1881	1943
Gaudron, Auguste	England	London ENG	1867	1913
Gaul, William H. aka William Gall	USA	Logansport IN	1871	1944
Gaylor, Helen	USA	PA	Abt. 1870	
Gilbert, Harry	USA	Cincinnati OH	1838	1892
Gillock, John L.	USA	Springfield IL	1862	1903
Gleason, Thomas C.	USA	Jackson MI	1859	1936
Gomes, James	USA	Springfield IL	1868	1909
Gomes, Joseph B.	USA	Springfield IL	1857	1919
Gould, William R.	USA	OH	1860	1944

Name	Career Region	Residence(s)	Born	Died
Graves, Estella stage name of Maud Shaw	USA	Kansas City MO	Abt. 1877	
Greenleaf, Thomas William	USA	Quincy IL	1866	1936
Gribble, James L. "Col. Jake"	USA	Louisville KY	1864	1922
Gribble, Stella nee Estella Belle Casteel	USA	Louisville KY	1877	1968
Gruber, Harry real name of Harry Jewell	USA	Philadelphia PA	1866	
Hagel, Frank	USA	Peoria IL	1862	1929
Hagel, Fred	USA	Peoria IL	1861	1938
Hagel, Harry	USA	Peoria IL	1870	1907
Hagel, Nellie W. (real name unknown)	USA	CA	**1862**	**1895**
Hagel, Otella "Tillie"	USA	Peoria IL	1873	
Hague, Paul R. real name of Prof. Zeno	USA	**Savannah, GA**	1875	1901
Hall, Edward Norris	USA	Portland OR	1876	
Hanner, Louise stage name of May Allison	USA	Cincinnati OH	1874	1896
Hanner, William H. "Kid"	USA	Cincinnati OH	1860	1900
Harding, Frederick real name of Jack Leroy	USA	Connersville IN	1872	1906
Harkes, Anne real name of Frankie Lavelle	USA	Cincinnati OH	1871	1891
Harrell, Frank C	USA	Indianapolis IN		
Hathaway, Ned stage name of Uel E. Hurd	USA	Springfield IL	1852	1909
Hawker, Ethel Harriet real name of Essie Viola	Australia, USA, New Zealand	San Francisco CA	1876	1935
Hawker, Lillian real name of Leila Adair	Australia, USA, New Zealand	San Francisco CA	1869	1933
Hawker, Ruby Marrania, real name of Millie (Mlle) Hawker	Australia, USA, New Zealand	San Francisco CA	1873	1935
Hawley, Mary Breed real name of Carlotta aka Mrs. Carl Myers	USA	Herkimer NY	1850	1932
Headley, (John) Daniel	USA	Springfield IL	1854	1941
Heid, Wilhelmina name of Victoria Leroy	USA	**Fremont OH**	**1870**	**1896**
Henden, Harry	England, Australia	Sydney NSW	1848	1937

Appendix: Notable Balloon-Parachute Era Aeronauts

Name	Career Region	Residence(s)	Born	Died
Hepner, Frank H.	USA	Sturgis MI	1869	1928
Hepner, Fredric J.	USA	Sturgis MI	1864	1905
Hibbard, George W.	USA	Jackson MI	1869	1956
Higgins, George	**England**	Haddenham ENG	**1851**	**1891**
Hill, Richard P.	USA	Emporia KS	1854	1926
Hogan, Edward D.	USA	**Jackson MI**	**1852**	**1889**
Hogan, John	USA	**Jackson MI**	**1854**	**1891**
Hogan, William	USA	Jackson MI	1843	1906
Hunt, Lottie stage name of Mrs. Oscar Hunt nee Elizabeth J. Clark	USA	Cleveland OH	1850	1923
Hunt, Oscar	USA	Cleveland OH	1854	1893
Hunt, William Leonard real name of Farini	England	Ontario CAN	1838	1929
Huonker, Lucy Alice real name of Madame Zeno	USA	Blairsville PA	1869	1964
Hurd, Uel Edward real name of Hathaway, Ned	USA	Springfield IL	1852	1909
Hutchison, Edmund Rane	USA	Elmira NY	1869	1950
Hutchison, Reta married name of Flora Ames aka Reta Danzelle	USA	Elmira NY	1880	1961
Irvin, Leslie L.	USA	Los Angeles CA	1895	1966
Ivy, William real name of Ivy Baldwin	USA	Alameda CA	1866	1953
Jacobs, Frank S.	USA	**Quincy IL**	**1867**	**1896**
Jaquins, Delia real name of Dot Zelno	USA	Charlotte NC	1876	1939
Jewell, Edward stage name of Edward Baltz	USA	Buffalo NY	1865	1928
Jewell, Harry stage name of Gruber, Harry	USA	Philadelphia PA	1866	
Jewell, Thomas	USA	Springfield IL	1859	1891
Jewell, Walter stage name of Walter Leonhauser	USA	Philadelphia PA	1895	1930
Johnson, Cora Etta real name of Madame Carmon	USA	Livingston IL	1880	1919
Johnson, Joseph real name of Charles Leroux	USA	**Waterbury CT**	**1856**	**1889**
Kabrich, Charles H.	USA	Sturgis MI	1861	Aft. 1935

Appendix: Notable Balloon-Parachute Era Aeronauts 203

Name	Career Region	Residence(s)	Born	Died
Kaiser, William aka Kiser, Kisser	USA	Louisville KY	1869	1891
Karletta stage name of Ellen Augusta Benjamin aka Helene Thiers	USA	Buffalo NY	1842	1893
Keesler, Eugene C.	USA	Marietta WI	1868	1939
Keifer, Frank	USA	Peoria IL	1869	1943
Keifer, May/Mamie married name of Amena May Lord	USA	Peoria IL	1871	1897
Kent, Cissie stage name of Cecelia C. Browning	England	London ENG	1868	1943
Keyes, Hazel	USA	Seattle WA	1864	1940
Killip, William Karl	USA	**Buffalo NY**	**1863**	**1893**
Knabenshue, Augustus Roy	USA	Los Angeles CA	1875	1960
Kray, Joseph real name of Joseph Laroux	USA	MA	1873	After 1937
Kulp, William H.	USA	Marshall MI	1859	1922
Kyle, Herr stage name of Peter Zimmerman	USA	Silver City NM	Abt. 1859	
La Petite Aerial stage name of Ada McDonald	England			
Lamont, Nellie stage name of Edith Rehahn	USA	Detroit MI	1872	1895
Langford, Thomas F.	USA	KS	1864	1927
Lapoint, Louis also known as Louis Bonette	USA	NH	1908	1969
Laroux, Joseph stage name of Joseph Kray	USA	MA	1873	After 1937
Lascelles, Prof., stage name of Daniel J. Maloney	USA	San Francisco CA	**1879**	**1905**
Lastrange, Charles J. stage name of Charles J. Peterson	USA	New York City NY		
Lavelle, Frankie stage name of Annie Harkes/Harkness	USA	Cincinnati OH	**1871**	**1891**
Law, Frederick Rodman	USA	Brooklyn NY	1885	1919
Lawrence, Hattie (Harriet) of Sisters Lawrence	USA ENG	London ENG	1855	
Lawrence, Jane (Jennie) of Sisters Lawrence	USA ENG	London ENG	1861	1894
Lawrence, Joseph real name of Joseph L. Van Tassel	USA	**Fort Scott KS**	**1865**	**1889**

Appendix: Notable Balloon-Parachute Era Aeronauts

Name	Career Region	Residence(s)	Born	Died
Le Voy, Mlle. Stage name of May Allison	USA	Cincinnati OH	**1874**	**1896**
Leach, Robert "Bobby"	USA	Ontario CAN	1857	1926
Lee, Eola stage name of Eola L. McKim	USA	Kansas City MO	1870	
Lee, Maud real name of Lillian Cody	USA	Norristown PA	1862	1947
LeFay, Lillian stage name of Adela Sowards aka Lillian Belmont	USA	MI	1880	1901
Leland, Jennie stage/maiden name of Mrs. Dewitt C. Ashmon	USA	Tacoma WA	1865	1947
Lempriere, George Philip	England	Birmingham ENG	1855	1949
Leon, Lottie stage name of Mrs. Oscar Hunt nee Elizabeth J. Clark	USA	Cleveland OH	1850	1923
Leonhauser, Walter S. real name of Walter Jewell	USA	Philadelphia PA	1895	1930
Leroux, Charles stage name of Joseph Johnson	USA	Waterbury CT	**1856**	**1889**
Leroy, Estella stage name of ? Hull	USA	Cleveland OH		
Leroy, Ida/Eva	USA	Quebec CAN	1877	
Leroy, Frank stage name of Emile Marcotte	USA	OH		
Leroy, Jack stage name of Frederick Harding	USA	Connersville IN	1872	1906
Leroy, Sadie stage name of Edith Finn	USA	Mt Vernon OH	1881	1941
Leroy, Victoria stage name of Wilhelmina Heid	USA	**Fremont OH**	**1870**	**1896**
Leroy, W.H. (Harry)	USA	IA		
Lochbaum, Otto real name of Otto Burke	USA	San Francisco CA	1874	1936
Lord, Amena May maiden name of May/Mamie	USA	Peoria IL	1871	1897
Love, Cora stage/married name of Cora Rolliston	USA	Indianapolis IN		
Love, William Z.	USA	**Indianapolis IN**	**1863**	**1899**
MacDonald, Ada real name of La Petite Aerial	England	London ENG	1858	
MacDonald, Marion L. real name of Daring Donald	USA	New Haven CT	1862	

Appendix: Notable Balloon-Parachute Era Aeronauts

Name	Career Region	Residence(s)	Born	Died
Madison, Nina stage name of Agnes Grace Stage	USA	Jersey City NJ	1876	1924
Maloney, Daniel J. real name of Prof. Lascelles	USA	San Francisco CA	1879	1905
Mansfield, Edward, Ltn.	England	Bombay India	1866	1891
Marcotte, Emile real name of Frank Leroy	USA	OH		
Markeberg, Emil	USA	San Francisco CA	1871	1900
Mars, James C. "Bud" stage/adopted name of James Cairn McBride	USA	CA	1875	1944
May, Rosa stage name of Juanetta Stobbs (Ashlock)	USA	Peoria IL	1872	
McBride, James Cairn real name of James C. "Bud" Mars	USA	CA	1875	1944
McClellan, Barton C.	USA	Spokane WA	1869	1946
McEwen, William W.	USA, South America	Jackson MI	1862	1930
McKim, Eola L. real name of Eola Lee	USA	Kansas City MO	1870	
McKim, Mortimer (Morton) real name of Harry Menier	USA	Missouri NY	1867	1911
McNeal, Louis N., real name of Hi Sidney Wallace aka Burr Robbins	USA	Mt Vernon OH	1875	1950
Mecklem, Llewelyn Guy	USA	Seattle WA	1882	1973
Melville, Emil Leandro	USA	San Francisco CA	1864	1934
Menier, Harry stage name of Mortimer McKim	USA	Missouri NY	1867	1911
Merton, Marie	England	London ENG		
Miss America stage name of May Allison	USA	Cincinnati OH	1874	1896
Miz(z)en, Walter	England	London ENG		
Mott, Justin B	USA	Glens Falls NY	1866	1906
Murray, John Henry real name of Charles Broadwick	USA	CA	1874	1943
Myers, Carl	USA	Herkimer NY	1842	1925
Myers, Carlotta stage name of Mary Breed Hawley aka Mrs. Carl Myers	USA	Herkimer NY	1850	1932
Northup, Edwin J.	USA	Quincy IL	1853	1920

Appendix: Notable Balloon-Parachute Era Aeronauts

Name	Career Region	Residence(s)	Born	Died
O'Dell, Leona married name of Emma Lou Penn	USA	GA	1877	1965
O'Dell, Leonidas Nichols	USA	IA	1864	1922
Odiva stage name of Mary Brown aka Alma Beaumont	England	London ENG; Brooklyn NY	1877	
Oliver, Charles real name of Charles Van Tassel	USA	CA		
Onzalo, Bertha stage name of Mrs. Arthur Cosgrove	USA	Bakersfield CA	1872	
Orton, Alfred Henry Joseph	England	London ENG	1852	1920
Owens, Mrs. D.W. married name of Ruby Deveau	USA	Missoula MT	1881	1966
Parker, Benjamin real name of Jack Dallas	USA	Rochester NY	1879	1940
Pate, Frederick H.	USA	**Battle Creek MI**	**1866**	**1895**
Paulus, Katharina "Käthe"	Germany	Frankfort GER	1868	1935
Penn, Emma Lou real name of Leona O'Dell	USA	GA	1877	1965
Perkins, Eugene	USA	Quincy IL	1873	1933
Perry, William K.	USA	**Birmingham AL**		**1889**
Peterson, Bertha L. real name of Nellie Woodall	USA	Everett WA	1876	Bef. 1940
Peterson, Charles J. real name of Charles Lastrange	USA	New York City NY		
Price, James W step-name of James W. Sisk	USA	Springfield IL	1862	1921
Price, Tillie aka Bell Price real name of Tillie Sibern	USA	**Richmond IN**	**1875**	**1894**
Prince Leo stage name of A. Leo Stevens	USA	Cleveland OH	1871	1944
Ralston, Walter stage name of John Walter Vandiver	USA	Norton County KS	1872	1919
Randall, Lulu stage name of Louise Rehahn	USA	**Detroit MI**	**1868**	**1894**
Redmond, Phinneas H.	USA	**Portland OR**	**1863**	**1890**
Rehahn, Edith real name of Nellie Lamont	USA	Detroit MI	1872	1895
Rehahn, Louise real name of Lulu Randall	USA	**Detroit MI**	**1868**	**1894**
Richmond, Charles	USA	**Springfield IL**	**1860**	**1893**

Appendix: Notable Balloon-Parachute Era Aeronauts 207

Name	Career Region	Residence(s)	Born	Died
Rice, George T.	USA	**Jackson MI**	**1857**	**1889**
Robbins, Burr stage name of Louis N. McNeal	USA	Mt Vernon OH	1875	1950
Rogers, George Augustus	USA	**Boston MA**	**1831**	**1892**
Rogers, William J.	USA	Seaman OH	1875	1924
Romig, James J.	USA	Oakland CA	1861	1937
Royale, Frederick H.	USA	Indianapolis IN	1874	1897
Rulison, Warren R.	USA	Herkimer NY	1853	1931
Rumary, Jane real name of Jeanette Van Tassel	India	Calcutta, India		1892
Russett, Frank	England	Nottingham ENG	1870	
St. Clair, W.E. stage name of Edward White	USA	Wichita KS	1864	1889
Sartell, L.A. stage name of Alfred L. Seeley, Jr.	USA	Traverse City MI	1884	1902
Scanlon, Robert Emmett	USA	**St. Louis MO**	**1871**	**1916**
Schroene, Louise Cody real name of Ruby Deveau	USA	Missoula MT	1881	1966
Seeley, Alfred L., Jr. real name of L.A. Sartell	USA	Traverse City MI	1884	1902
Shannon, Grace	USA			
Shepherd, Elizabeth "Dolly"	England	London ENG	1886	1983
Shaw, Maud real name of Estella Graves	USA	Kansas City MO	Abt. 1877	
Shipley, William Hetherington	England	South Shields ENG	1853	1929
Sibern, Tillie stage name of Bell "Tillie" Price	USA	**Richmond IN**	**1875**	**1894**
Simmons, Harry T.	USA	Indianapolis IN		
Sisk, James W. real name of James W. Price	USA	Springfield IL	1862	1921
Smith, William M.	USA	Springfield IL		
Snyder, Charles Henry "Harry"	USA	Dayton OH	1877	
Soper, Alfred H.	USA	Saginaw MI	1845	1904
Sowards, Adela real name of Lillian Belmont	USA	MI	1880	1901
Spencer, Arthur	England	London ENG	1866	1922

Appendix: Notable Balloon-Parachute Era Aeronauts

Name	Career Region	Residence(s)	Born	Died
Spencer, Charles Green	England	London ENG	1837	1890
Spencer, Percival	England	London ENG	1864	1913
Spencer, Stanley	England	London ENG	1868	1906
Spencer, Viola stage name of Edith M. Cook	**England**	**Ipswich ENG**	**1878**	**1910**
Sprague, Eugene	USA	Ionia MI	1881	1899
Squires, Frank Albert	USA	Galesburg IL	1864	1940
Stackhouse, Jerry	USA	Marshall MI	1858	1891
Stage, Agnes Grace real name of Nina Madison	USA	Jersey City NJ	1876	1924
Stevens, Albert Leo real name of Prince Leo	USA	Cleveland OH	1871	1944
Stevens, Don Carlos stage name of Frank Stevens	USA	Cleveland OH	1875	1958
Stevens, Frank H. real name of Don Carlos Stevens	USA	Cleveland OH	1875	1958
Steward, William S.	USA	Quincy IL	1873	1917
Stobbs, Juanetta real name of Rosa May	USA	Peoria IL	1872	
Stokes, John Henry real name of King Burke	USA	Cleveland OH	1867	1932
Streif, Harry	USA	Sioux City IA	1872	1914
Stuart, Adaline real name of Leona Dare	USA	New York City NY	1854	1922
Swearingen, Chester A. real name of Chet Baldwin	USA	Quincy IL	1868	
Thayer, Willard A.	USA	Sparta MI	1866	1899
Thiers, Helene stage name of Ellen Augusta Benjamin aka Karletta	USA	Buffalo NY	1842	1893
Thompson, Frederick Leroy	USA	Quincy IL	1864	1948
Thompson, Georgia Anne real name of Tiny Broadwick	USA	CA	1893	1978
Tisdell, Tracey A. real name of Leon Dare	USA	Brooklyn NY	1866	1938
Tolbert, Albert L.	USA	Daviess IN/ Kankakee IL	1856	1900
Townsend, William E.	USA	PA	1872	1914
Trautwein, Lillian real name of Josie Carmo	USA	Toledo OH	1877	

Appendix: Notable Balloon-Parachute Era Aeronauts

Name	Career Region	Residence(s)	Born	Died
Unger, Edward P.	USA	Los Angeles CA	1885	1973
Van Dresen, Ella Beatrice real name of Beatrice Von Dressden	USA	Frankfort NY	1875	1894
Van Tassel, Charles stage name of Charles Oliver	USA	CA		
Van Tassel, Gladys stage name of Gladys Freitas	Australia	Sydney NSW		
Van Tassel, James P. stage name of James W. Price	USA	Springfield IL	1862	1921
Van Tassel, Jeanette stage name of Jane Rumary	**India**	Calcutta, India		1892
Van Tassel, Joseph L. stage name of Joseph Lawrence	USA	Fort Scott KS		1889
Van Tassel, "Mrs." nee Clara Coykendall	USA	San Jose CA	1861	
Van Tassel, Parker A.	USA, Australia, Asia	San Francisco CA	1853	1930
Van Tassel, Valerie stage name of Valerie Grace Freitas	Australia	Sydney NSW		
Vandegrift, Hubbard F. "Frank"	USA	Cleveland OH	1864	1888
Vandell, Elsey (stage name of Isabelle Acker)	USA	Cleveland OH		
Vandiver, John Walter real name of Walter Ralston	USA	Norton County KS	1872	1919
Viola, Essie stage name of Ethel Harriet Hawker	Australia, USA, New Zealand	San Francisco CA	1876	1935
Viola, Millie stage name of Ruby Marrania Hawker	Australia, USA, New Zealand	San Francisco CA	1873	1935
Viola, Millie stage name of Ida Bozarth	USA	Clinton MO	1867	1889
Von Dressden, Beatrice stage name of Ella Beatrice VanDresen	USA	Frankfort NY	1875	1894
Waite, Charles Fremont	USA	Jackson MI	1861	1947
Walcott, Charles	USA	Jackson MI	1870	1908
Walker, Bert/Burt (John Adelbert)	USA, Southeast Asia	Adrian MI	1870	1951
Wallace, Hi Sidney stage name of Louis N. McNeal	USA	Mt Vernon OH	1875	1950
Walrath, Edward M.	USA	**Ilion NY**	**1867**	**1889**
Ward, Warren Albert	USA	Sioux City IA	1858	1906

Appendix: Notable Balloon-Parachute Era Aeronauts

Name	Career Region	Residence(s)	Born	Died
Warner, Harry stage name of John Wesley Biggerstaff	USA	New Orleans LA	1855	1897
Watkins, Ulysses S. Grant	USA	Indianapolis IN	1880	
Weston, George stage name of George Weston Daggett	USA	San Francisco CA	1871	1897
Wheeler, Nellie stage name of Jennie C. Crockett	USA	Boston MA	1857	1891
Wheeler, Viola Mary	USA	Springfield IL	1872	1948
Whelan, James Augustus	England	Yorkshire ENG	1848	1893
White, Edward real name of W.E. St. Clair	USA	Wichita KS	1864	1889
Whorter, John Hunter real name of Prof. Zeno (I)	USA	Shelby TN	1855	1942
Wild, Horace B.	USA	Chicago IL	1878	1940
Williams, Charles W.	USA ENG	Cincinnati OH	1864	1912
Williams, John T.	Australia	Sydney NSW	1855	1920?
Williamson, C.W. alter ego of Charles W. Williams	USA ENG	Cincinnati OH; New York City NY	1864	1912
Wilson, William real name of Del. Dare	USA	Deposit NY		
Wood, Eleazer Mattison	USA	Springfield IL	1863	1917
Woodall, Frederick J.	USA	Dayton OH	1875	1940
Woodall, Harriet "Jennie" aka Harriet S. Bonham	USA	Terre Haute IN	1868	1945
Woodall, John William	USA	Terre Haute IN	1862	1934
Woodall, Nellie stage name of Bertha L. Peterson	USA	Everett WA	1876	Bef. 1940
Woodall, William J.	USA	Snohomish WA	1863	1941
Young, Samuel C	USA ENG	Cincinnati OH	1860	1892
Zelno, Dot stage name of Delia Jaquins	USA	Charlotte NC	1876	1939
Zelno, Jessie stage name of Jessie Brown	USA	Marietta GA	Abt. 1875	
Zelno, Marion Frank stage name of Marion Francis Ezzell	USA	IL	1872	1926

Appendix: Notable Balloon-Parachute Era Aeronauts **211**

Name	Career Region	Residence(s)	Born	Died
Zeno, Madame stage name of Lucy Alice Hounker	USA	Blairsville PA	1869	1964
Zeno, Prof. (I) stage name of John Whorter	USA	Shelby TN	1855	1942
Zeno, Prof. (II) stage name of Paul R. Hague	USA	**Savannah GA**	**1875**	**1901**
Zimmerman, Peter real name of Herr Kyle	USA	Silver City NM	Abt. 1859	

Chapter Notes

Preface

1. Many balloon-trapeze and balloon-parachute performers used a safety-line that would hold them to their perch if their hands slipped; incredibly, a few did not.
2. "Ascensionist" is perhaps the most charming name given to both balloonists and parachutists.
3. The Early Birds of Aviation was an honorary society of 598 gas balloon, glider, or airplane pilots who flew solo prior to December 17, 1916. Those who only performed with hot-air balloons were not included.

Chapter One

1. Joseph-Michel Montgolfier (Jacques-Étienne's brother) was among the witnesses to see Lenormand's jump.
2. This was the same action that culminated the 2019 movie *The Aeronauts*.
3. Jacob Hervey Family Papers, New York Historical Society.
4. "Balloon Ascension and Parachute Descent at Lemon Hill," *Philadelphia Public Ledger*, Sept. 8, 1857.

Chapter Two

1. "Daring Adventure," *Altoona (PA) Tribune*, July 14, 1866.
2. "Ha! Ha! Ha!—Laugh and Grow Fat" (Classified Advertisement), *Philadelphia Public Ledger*, April 24, 1858.
3. The feat of crossing the Atlantic by balloon was not to be realized for over a hundred years, until 1978.

Chapter Three

1. "Blind Veteran to Raise Flag Memorial Day," *Buffalo Courier*, May 14, 1916.
2. "Highland House" (Classified Advertisement), *Cincinnati Enquirer*, July 7, 1883.
3. "Up in a Balloon," *Cincinnati Enquirer*, June 29, 1886. Lulu Bates' real name is unknown, as is her death date and burial place.
4. "Courting the Clouds," *Cleveland Leader*, June 30, 1883.
5. "By Air Ship," *Cleveland Leader*, Sept. 30, 1897.
6. "Matters in the Courts," *Philadelphia Inquirer*, Oct. 4, 1875.
7. "A Boy's Brutal Master," *New York Times*, Nov. 8, 1875.
8. "Will Drop," *Bay City Times*, Oct. 1, 1889.
9. "Brady's Adventures," *Washington Star*, Feb. 7, 1889.
10. "A Balloonist's Wild Trip," *Buffalo Express*, Sept. 18, 1884.
11. "Every Star an Artist" (Advertisement), *Columbus Courier*, April 27, 1882.
12. "Casualties: Frightful Fall from a Balloon," *St. Louis Globe-Democrat*, Sept. 1, 1887.
13. An odd coincidence occurred in the careers of Price, Hathaway and Gomes. Once each young man acquired limited fame as dashing aeronauts, they

all got in romantic trouble with young women, causing them more grief than any aerial stunts. As Ned Hathaway's career was beginning, he divorced his first wife for adultery; then, two years later, he eloped with a 15-year-old girl and was arrested for abduction. Similarly, in 1886, Gomes ran off from Springfield with Goldie Levi, a young Jewish woman who was rebelling from an arranged engagement. Gomes and Levi were discovered and returned to Springfield, but they ran off a second time and found a Justice of the Peace to marry them. The same impulsiveness that caused marital problems for Price, Hathaway and Gomes was likely an advantage when expressed differently in their careers as daredevils.

14. "The El Paso Suicide," *Bloomington Pantograph*, July 21, 1885.

15. "Balloon Tragedy," *Philadelphia Inquirer*, Aug. 3, 1885.

16. Only a few brief notes in newspapers attest to Van Tassel's position with Forepaugh. One example can be found in "Something Extraordinary," *Leavenworth Times*, June 1, 1877. Van Tassel managed the advertising railcar of the Forepaugh Circus, which was noted for its extravagant features.

Chapter Four

1. Van Tassel became a frequent drinking companion of Denver's infamous saloon owner and racketeer, Lou Blonger; that ended in a drunken row with Blonger over a slight made against a woman.

2. With typical show puffery, Melville claimed to be a famous French scientific balloonist. In truth, he was born in San Francisco. Melville went on to have a long career as an acrobat with the Barnum & Bailey circus and was still performing in his 60s.

3. "May-Day at Capitola," *Santa Cruz Sentinel*, May 2, 1886.

4. A good summary of Van Tassel's side of the dispute can be found in Gary B. Fogel's *Sky Rider, Park Van Tassel and the Rise of Ballooning in the West*.

5. "Daring Jumps," *San Francisco Examiner*, Jan. 22, 1887.

6. "Bush-Street Theater," *San Francisco Examiner*, Jan. 9, 1887.

7. The man referred to was Auguste Buislay.

8. "A Thrilling Descent," *San Francisco Examiner*, Jan. 31, 1887.

9. "An Aeronaut Leaps One Thousand Feet," *Rockford Daily Gazette*, Jan. 31, 1887.

10. "Wonderful Leap," *Cincinnati Commercial Tribune*, July 5, 1887.

11. "A Parachute Craze," *New York Sun*, Aug. 7, 1887.

Chapter Five

1. "Terrible Drop," *Cincinnati Commercial Tribune*, July 31, 1887.

2. "Prof. Baldwin and His Parachute," *New York Sun*, Sept. 23, 1887.

3. "Mount Morris Fair," *Livingston Democrat*, Sept. 28, 1887.

4. "The Balloon Ascension and Races," *Atlanta Constitution*, Sept. 23, 1887.

5. "Up In a Balloon," *Buffalo Express*, Aug. 4, 1889.

6. "The Balloon Episode," *Potsdam Courier*, Sept. 28, 1887.

7. "Sidney, Ohio," *Cincinnati Enquirer*, July 5, 1888.

8. "News of the State," *Indianapolis News*, June 18, 1888.

9. "Tight Rope Walker," *Minneapolis Star*, Oct. 1, 1888.

10. "Up In a Balloon," *Wichita Star*, Aug. 15, 1888.

11. Harry Hill's Historical Oklahoma Wild West show featured two trick shooters with ties to aviation: Samuel F. Cody and his wife, Maud Lee. Maud Lee would go on to make a few parachute jumps for William Z. Love in Indiana in 1895, and Samuel F. Cody moved to England and experimented with man-carrying kites and airships; he was the first man to fly an airplane in Great Britain.

12. "Medicine Men," *Illinois State Journal*, May 17, 1887.

13. "The Jump," *Natchez Democrat*, April 18, 1888.

14. "The Parachute Play," *Springfield Republic*, April 27, 1888.

15. "Oakland Garden" (Advertisement), *Boston Globe*, June 10, 1888.

16. "A Nervy Aeronaut," *St. Louis Globe-Democrat*, May 24, 1891.
17. "Shocked Her Fiancée," *Chicago Inter-Ocean*, Mar. 9, 1886.
18. "The Balloon Ascension," *Butte Miner*, July 6, 1888.
19. "Fell from a Balloon," *Benton Harbor Palladium*, July 3, 1892.
20. "The Aeronaut in a Dangerous Condition," *Charlotte Observer*, Aug. 13, 1889.
21. "The Balloon Ascension," *Clinton Advocate*, July 9, 1885.
22. "Jesting with Death," *Chicago Tribune*, July 22, 1888.
23. "Another Parachute Operator," *Chicago Tribune*, May 5, 1888.
24. Stokes took his stage name "King Burke" from the name of a popular 1880s circus, King, Burke & Co.
25. Mary Butler, "Balloons Over Battle Creek," *Scene Magazine* 37, no. 7 (2012): 18.
26. "Hogan's High Hop," *Topeka Capitol*, April 5, 1888.
27. Bartholomew had returned to Michigan from Quincy but had been born and raised in a small town about 75 miles distant from Jackson and Sturgis, Michigan—a fact interesting to note, since it associates Bartholomew with three centers of parachuting activity: Quincy, Jackson, and Sturgis.
28. "Killed at a Balloon Ascension," *Rock Island Argus*, Aug. 20, 1888.
29. "Lassoed By a Guy Rope," *Alton Telegraph*, Sept. 21, 1888.
30. The identity of Charles Van Tassel was researched by Gary B. Fogel in his excellent 2021 biography of Park Van Tassel, *Sky Rider*.
31. "A Woman's Jump," *Los Angeles Herald*, July 6, 1888.
32. "An Aeronaut's Fate," *Maysville Bulletin*, Nov. 24, 1888.

Chapter Six

1. The *Pall Mall Budget* article was reprinted in "A Quincy Boy in London," *St. Joseph Herald*, Aug. 23, 1888.
2. "Conscience Money Extraordinary," *Aberdeen Journal*, Oct. 4, 1888.
3. Howard Lee Scamehorn, "Thomas Scott Baldwin: The Columbus of the Air," *Journal of the Illinois State Historical Society* 49, no. 2 (Summer 1956): 163–189.
4. Several secondary sources cite Balleni's death date as 1888, which may be wishful thinking on the part of the abandoned wife and family. However, he can be found living with Ada MacDonald in the 1891 and 1901 census records.
5. "Shocking Ballooning Disaster at Leeds," *Middlesbrough Northeastern*, Aug. 10, 1891.
6. "Miss Jessie Dene [sic]," *London Era*, May 19, 1894.
7. "Olympia—Parachute Descent" (Advertisement), *London Times*, Jan. 1, 1889.
8. "Daring Feat of a Nottingham Aeronaut," *Sheffield Telegraph*, Apr. 27, 1889.
9. "Accident to an Aeronaut," *London Standard*, June 4, 1889.
10. "Fete at the Botanic Gardens," *Belfast News*, Apr. 23, 1889.
11. "Professor Charles Baldwin" (Advertisement), *London Era*, Oct. 3, 1891.
12. "A Secret No Longer" (Advertisement), *London Era*, July 3, 1897.
13. The real names of the Brooks sisters are not known, nor is there verification of their relationship as siblings.
14. "Police Intelligence," *London Standard*, Oct. 29, 1896. Beaumont's accusation of desertion, as well as her livelihood, was mocked by the court.
15. "The Death of a Girl Parachutist," *Lloyd's Weekly Newspaper*, Aug. 2, 1896.

Chapter Seven

1. Morton was also a mentor to a later British balloon impresario, George P. Lempriere.
2. Keith Isaacs, "The Signal Exploits of Mr H. Hendon, Aeronaut," *Canberra Times*, Jan. 14, 1984, p. 15.
3. "A Drop from the Clouds at Bombay," *Scientific American*, April 13, 1889.
4. "Ballooning and Parachuting in Calcutta," *Aberdeen Journal*, April 17, 1889.
5. In 1989, on the one-hundredth anniversary of Leroux's death, a

sculpture in his honor made by noted Estonia sculptor Matu Karmin was unveiled in Tallinn.
6. "Parachutist Tom Baldwin," *New York World*, Aug. 21, 1889.
7. "Ballooning in Asia," *Canton Press*, June 19, 1891
8. "A Horrible Death," *Fort Scott Tribune*, Dec. 4, 1889.
9. "What Else Could Be Expected?" *Salt Lake Herald*, July 30, 1889.
10. The Freitas name was often spelled as Frietas, and it is unclear which spelling was preferred by the sisters. "Freitas" is the much more prevalent spelling worldwide.
11. The author is indebted to writer Catherine Clarke for her aid in sorting out the identities of the Freitas and Hawker sisters, who not only adopted stage names, but had those stage names used by others. At various points both the Freitas and Hawker sisters claimed to have come from the United States to Australia, but there is no evidence of this. The Hawker women were natives of New South Wales, while the Freitas sisters apparently arrived in Australia as members of a family of performers touring Southeast Asia.
12. "Passengers by the R.M.S. Miowera," *Sydney Telegraph*, Jan. 25, 1896.
13. "A Woman's Wild Dive for Fame," *San Francisco Examiner*, May 17, 1896.
14. "Fatal Accident at Breakfast Creek," *Brisbane Courier*, May 27, 1890.
15. "Aeronaut Van Tassel Still Alive," *Chicago Tribune*, Sept. 14, 1891.
16. "Fatal Accident to a Female Parachutist," *London Post*, March 19, 1892.
17. "Betrothed in the Air," *San Francisco Chronicle*, Aug. 28, 1892.
18. "Burt Walker," *Adrian Daily Telegram*, Oct. 8, 1901.

Chapter Eight

1. "'Daring Donald' Will Try Again," *New York Herald*, July 25, 1891.
2. "One Way to Die," *Boston Post*, Dec. 14, 1895.
3. "Up in a Balloon," *Buffalo Express*, Aug. 8, 1889.

4. "6/28/1889," *Ilion History* 3, p. 41.
5. "To Dive for an Aeronaut's Body," *Troy Times*, Oct. 10, 1889.
6. "Seen from the Clouds," *Brookfield Courier*, Nov. 30, 1896.
7. A dozen years later, in 1910–11, Llewellyn Guy Mecklem made the same transition from aeronaut to deep-sea diver.
8. "Fell a Mile!" *Buffalo Sunday Morning News*, Oct. 7, 1894.
9. "Fell from the Clouds," *Buffalo Morning Express*, Oct. 14, 1894; "Danger in Parachutes," *Rome Sentinel*, Aug. 9, 1906.
10. "Aeronaut Meets Death in the Ohio," *Indianapolis Journal*, Oct. 8, 1889.
11. "An Awful Plunge," *Detroit Free Press*, Aug. 31, 1891.
12. Walcott bridged the two aeronaut capitals of Springfield, Illinois and Jackson, Michigan. Born in Jackson, he undoubted knew and worked with Edward Hogan but in the mid–1880s also performed the balloon-trapeze act with Springfield's senior balloonist, Daniel Headley. Later in his career, Walcott would be a member of the Weehauken Eldorado aeronaut colony. He likely knew every aeronaut of note.
13. "Balloon Accident," *Boston Advertiser*, Aug. 3, 1894.
14. "A Cold Journey," *Jackson Citizen*, July 20, 1891.
15. "Aerial Navigation Scheme," *Omaha World Herald*, April 12, 1892.
16. "To Shoot Niagara," *Warren Semi-Weekly Ledger*, Aug. 2, 1895.
17. "Detroit Gambler Drowns in South," *Detroit Free Press*, Oct. 16, 1913.

Chapter Nine

1. McDonald appears to have done most of the leaps, which was perhaps a sore point that led to his fistfight with McKim in 1893.
2. "He Descended to Death," *Brooklyn Citizen*, Sept. 11, 1891.
3. "Wanted to Outdo Brodie," *New York Sun*, Oct. 14, 1894.
4. "New Balloon Enterprise," *Chicago Tribune*, Nov. 4, 1894.

5. A name adopted, apparently, in honor of a French chocolatier and adventurer, Henri Menier.
6. "Lucky Menier, Bridge Jumper," *New York Herald*, Nov. 28, 1894.
7. "Menier Takes Another Leap," *New York Herald*, Dec. 26, 1894.
8. "Miss Nina's Jump," *Buffalo Enquirer*, Jan. 7, 1895.
9. "From the Brooklyn Bridge," *San Francisco Call*, Oct. 20, 1897.
10. The New York Balloon Company continued to make ascension engagements into the first years of the twentieth century, but without its founding members.

Chapter Ten

1. "Frank Jacobs' Funeral," *Quincy Journal*, Aug. 18, 1896.
2. "Swearingen's Foul Play," *Quincy Journal*, July 28, 1893; "That Salting Scrape," *Quincy Herald*, July 29, 1893.
3. "Personal," *Wisconsin Leader Telegram*, April 9, 1905.
4. "Flying Baldwins Caught on Big at Edina, Mo.," *Quincy Journal*, Oct. 29, 1906.
5. Ken Gaunt, "Daredevil Ivy Baldwin | Airport Journals," http://airportjournals.com/daredevil-ivy-baldwin/. Accessed Sept. 6, 2021.
6. "Murder Trial at Springfield," *Decatur Republican*, Dec. 21, 1891.
7. "A Fearful Drop to Death," *Lancaster Examiner*, June 7, 1893.
8. "Peddled Drugs, Charge." *Buffalo Enquirer*, March 29, 1918.
9. "Leaps to Death as Parachute Fails," *Wilmington News Journal*, Aug. 25, 1930.
10. "Balloon Thrills Carded at Fair," *Trenton Times*, Sept. 19, 1933.
11. For a full profile of the Allen Family, see Arch Merrill's *Shadows on the Wall*, 1994.
12. Hogan's side of the story is told in "A Tale of Hard Luck," *Helena Independent Record*, Oct. 16, 1899.
13. "Superstitious, But Plucky," *St. Louis Globe*, Aug. 30, 1896.
14. Newspaper accounts concerning Eva Leroy often referred to her as Ida Leroy, but they appear to be the same person; she gave the name "Eva Leroy" in the 1900 U.S. Federal Census.
15. "Woman Aeronaut Talks Interestingly of Her Calling," *Des Moines Daily News*, Oct. 4, 1899.
16. "They Feared a Lynching," *East Liverpool News*, Oct. 8, 1894.
17. "Prisoner Tells His Life Story," *Huntington Daily News-Democrat*, Oct. 22, 1907.
18. "Drop From the Clouds," *San Francisco Examiner*, Oct. 18, 1891.
19. "Aeronautical Experiment," *Nashville Tennessean*, Oct. 31, 1889.
20. "An Aeronaut's Fall," *Eufaula Times*, June 18, 1890.
21. Grace Shannon's origins and fate remain as one of the biggest mysteries of the balloon-parachute act, since the troupe with her name performed more jumps than any other group.
22. The manufacture of parachutes likely represented only a small percentage of the awning business; this was an era where every storefront in every town and city was likely to sport an awning. Numerous balloonists operated awning businesses.
23. "Girl Dies in Stunt Boarding Airplane From Running Auto," *New York Times*, Dec. 5, 1921.

Chapter Eleven

1. "Parachute Jump Safe as Crossing City Street," *St. Johnsbury Caledonian*, July 29, 1943.
2. "Plan Parachute Jumps for Fair," *Northfield News*, July 16, 1929.
3. "A Chat with Carlotta," *Hornellsville Evening Tribune*, Aug. 21, 1893.
4. "A Woman of Nerve," *Buffalo Express*, Oct. 8, 1893.
5. "How Karl Killip Died," *Buffalo Express*, Jan. 28, 1894.
6. Pilot Ruth Law was the sister of daredevil Frederick Rodman Law, who will be mentioned in a later chapter.
7. "Kneeling, She Begged Him to Marry Her," *Cincinnati Enquirer*, Aug. 20, 1891.
8. "Fell Two Thousand Feet," *St. Louis Globe*, Sept. 22, 1895.
9. "Aeronaut Drowned, *Baltimore Sun*, May 27, 1896.

10. "Balloonist Fell to His Death," *Maysville Public Ledger*, Oct. 2, 1900.
11. "She Rode with the Birds Before the Wright Brothers," *Long Beach Independent*, Oct. 4, 1955.
12. "'Prof. Zeno' Dies At 86 Years of Age," *Jackson Sun*, Oct. 28, 1942.
13. Kim Kincaid, "Final Flight on a Warm Autumn Day," *Lima News*, Sept. 29, 2004.
14. "She Rode with the Birds Before the Wright Brothers," *Long Beach Independent*, Oct. 4, 1955.
15. "A Gritty Woman," *Bedford Mail*, Oct. 17, 1890.
16. Maud Lee's adventurous, sad life is featured in my previous book, *A Pair of Shootists: The Wild West Story of S. F. Cody and Maud Lee* (Norman: University of Oklahoma Press, 2010).
17. "Met Her Death," *Richmond Item*, Aug. 2, 1894.
18. "Parachute Leap Features Klan Celebration," *Fiery Cross* (Indianapolis), Aug. 24, 1924.
19. "Balloonist Harrell," *Logansport Pharos*, Sept. 2, 1895.
20. "Royal Is Dead," *Logansport Tribune*, July 10, 1897.
21. "Claims 30 Cent Jackpot; Is Shot Through Heart," *Chicago Tribune*, May 9, 1904.
22. "Asks Thousands," *Logansport Reporter*, May 20, 1899.
23. William P. Dennis was unrelated to the Franklin, Indiana, jumper D. Luther Dennis. Also, John Woodall was unrelated to Dayton, Ohio's young parachutist of the 1890s, Fred Woodall, and also unrelated to William M. Woodall and his wife Nellie, 1890s parachutists of the Pacific Northwest.
24. "Far Up in the Air," *Richmond Palladium*, Sept. 29, 1900.
25. All through the period of the balloon-parachute act, there was a common belief that a prolonged freefall would kill you before you hit the ground, by "taking away" your breath and rendering you unconscious. It was not until the parachute pack was developed that this myth was dispelled. Though it is not advised to open your mouth facing downward while falling, falling itself does not prevent the act of breathing. It is still possible to pass out from fear.
26. "Mrs. Crawford was Sick," *St. Louis Globe Democrat*, July 6, 1892.
27. "For Scientific Points," *St. Louis Post*, Aug. 13, 1892.
28. "Bozarth Has a Tumble," *Henry County Democrat*, Oct. 5, 1900.
29. "Parachute Jumper Killed," *Kansas City Journal*, Oct. 2, 1896.
30. "R.P. Hill, Father of Ferris Hill, Made Emporia's First Balloon Ascension at a County Fair in 1890," *Emporia Gazette*, Aug. 18, 1951.
31. "Famous Aeronaut Dead," *Emporia Republican*, Oct. 20, 1898.
32. "Leap from a Balloon," *Lexington Leader*, Oct. 13, 1890.
33. "Preparing for a Jump," *Meriden Journal*, July 16, 1895.
34. "The Plunge of a Human Meteor," *Rochester Democrat and Chronicle*, Nov. 29, 1896.
35. "Professor Ward Killed," *Downs Times*, July 19, 1906.
36. "She Jumped 3000 Feet," *Tacoma Ledger*, Aug. 21, 1893.
37. "Ballooning at Edison," *Tacoma Ledger*, Oct. 30, 1893.
38. "Shoot the Chutes" (Advertisement), *San Francisco Chronicle*, Jan. 3, 1896.
39. "Came to Grief," *Sacramento Record Union*, July 7, 1897.
40. "A Perilous Descent," *Buffalo Courier*, July 5, 1896.
41. "A Thrilling Experience," *Morning Oregonian*, Sept. 9, 1889.
42. "Death of a Balloonist," *San Francisco Examiner*, May 31, 1890.
43. "Did He Commit Suicide?" *Morning Oregonian*, Aug. 13, 1890.
44. "Flung to the Earth," *Seattle Post*, Aug. 16, 1891.
45. "Spurious Money," *Davenport Republican*, Nov. 20, 1895.
46. "Balloon Ascension," *San Francisco Call*, Nov. 17, 1890.
47. "Rescued From the Masts," *San Francisco Examiner*, June 5, 1893.
48. "Was Jealous of Her," *San Francisco Examiner*, Sept. 25, 1895.
49. "Cheats Gallows by Death from Influenza," *San Bernardino Sun*, Oct. 23, 1918.
50. "Sand-Lot Queen Fined at Beach," *Los Angeles Times*, Sept. 1, 1915.

Chaper Twelve

1. "Aeronaut Luck," *Davenport Democrat*, Feb. 7, 1888.
2. "A Colored Aeronaut Now," *Quincy Herald*, July 26, 1893.
3. Mary Butler, "Balloons Over Battle Creek" *Scene Magazine* 37, no. 7, (2012): 18–22.
4. "Balloon Man, Known Here, Dies at Seaman," *Wilmington News Journal*, Nov. 24, 1924.
5. "Black King of Air to Go with Wright," *Portsmouth Times*, Sept. 6, 1912.
6. "Eloped with Aeronaut," *Cincinnati Tribune*, Nov. 8, 1902.
7. "They Pelted the Aeronaut," *Pittston Gazette*, May 22, 1888.
8. "Attack on a Lady Parachutist," *Reynolds Newspaper* (London), Aug. 12, 1894.
9. "Roughs Do Up a Circus," *St. Louis Globe*, Aug. 7, 1890.
10. "A Monkey Baldwin," *Pall Mall Gazette*, Dec. 7, 1888.
11. In World War II, the British Army employed parachuting dogs during the Normandy invasion. Also, during World War II the United States military trained dogs for search and rescue of downed pilots in isolated areas.
12. "The Parachutist," *Buffalo Express*, Sept. 8, 1889.
13. "Song of the Parachute," *Current Literature* 1, no. 3 (Sept. 1888): 270.
14. "Look at That, Now!" *Rolla Herald*, Oct. 15, 1891.
15. "Mistaken for the Lord," *Buffalo Enquirer*, Oct. 15, 1897.

Chapter Thirteen

1. "Heavenward on a Kite," *Chicago Tribune*, Aug. 2, 1889.
2. "Took Ascension Beneath a Kite," *Boston Globe*, June 21, 1897.
3. More detail on the aeronautical projects of S.F. Cody can be found in my previous book, *A Pair of Shootists: The Wild West Story of S. F. Cody and Maud Lee* (Norman: University of Oklahoma Press, 2010).
4. "First Man to Fly Describes His Sensation," *San Francisco Examiner*, Apr. 30, 1905.
5. "Balloon Ascension," *Montpelier Examiner*, Sept. 29, 1905.
6. Some sources misattribute the Campbell pilot as James A. Allen, not his son James K. Allen. James A. Allen was an associate of balloonist Samuel King and also served in the Balloon Corps of the Union Army during the Civil War. These Rhode Island Allens may have been cousins to the New York Allen family of parachutists but were not directly related.
7. "Far Out at Sea," *Boston Globe*, July 18, 1889.
8. "A Cold Journey," *Jackson Daily Citizen*, July 20, 1891.
9. "A Practical Aeronaut Who Says the Dirigible Airship Is an Impossibility," *Detroit Free Press*, April 9, 1905.
10. "Aerial Honors Even," *Brooklyn Times Union*, Oct. 1, 1902.
11. "Building an Airship in the Garden City," *San Francisco Call Bulletin*, Oct. 23, 1902.
12. "Sails Around Over City," *Omaha Bee*, Oct. 19, 1903.
13. "Airship Disabled," *Newark Evening Star and Advertiser*, Aug. 8, 1907.
14. Although there is no documentation that John Berry parachuted, another St. Louis balloon-parachutist, Robert E. Scanlon, claimed that he got his start when both he and Berry made jumps.
15. In a Jan. 7, 1911, interview in the *Detroit Free Press*, Goodale mentioned that he had jumped from hot-air balloons with a parachute; however, the specifics are unknown. It likely happened between 1907 and 1910. In 1909–1911, Goodale worked for Palisades Park, an amusement park overlooking Manhattan. He made headlines there for several unannounced airship passes over major New York City landmarks: Grant's Tomb, the *New York Times* building, Battery Park, etc. In 1911, Goddale ascended in his airship from Palisades Park and climbed into the clouds, then made a hurried, unexpected landing. He emerged from the airship looking pale and frightened, and told reporters that he had been forced out of the air by an enormous, green, winged "air-serpent." As expected, headlines carried the story the next day. Goodale never recanted, but decades

later a publicity agent admitted that he had devised the prank. This hoax represents the only occasion when a balloon-parachutist or airship pilot reported seeing anything supernatural in the sky; though several balloonists have reported seeing a strange optical illusion of their own balloon projected in a different part of the sky.

16. "Jack Dallas" was the stage name of Benjamin Parker of Rochester, New York. In a 1907 interview, Parker stated: "I began my career as an aeronaut by ballooning and parachute leaping several years ago, and have travelled in China, Japan, and the Philippines with the balloon. I have made an ascension from the main plaza in Manila and as you know the islands are very close to another in the Philippines. I was once carried from Manila to a neighboring island. When I leaped from the balloon the natives took to their heels in fright." Aside from this interview, the prior ballooning experience of Dallas remains unconfirmed. His brother Evan Parker also had a career as a dirigible pilot.

Chapter Fourteen

1. Mecklem's autobiographical quotes are taken from interviews conducted with Mecklem. Don Ecklund used this material to produce *Washington's "Wild Scotsman": The Early Aeronautical Adventures of L. Guy Mecklem, 1897–1910* (Bellingham: Center for Pacific Northwest Studies, Western Washington State College, 1974). The original transcribed interviews were bound in a volume "Autobiographical materials concerning L. Guy Mecklem," which is held by the Seattle Public Library. Those original interviews were again transcribed for publication on the Internet by Anya Woodhouse and Todd Mecklem and can be found online at Todd's site: http://toddmecklem.com/lgmecklem.pdf (accessed 10/8/2021).

2. Little is known about this aeronaut, but he performed as Arthur W. Sylvan from British Columbia. He performed regularly at Seattle's Luna Park in 1909.

3. Mecklem was likely at Chutes during its 1904–1905 season.

4. "Venice of America" opened on July 4, 1905.

5. This was Tom Baldwin with a smaller airship, which first appeared at Chutes in February 1905 and was shown there at times for the next year.

Chapter Fifteen

1. Many secondary sources suggest that Charles K. Hamilton was a balloon-parachutist and cite as evidence references to "Professor Hamilton" who was active in the San Francisco-Oakland area from 1906 to 1913. However, this California aeronaut was Frank J. Hamilton (1878–1924). Frank J. Hamilton operated the balloon from which Daniel J. Maloney was dropped in John J. Montgomery's glider. He also tried to build a copy of Montgomery's glider and was sued by Montgomery. Charles K. Hamilton, on the other hand, at about the same time (1905) was piloting the kite-gliders of New York lawyer-inventor Israel Ludlow. Hamilton later piloted Baldwin's California Arrow and other airships. If Charles K. Hamilton was a balloon-parachutist, the documentation is elusive.

2. One practitioner of the two-parachute drop was Clarence C. Bonette, according to the April 11, 1902, edition of the *St. Albans Daily Messenger.*

3. "Skyrocket Flying Machine," *Cincinnati Enquirer,* Apr. 5, 1913.

4. Law and Stevens were not the only parachute aeronauts to tinker with rockets. One of the Jackson, Michigan aeronauts, William W. McEwen, invested in one of the more quixotic projects in aeronautical history. In 1896, he started construction of a sixty-foot-long aluminum and bronze rocket, with the intention of propelling a manned-observation platform miles above the earth, where (McEwen thought) the pull of gravity greatly lessened. It would return to earth by deploying a parachute. How far the project progressed is not known, but the year after publicizing the idea, McEwen returned to the balloon-parachute act for another year, then retired to the film

industry and went on to live a full life, but still died violently in a car accident in 1930 when he tried to beat an oncoming train past a rail crossing.

5. The Germans, on the other hand, had made significant improvements in their parachute packs, and were using them in airplanes.

6. Interestingly, Harry Eibe's mentor, Felix J. Coughlin, filed a patent on April 30, 1919, for a parachute packing system. It appears many on Hoffman's panel wanted a share of the intellectual property of the new parachute design.

Bibliography

Amick, M.L. *History of Donaldson's Balloon Ascensions: Laughable Incidents, Frightful Accidents, Narrow Escapes, Thrilling Adventures, Bursted Balloons.* Cincinnati: Cincinnati News Company, 1875.
Baldwin, Thomas S. *Dean of the Aviators: Capt. Thomas S. Baldwin and His Most Successful Flyers, Excerpts from His Biography.* Ewing: Hall's Mill Farm, 1986.
Clarke, Catherine. *The Only Living Lady Parachutist.* Lower Hutt: Idle Fancy Press, 2021.
Crouch, Tom D. *A Dream of Wings: Americans and the Airplane, 1875–1905.* New York: Norton, 1989.
Crouch, Tom D. *The Eagle Aloft: Two Centuries of the Balloon in America.* Washington, D.C.: Smithsonian Institution Press, 1983.
Crouch, Tom D. *Lighter Than Air: An Illustrated History of Balloons and Airships.* Baltimore: Johns Hopkins University Press, 2009.
Eklund, Donald Dean. *Captain Thomas S. Baldwin: Pioneer American Aeronaut.* Ann Arbor: University Microfilms, 1972.
Eklund, Donald Dean. *Washington's "Wild Scotsman": The Early Aeronautical Adventures of L. Guy Mecklem, 1897–1910.* Bellingham: Center for Pacific Northwest Studies, Western Washington State College, 1974.
Fogel, Gary B. *Sky Rider: Park Van Tassel and the Rise of Ballooning in the West.* Albuquerque: University of New Mexico Press, 2021.
Fortier, R. "Tout le monde à bord pour le Klondike: Le merveilleux aéronautique et quelques projets de vols vers les gisements aurifères du nord canadien, 1897–1898." *Scientia Canadensis* 38, no. 2 (2015): 57–77. https://doi.org/10.7202/1037947ar.
Harwood, Craig S. *Quest for Flight: John J. Montgomery and the Dawn of Aviation in the West.* Norman: University of Oklahoma Press, 2019.
Hearn, Peter. *Sky High Irvin: The Story of a Parachute Pioneer.* London: R. Hale, 1983.
Hearn, Peter. *The Sky People: A History of Parachuting.* Shrewsbury: Airlife, 1990.
Holmes, Richard. *Falling Upwards: How We Took to the Air.* New York: Pantheon, 2013.
Horan, Michael, and Linda H. Druskis. *Parachuting Folklore: The Evolution of Freefall.* Richmond: Parachuting Resources, 1980.
Kotar, S.L., and J.E. Gessler. *Ballooning: A History, 1782–1900.* Jefferson: McFarland, 2011.
Lamster, Mark. *Spalding's World Tour: The Epic Adventure That Took Baseball Around the Globe and Made It America's Game.* New York: Public Affairs, 2006.
Merrill, Arch. *Shadows on the Wall.* Interlaken: Empire State Books, 1994.
Moffett, Cleveland. *Careers of Danger and Daring, by Cleveland Moffett. With illustrations by Jay Hambidge and George Varian and Others.* New York: 1879–80. Special Collections Research Center, Syracuse University Libraries.
Murphy, Charles John Vincent. *Parachute.* New York: G.P. Putnam's Sons, 1930.
Myers, Carl E. *Carl and Carlotta Myers Ballooning Collection*, 1879–80. Special Collections Research Center, Syracuse University Libraries.

Raab, James W. *Daredevil Balloonist: W.H. Donaldson, 1840–1875*. West Conshohocken: Infinity, 2010.
Read, Richard T., and David Rambow. "Hydrogen and Smoke: A Survey of Lighter-Than-Air Flight in South Dakota Prior to World War I." *South Dakota History* 18, no. 3 (1988).
Rechs, Robert J. *Who's Who of Ballooning*. Indianola: R.J. Rechs, 1983.
Rechs, Robert J. *An Introduction to Muscle Powered Ultra-Light Gas Blimps: In All Their Glory*. Chula Vista: Rechs, 1998.
Ritter, Lisa. "Pack Man: Charles Broadwick Invented a New Way of Falling." *Air & Space Magazine,* May 2010. https://www.airspacemag.com/history-of-flight/pack-man-10601089/ Retrieved 9/17/2021.
Rolt, Lionel Thomas Caswall. *The Aeronauts: A History of Ballooning, 1783–1903. L.T.C. Rolt.* London: Longmans, 1966.
Shepherd, Dolly, Peter Hearn, and Molly Sedgwick. *When the 'Chute Went Up: Adventures of a Pioneer Lady Parachutist*. Amberley: Skyline, 1996.
Smith, Jacob. *The Thrill Makers: Celebrity, Masculinity, and Stunt Performance*. Berkeley: University of California Press, 2012.
Tait, Peta. *Circus Bodies: Cultural Identity in Aerial Performance*. Abingdon: Routledge, 2005
Tobin, James. *To Conquer the Air: The Wright Brothers and the Great Race for Flight*. New York: Free Press, 2004.
Wright, Sharon. *Balloonomania Belles: Daredevil Divas Who First Took to the Sky*. Barnsley: Pen and Sword History, 2018.

Index

Acker, Isabelle *see* Vandell, Elsie
Adair, Leila 74–75
Adair, Madame *see* Denton, Alfretta
African Americans 102, 145–147, 166
Alexandra Palace, London 55–57, 62, 64
Allen, Arlene 106
Allen, Comfort "Curt" 27, 105
Allen, Edward 105–106
Allen, Edward, Jr. 105–106
Allen, Florence 105–106
Allen, Gloria 105
Allen, Ira 27, 44, 105
Allen, James K. 159–160, 219*ch*13*n*6
Allen, Martin 27, 44, 105
Allen, Warren "Speck" 105
Allen, Warren, Jr. 105–106
Allison, May 124
Ammons, Anna 127
Ammons, Claude 127
Anderson, George 132
Armstrong, James 147
Ashlock, Estes 113
Australia 58, 66–67, 69, 73–76, 138, 148, 154, 216*ch*7*n*11

Baird, George W. 29
Baldwin, Charles 63
Baldwin, Chet *see* Swearingen, Chester
Baldwin, Clarence Earl 116–117
Baldwin, Ivy *see* Ivy, William
Baldwin, Richard J. 63
Baldwin, Samuel Y. 45, 70, 101–103, 135
Baldwin, Thomas S. 1–3, 30–32, 34, 36–41, 44–45, 55–58, 66, 69–71, 103, 151–154, 162–163, 165, 167, 174, 183–184, 220*ch*14*n*5
Balleni, Henri 58, 60, 215*ch*6*n*4
Baltz, Edward 49, 103–104
Barnell, Dan 135
Barnum, P.T. 25

Bartholomew, Coryell 41, 51–53, 66–67, 76, 82–83, 88–89, 160, 215*n*27
Barton, Francis 164–165
Bates, Louise "Lulu" 28, 45, 96, 98, 125, 213*ch*3*n*3
Beachey, Lincoln 163, 167
Beaumont, Alma 60–62, 64, 215*n*14
Belmont, Cleo 117
Belmont, Lillian *see* Sowards, Adela
Belmont, Lucielle 117–118
Belmont, Madeline *see* Davis, Madeline
Belmont Sisters 116–118
Berry, Bertram "Bert" B. 166, 186–187, 219*ch*13*n*14
Berry, John 89, 166, 186, 219*ch*13*n*14
Bickford, Frederick W. 154
Biggerstaff, John Wesley *see* Warner, Harry
Blake, Louis B. 147
Blanchard, Jean Pierre 9
Blanchard, Sophie 9
Blondin, Charles 18–19, 21
Boland, Edward 192
Bonette, Clarence C. 119–121, 185, 220*ch*15*n*2
Bonnet, Frédéric 189
Bottreil, Ralph 192
Boyce, Edward C. 162
Bozarth, Ida "Mlle. Viola" 50
Bozarth, Joseph W. "Montz" 50, 132–133, 186
Bradford, Fred L. 147
Brady, Owen J. 29, 54
Brayton, Nell 227
Bready, Owen *see* Brady, Owen
Broadwick, Charles 2, 189–190
Broadwick, Georgia "Tiny" 189–190
Brooks, Edith 63, 215*n*13
Brooks, Maude 63, 215*n*13
Browning, Cecilia *see* Kent, Cissie
Buckner, Cora 147

225

Index

Buislay, Adolphe 19
Buislay, Auguste 19, 214*ch*4*n*7
Burke, King 51, 215*n*24
Burke, Otto 138
Burns, Wilfred 75
Bush, Louis R. 123
Byrd, John 145–146

Campbell, Peter C. 159–161
Campbell-Myers Airship 3, 159–161
Carman, Cora Johnson "Madame Carmon" 116
Carmo, Gertie *see* Clausen, Gertrude
Carrow, William E. 116–117
Carton, Emile 95
Cash, T.I. 48
Cayley, George 13, 15
Chanute, Octave 5, 154
Charles, Jacques 8–9
Chutes Park, Los Angeles 168, 171–174, 187, 220*ch*14*n*3
Chutes Park, San Francisco 138
Cincinnati, OH 27, 42–43, 45, 50, 102, 124–126
Claridge, Edwin 27, 44, 122
Clausen, Gertrude 76, 83, 160
Cleveland, OH 29, 54, 162
Cliff House, San Francisco, CA 35–36
coal gas 1, 16, 26, 148, 182
Cocking, Robert 13–15
Cody, Lillian 126, 154, 214*ch*5*n*11, 218*n*16
Cody, Samuel F. 64, 126, 154–155, 165, 185, 214*ch*5*n*11, 219*ch*13*n*3
Colby, Charles E. 47–48
Cole, Edward 88
Coney Island, NY 156, 160, 162
Coney Island, OH 42–43, 45, 123
Conlon, Charles T. 155–156
Cook, Edith M. 64–65
Cooke, James 36
Coughlin, Felix 109, 221*n*6
Coughlin, John J. 109
Courtland Beach, Omaha, NE 135–135
Coykendall, Clara *see* Van Tassel, Clara
Craig, Edward E. 83, 108–110
Crawford, Elizabeth C. 129–132
Crosby, Jack 135
Cuba 103, 122
Curtiss, Glenn 163, 183–184

Daggett, George Weston *see* Weston, George
Dallas, Jack 167, 220n*16*
Danzelle, Reta 115
Dare, Del *see* Wilson, William

Dare, Leona 19, 21
Darnell, Rodney 141
Dashiell, Lucielle *see* Belmont, Lucielle
Davis, Madeline 118
Davonda, Dorothy 116–117
Deering, John 142
DeHaven, George 30
DeHaven, Maud 96, 150
De Lamond, Cora "Madame Cora" 74
Delmore, Clara 96
Dene, Jenny 59–60, 62–63
Dennis, D. Luther 127
Dennis, William 128–129
Denton, Alfretta 131–132
Deveau, Ruby 115
Devoy, Emmie *see* Dovey, Emily
Dixon, Cromwell 166
dogs, parachuting 9, 18, 36, 96, 134, 138, 150, 219*ch*12*n*11
Donaldson, Washington H. 20–22, 24–25, 34
Dovey, Emily 59, 63

Earlston, Robert J. 138–139
Eckhart, Clarence G. 122
Eddy, Charles J. 102, 135
Eddy, William Abner 154
Eibe, Harry 109, 192–193, 221*n*6
Elder, Ray 132
Eldorado resort, Weehawken, NJ 91–100
Engelhardt, Helen 92, 96
Evans, Louisa Maud "Mlle. Albertina" 64
Everett, Edith 114
Ezzell, Marion Francis *see* Zelno, Frank

Farini, the Great 55
Finn, Edith 107–108
fireworks 9, 43, 115, 136, 192
Fisk, Ira N. 32–33, 47, 49–50, 114
Flying Allens 105–106
Flying Baldwins 103
Forepaugh Circus 27, 34, 214*n*16
Forsman, Milton M. 110–113
Frankfort, NY 27, 81
Freitas, Gladys 73–75, 216*ch*7*n*10
Freitas, Valerie 73–75, 216*ch*7*n*10
Frisbie, John J. 27, 105, 185
Frost, Frank 71–73

Garnerin, André-Jacques 9–12
Garnerin, Élisa 12–13
Gates, Dorothy *see* Davonda, Dorothy
Gaudron, Auguste 60, 64, 154, 163–164
Gaul, William 127
Gaylor, Helen 107

Giffard, Henri 17
Gilbert, Harry 22, 27, 42, 96, 122
Gillock, John L. 32–33, 47–48
Glasgow, A.T. 133
glider-parachutes 100, 104, 157–158
gliders, unpowered 153–158
Godard, Auguste 18
Godard, Eugène 15–18
Godard, Marcel Andre 15
Gomes, Joseph B. 32–33, 46–49, 110, 124, 214*ch*3*n*13
Goodale, Frank W. 167, 219–220*ch*13*n*15
Gould, William R. 134–136
Graves, Estella 107
Green, Charles 13–17
Greenleaf, Thomas 102–103
Greth, August 162–163
Gribble, Estella "Belle" 135
Gribble, James L. "Jake" 134–135, 166
Griffin, Archie 166
Grimley, Charles H. 27
Gruber, Harry 49, 103–105
Guillé, Louis Charles 12–13

Hagel, Frank 113
Hagel, Fred 113
Hagel, Harry 110, 113
Hagel, Nellie 113
Hagel, Tillie 113
Hague, Paul 125
Hall, Edward N "Eddie" 139–141
Hamilton, Charles K. 156, 167, 183, 220*ch*15*n*1
Hamilton, Frank J. 220*ch*15*n*1
Hampton, John 15–16
Hanner, William 49, 124–125
Harding, Frederick A. *see* Leroy, Jack
Hargrave, Lawrence 5, 154
Harkes, Anna *see* Lavell, Frankie
Harrell, Frank 127–128
Hathaway, Ned 32–33, 46–48, 214*ch*3*n*13
Haverly's Mastodon Minstrels 49
Hawker, Ethel *see* Viola, Essie
Hawker, Lillian *see* Adair, Leila
Hawker, Ruby *see* Viola, Millie
Headley, J. Daniel 32–33
Heid, Wilhelmina 107
Hendon, Harry 67
Hepner, Frank 109
Hepner, Fred 109
Hibbard, George W. 99, 106–107
Higgins, George 58–59
highwire *see* tightrope acts
Hill, Richard P. 134, 150

Hoffman, Edward L. 192–193
Hogan, Augustina 82
Hogan, Edward D. 3, 30, 51, 148, 160
Hogan, Ernest 166
Hogan, John 30, 82
Hogan, John B. 106, 217*ch*10*n*12
Hogan, William 30
Hunt, Elizabeth Clark "Lottie Leon" 29, 50
Hunt, Oscar 28, 50–51
Hunt, William Leonard *see* Farini, the Great
Huonker, Alice 125–126
Hurd, Uel E. *see* Hathaway, Ned
Hutchison, Edmund R. 114–115

Irvin, Leslie 2, 190, 193
Ivy, William 70, 102–103, 167, 185

Jackson, MI 30, 41
Jacobs, Frank 102
Jannus, Tony 186
Japan 67–68, 70, 75–76, 154, 183
Jaquins, Delia *see* Zelno, Dot
Jewell, "Daring Dan" 105
Jewell, Edward *see* Baltz, Edward
Jewell, Harry *see* Gruber, Harry
Jewell, Thomas 32–33, 48, 103–104
Jewell, Walter *see* Leonhauser, Walter S.

Kabrich, Charles H. 83–84
Kent, Cissie 63
Keyes, Edward S. 142–144
Keyes, Hazel 141–144, 150
Killip, W. Karl 122
King, Kitty 63
King, Samuel A. 47
Kiralfy, Bolossy 91–92, 95
kites 153–155, 220*ch*15*n*1
Knabenshue, A. Roy 163, 166–167
Kotelnikov, Gleb 188–189
Kreig, Peter 183
Kyle, Herr *see* Zimmerman, Peter

La Loubère, Simon de 7
Lamont, Nellie 83
LaMountain, John 22
Lamson, Charles H. 154
Langford, Thomas F. 46
Langley, Samuel 5
Lapham, Arthur 192
Lapoint, Louis 121
Laroux, Joseph 154
Lastrange, Charles 96–100, 158
Lavell, Frankie 123

228　Index

Law, Frederick Rodman 190–192
Law, Ruth 118, 123, 217*ch*11*n*6
Lawrence, Joseph 71–72
laws against parachuting 149
Leach, Robert "Bobby" 115, 190
Lee, Maud *see* Cody, Lillian
LeFay, Lillian *see* Sowards, Adela
Leland, Jennie 137–138
Lempriere, George Philip 63–64
Lenormand, Louis-Sébastien 7–8
Leonhauser, Walter S. 104
Leroux, Charles 3, 37–38, 55, 67–68, 215–216*ch*7*n*5
Leroy, Eva 107–108, 217*n*14
Leroy, Frank 108
Leroy, Jack 108
Leroy, Sadie *see* Finn, Edith
Leroy, Victoria *see* Heid, Wilhelmina
LeRoy, W.H. "Harry" 45–46, 106
Leslie, Harry 19–20
Levoy, Mlle. 124
Lewis, William 126–127
Lilienthal, Otto 5
Loomis, John 135
Louis, Elmer 123
Love, William Z. 126–127
Lowe, Thaddeus 19–20, 23
Ludlow, Israel 156, 220*ch*315*n*1

MacDonald, Ada 59–60
Madison, Nina 96, 98–99, 135
Maloney, Daniel J. 3, 155–157, 220*ch*15*n*1
Markeberg, Emil 138
Mars, James C. "Bud" 2, 156–158, 167, 183, 185–186
Martin, Glenn 190
May, Rosa *see* Stubbs, Juanetta
McBain, Pearl 27
McClellan, B.C. 185
McDonald, Marion L. "Daring Donald" 92, 95, 216*ch*9*n*1
McEwen, William W. 51, 82, 220–221*ch*15*n*4
McKim, Eola Lee 96
McKim, Mortimer 78, 92–99
McNeal, Louis N. *see* Wallace, Hi Sidney
Mecklem, L. Guy 168–182, 216*ch*14*n*1
Melville, Emil Leandro 35, 214*ch*4*n*2
Melvin, Nina 114
Merton, Marie 63, 148
Mizen, Walter 59
monkeys, parachuting 35, 141–143, 149–150
Montgolfier, Jacques-Étienne 7

Montgolfier, Joseph-Michel 7–8, 213*ch*1*n*1
Montgomery, John J. 3, 5, 155–157, 163, 220*ch*15*n*1
Morton, John 67, 215*ch*7*n*1
Morton, William "Grant" 186–187
Myers, Carl E. 2, 27, 44, 79–82, 159–162
Myers, Mary "Carlotta" 27–28, 44

Nantasket Beach MA 48
Niagara River Gorge 19, 30, 58, 88, 110, 115, 190
Norin, Oscar 136
Northup, Edwin J. 92

O'Dell, Leona 115
O'Dell, Leonidas N. 115
Odiva *see* Beaumont, Alma
Oliver, Charles 52, 71
Omaha, NE 134–135, 167
Onzola, Bertha 140–141
Orton, Alfred D. 58

Parker, John E. 140–141
Parks, George "J.P." 166
Passaic, NJ 37, 148
Pate, Fred 146–147
Paulhan, Louis 179–181
Paulus, Katharina "Käthe" 187–188
Pedanto, Signor 27
Peoria, IL 49, 110–113
Perkins, Eugene "Gene" 102, 146
Perry, William K. 49
Poitevin, Eugene 17–18
Poitevin, Louise 17–18
Price, James W. 29, 32, 50–51, 71, 73–75, 167
Price, Tillie 126–127

Quincy, IL 41, 45

racism 102, 145, 186
Radford, E.L. 147
Ralston, Walter 185
Randall, Lulu 83
Redmond, Phineas H. 139–140
Rehahn, Edith *see* Lamont, Nellie
Rehahn, Louise *see* Randall, Lulu
Rice, George T. 82
Richmond, Charles 49, 103–104
Ringling Brothers Circus 27, 51
Robinson, Hugh 184
Rockaway Beach, Queens, NY 44, 51, 91, 160
Rogers, George A. 47
Rogers, William J. 147

Index

Rolliston, Cora 126–127
Romig, James J. 140–144
rope walking *see* tightrope acts
Ross, Duncan C. 92, 96, 98
Royale, Fred 127–128
Rulison, William 27, 44, 80–81
Rumary, Jane 75
Russet, Frank 60

St. Clair, W.E. 45–46
San Francisco, CA 34, 35–40, 52, 69, 71, 75, 103, 113, 138, 140–142, 155–156, 158, 220*ch*15*n*1
Santos-Dumont, Alberto 162–163
Sartell, L.A. *see* Seeley, Alfred J.
Scanlon, Robert E. 89–90
Schafer, Claude 183
Seeley, Alfred J. 117
Sells-Floto Circus 51
Shannon, Grace 49, 114–115, 217*n*21
Shaw, Maud *see* Graves, Estella
Shepherd, Dolly 64–65
Simmons, T. Harry 127–128
Smith, C.O. 147
Smith, Floyd 192–193
Smith, William M. 32–34, 48
smoke balloons 1, 66, 81, 85, 93–95, 147, 170
Snyder, Charles Henry "Harry" 107–108
South Africa 58, 66, 74, 135
Sowards, Adela 117
Spalding, Albert 52, 66–67
Spencer, Arthur 60
Spencer, Charles Green 60, 64
Spencer, Edward 13–15
Spencer, Henry 164
Spencer, Percival 60–62, 64, 67–68, 70
Spencer, Stanley 60–62, 64, 163–164
Spencer, Viola *see* Cook, Edith M.
Sprague, Eugene 116
Springfield, IL 32–33
Stevens, Albert Leo "Prince Leo" 2, 4, 96–100, 158, 162, 165, 190–193
Stevens, Frank "Don Carlos" 29, 97–99
Stevens, Julia 4
Steward, William S. 102
Stokes, John *see* Burke, King
Stroebel, Charles J. 166–167
Stubbs, Juanetta "Rosa May" 113, 131
Sturgis, MI 83
Swearingen, Chester 102
Sylvan, Arthur W. 170–171, 220*ch*14*n*2
Sylvon *see* Sylvan, Arthur W.

Temple, Lillian 99
Thayer, Willard A. 116

Thiers, Helene A. "Karletta" 27, 121–122
tightrope acts 18–22, 29–30, 32, 36, 50, 103, 106, 122
Tolbert, Albert L. 33–34, 45, 126
Townsend, William E. 81–82
Trainer, Patrick 125
trapeze-balloon act 2, 18–20, 24, 26–27, 29–30, 32–38, 42, 44, 46–47, 50, 74, 80, 103, 121–122, 125, 132, 136, 139, 170–171, 216*ch*8*n*12
Trautwein, Lillian 88

Unger, Edward 193
Union Army Balloon Corps 19, 23, 219*ch*13*n*6

Vandell, Elsie 51
Vandergrift, Hubbard "Frank" 29, 54
VanDresen, Ella Beatrice 81
Van Tassell, Charles *see* Oliver, Charles
Van Tassel, Clara 53
Van Tassel, Gladys *see* Freitas, Gladys
Van Tassel, James P. *see* Price, James W.
Van Tassel, Jeanette *see* Rumary, Jane
Van Tassel, Joseph *see* Lawrence, Joseph
Van Tassel, Parker A. "Park" 34–41, 52–53, 71–76, 193, 214*ch*3*n*16, 214*ch*4*n*1
Van Tassel, Valerie *see* Freitas, Valerie
Viola, Essie 74, 138
Viola, Millie 74

Walcott, Charles 32, 83–88, 97–99, 216*ch*8*n*12
Walker, John Adelbert "Burt" 76–77, 83
Wallace, Hi Sidney 107–108
Walrath, Edward 80–81
Ward, Warren A "Bert" 136–137
Warner, Harry 29, 46
Watkins, U.S. Grant 147
Weehawken, NJ 91–100
Weston, George 138
Wheeler, Viola 49
Whelan, James 62–63
White, Edward *see* St. Clair, W.E.
Whorter, John Hunter 125
Wild, Horace B. 2, 166
Williams, Charles W. 27, 42–45, 62, 96, 98, 184
Williams, John T. 67
Wilson, William "Del Dare" 27, 44
Wise, John 9, 18, 22–24
Wise, Lizzie Ihling 27
Wood, Eleazer M. 32–33, 48
Woodall, Fred 218*n*23

Woodall, Gus *see* Hall, Edward N.
Woodall, Harriet "Jennie" 128–129
Woodall, John 128*n*23
Woodall, Nellie 141
Woodall, William 140–141
Wright Brothers 5, 154

Young, Samuel C. 27, 42–45, 62

Zelno, Dot 114–115
Zelno, Frank 114–115, 135
Zelno, Jessie 115, 135
Zeno, Madame *see* Huonker, Alice
Zeno, Professor *see* Whorter, John Hunter
Zeno, Professor *see* Hague, Paul
Zimmerman, Peter "Herr Kyle" 106